RUSSIA THROUGH EUROPEAN EYES No. 11

General Editor:
Dr. A. G. CROSS, University of East Anglia

A Tour of Russia, Siberia and the Crimea 1792-1794

RUSSIA THROUGH EUROPEAN EYES

A Tour of
Russia, Siberia
and the Crimea
1792-1794

John Parkinson

Edited with an introduction by:
William Collier, M.A., F.S.A.

FRANK CASS & CO. LTD.
1971

First published in 1971 by

FRANK CASS & COMPANY LIMITED

67 Great Russell Street, London WC1B 3BT

Introduction Copyright © 1971 William Collier

ISBN 0 7146 2597 3

Printed in Great Britain by
Clarke, Doble & Brendon, Ltd.,
Plymouth

Contents

v

Illustrations

Map

Acknowledgments

I am most grateful to Mrs. Robinson for consigning to my care the diaries of her distinguished ancestor and for her help and encouragement in editing them.

Mr. George Dixon kindly told me of the existence of the diaries. Mr. Peter McWhirr gave generous assistance in checking Russian sources for the notes; and Mrs. Irene Gladwyn answered a number of difficult queries.

In typing the text, with its many hazards of archaic spelling and unexpected capitals, my wife undertook a large share of the work.

Richmond,   WILLIAM COLLIER
October, 1970

Introduction

Russia has long been a source of fascination for the westerner. As now, so in the 18th century the Russian people intrigued foreigners by their remoteness and their unpredictable attitude towards the West. There was for much of the century and especially at the time of the French Revolution, an implied contradiction between the Russian desire to take what the West could offer, whether French or German savants, English sailors or Italian artists, and the strong patriotism which hated and feared ideas that might weaken the Russian state. More than patriotism, there was under Catherine the Great a chauvinism which insisted on Russian pre-eminence in fields where the West had excelled, combined with a refusal to admit the very serious defects of Russian society. Attention was distracted from poverty and lack of freedom by a cautiously aggressive foreign policy against the weaker states of eastern Europe. It was a situation which is familiar again today and which we can here see mirrored in the writings of an educated and intelligent traveller of that time.

John Parkinson gave his travel diaries for the years 1792 to 1794 the title 'Northern Tour'. The journey, in everything except its route, was typical of the traditional Grand Tour. Parkinson, an Oxford don, was acting as companion to a rich scion of the landed gentry, Edward Wilbraham-Bootle, later first Lord Skelmersdale, who had just come down from Oxford and was to embark on a political career soon after their tour round Europe.

To a student of politics, the usual route through France and Italy would have been fascinating but highly dangerous with the French Revolution in full spate. Northern and central Europe could offer compensating advantages, for by the later 18th century a change had come over the balance of power, shifting the centre of gravity north and east away from the declining Mediterranean states to the growing powers of Prussia, Austria and Russia. Sweden, for some decades in eclipse, was again a force to reckon with under the vigorous autocracy of Gustavus III, assassinated only a few months before John Parkinson passed through Stockholm on his way to Russia.

One or two adventurous young Englishmen on the Grand Tour

had already included Russia in their itinerary, notably Lord Herbert, who, accompanied by the Reverend William Coxe, had visited St. Petersburg and Moscow in 1776. More often Russia had attracted people like the notorious Duchess of Kingston and the adventurer Semple Lisle, who might hope that their reputations, bad enough in western Europe, had not come so far afield: or enterprising Scottish doctors and naval officers, welcomed by Catherine the Great for their skill and integrity, such as Admiral Greig, who helped to destroy the Turkish fleet at Chesme, or her own physician Rogerson, medical examiner of prospective favourites. Travellers on the Grand Tour only really started to arrive in the 1780s. By 1792, when the Terror had broken out in France, Edward Wilbraham-Bootle found four other wealthy young Englishmen in St. Petersburg: Sir Watkin Williams Wynn, Lord Dalkeith, eldest son of the Duke of Buccleugh, Lord Borringdon, later first Earl of Morley, and Lord Granville Leveson-Gower, afterwards ambassador to St. Petersburg and Paris. All five were born within a few years of each other and all except Borringdon, already a member of the House of Lords, became M.P.s on their return to England. They supported the policies of the younger Pitt and formed a group of young Tories to which Dalkeith's travelling companion, William Garthshore, tutor at Christchurch, was recruited as an additional member.

At St. Petersburg they were introduced to Russian politics by the British Ambassador, Charles Whitworth. His abilities and exceptional good looks were being put to good use at court, where, by a liaison with the sister of the imperial favourite, he was laying the foundations of the Anglo-Russian alliance of 1795. But his English guests may have received stronger impressions from Russian society, which, despite the similar diversions of Catherine the Great and the Prince of Wales, was very different not only from English life but also from that of western Europe. Almost the sole original counterpart of a French *philosophe* was the writer Radishchev, exiled to Siberia; and the small group of Free Masons was being persecuted by that former friend of *philosophes*, the Empress, to whom the French Revolution was causing serious misgivings. The capital might seem to John Parkinson a modern Athens, but it was less the creation of native Russians than of foreign architects and artists. Young Englishmen could be excused for seeing in Russian society only a mixture of corrupt upper classes, ignorant and downtrodden serfs, and merchants—often foreigners and without influence. It was enough to make these Milords complacent about their native land and their own beneficent role in its government.

Most British visitors saw just St. Petersburg, Moscow and the countryside on the way to and from these towns. Only a few ventured farther south, among them Lady Elizabeth Craven, who published her letters from the Crimea in 1786. Maria Guthrie, a Frenchwoman married to a Scottish doctor in St. Petersburg, wrote about her journey there ten years later. Even fewer travellers attempted to go east from Moscow across the Volga and into Siberia, journeys still regarded as exploration by western Europeans. Louis XV had specially commissioned the Abbé Chappe d'Auteroche to write his *Voyage en Siberie* in 1761. Two Scotsmen, John Bell and John Cook, had published accounts of journeys, the first to Pekin in 1719 by way of Siberia, the second in a book of 1770 about a voyage some years earlier down the Volga and across the Caspian to Persia. Between these and the next description of Siberia by an Englishman there is a long gap, broken only by the diaries of Jeremy Bentham's brother Samuel, a splendid eccentric whose account of his expedition to Tobolsk in 1789 is unfortunately fragmentary. No more eye-witness accounts of Siberia in English, other than translations, such as of von Kotzebue's book about his exile there in 1800, appeared until 1802, when Martin Sauer published his narrative of the English naval expedition of 1785–94 along the Siberian north-east coast. The interior of Siberia was described again in 1820 by Captain John Dundas Cochrane, R.N., who walked, with occasional lifts, from Boulogne over Europe to Russia and thence across Russia and Siberia to the Pacific. There in Kamchatka he married a Russian girl and they travelled back together by horse sleigh and carriage. Cochrane, for all his bluff, matter-of-fact recital of hardships and dangers, admitted to feeling unreasonably nervous on walking over the Urals into Siberia, not about the hazards of journeying across difficult country but because he was approaching 'such a supposed scene of cruelty and misery'.

Siberia's reputation was of long standing. It is all the more remarkable and valuable to have John Parkinson's account of 1793, the year when he and his companion diverged so far from the normal routes of the Grand Tour as to get to Tobolsk. They had come to Russia by way of Scandinavia and stayed longer than usual in St. Petersburg and Moscow preparing for the journey east. Discouraged by the Princess Dashkova from the idea of getting to China (the American John Ledyard had been arrested in eastern Siberia only five years earlier), they decided on a round trip, turning south from Tobolsk to the Caspian and the foothills of the Caucasus, thence across to the Crimea and back north over the Ukraine to Moscow and the capital. They spent the whole of the spring, summer and autumn of 1793 on the journey, remaining most

of the next winter in St. Petersburg. In the spring of 1794 they set
off for England, taking in on their way Vienna, Dresden, Berlin,
Brunswick and Hamburg.

The detailed account of this long and very unusual version of
the Grand Tour is contained in Parkinson's diary. It tells us much
about Russia and the Russians, less about the diarist. Every so
often one comes across a spontaneous explosion of irritation, but
for the most part he seems to have been a sociable and longsuffering man, as befitted a bear-leader, and his comments are only
implied. This makes for some excellent reporting, set down very
soon after the events or conversations described, without conceal-
ments or moralizings. Indeed some of his stories would hardly have
been publishable in his own day and his elegant Jane-Austenish
diction is oddly employed describing occasions which Jane Austen
would never have mentioned.

This worldliness, in a don who was also a clergyman, arose partly
from his position in society. Although of fairly prosperous farming
stock, and combining a Fellowship of Magdalen College, Oxford,
with a rectory at Brocklesby in his native Lincolnshire, he lacked
influential connections to provide advancement. Behind what his
epitaph describes as 'the modest stillness of his demeanour' and
'the suavity of his manners', there lay hid a determination to become
either a dignitary of the Anglican church or President of his college.
To gain clerical preferment he must, like Mr. Collins in *Pride and
Prejudice*, think of who had more to give. Seeking the company of
the upper classes without belonging to their number, he had taken
to writing frankly about them in his diary. Besides mixing in
London society, he accompanied young graduates on tours of
Switzerland, Italy and Holland, but without ever finding a patron
who would present him with a valuable living. In 1791 occurred
the crisis of his career: Magdalen was to elect a new President.
There were only two candidates: John Parkinson, who had been
appointed Bursar of the college four years earlier, and Dr. Routh.
The election took place in April and Routh triumphed by a single
vote. It must have been with relief that John Parkinson left in the
following spring on the long journey that would take him to
Scandinavia, Russia, Siberia and central Europe.

Though he had written diaries of travels before, they had tended
to describe things he had seen. The Northern Tour tells us as much
about Russian society as about the country. Writing for himself,
he had no axes to grind, unlike authors of books on Russia who
must choose a point of view to explain the strange phenomenon
of a partly westernized, partly Byzantine society filled with
anachronisms and odd juxtapositions. William Coxe had decided

that the main trouble lay in the 'vassalage of the peasants', while Edward Clarke was to put the blame on 'the Russian character', adding firmly that 'those Authors who endeavour to present a favourable view of the Russian people, and who strain every effort to accomplish the undertaking, are continually betraying the hidden reality'. Even foreigners writing home tended to dogmatize on Russian life according to where they were living and the amount of strain that involved. Diplomatists in St. Petersburg, where life for the upper classes was comfortable and entertaining, would comment favourably, Sir George Macartney maintaining early in Catherine's reign that 'to despotism Russia owes her greatness and her dominions'. The court painter Robert Porter, after residing three years in the capital, wrote of the Russian serfs that 'their comforts are very properly attended to; and cruelty and oppression is very seldom suffered to embitter their existence'. The letters of the Wilmot sisters, guests of the Princess Dashkova, changed from appreciation of Russia to strong dislike when they found that the Princess's family resented their influence. A balanced outlook on Russia was in fact a difficult achievement for foreigners.

The only way of summarizing the Russia of Catherine the Great was to insist on its variety and size, its lack of shape and consistency, in fact on its refusal to be summarized. It was an empire sometimes appearing sharply cut off from other countries, sometimes fading away at the edges like a bad photograph. John Parkinson recorded the capital and court, where one could not but believe in the Russian state, in its splendour and corruption. But he also brings to light those places where the Empress was so distant and unconvincing a figure that it was easier for Russians to accept the fables of the adventurer Pugachov, that he was their Emperor, Peter III, alive after all and escaped from the wicked Empress's prison. This was the reverse side of the imperial coin which the diplomatists in St. Petersburg never saw. By the time John Parkinson reached eastern Russia, the cowed peasantry had been taught which was fable and which reality. At Tobolsk he noted the life of the malcontents in exile and on the Caucasian frontier the military basis of autocratic power. What happened when this foundation gave way he learnt later from an eye-witness of the uprising against the Russian garrison in Warsaw.

Yet these instances alone over-simplify. There were no two clearly defined classes, rulers and ruled, or even two extremes of autocrat and subject with gradations in between. Russia contained an extraordinary variety of semi-independent classes and communities: Orthodox monasteries and great landowners; half foreign trading centres like Astrakhan, with its Persian and Indian immigrants;

foreign settlers on the land, such as the Moravian Brethren at Sarepta; English merchants and Scottish naval officers; Kalmyk and Circassian chiefs and tribesmen of uncertain allegiance. Each of these John Parkinson was able to visit and describe.

His manuscript diary runs to six volumes. Its guide book inventories of paintings and architecture can be found elsewhere and have been omitted from these extracts, as have his notes of daily happenings that are irrelevant to the narrative or to his picture of Russian life. No change has been made in his use of capital letters or in his spelling (apart from correction of mistakes and inconsistencies), though the notes, marked in the text by asterisks, give one of the usual modern transliterations of Russian words. In this way, it is hoped, the essential flavour of the diary has been kept despite condensation from four volumes to one, the other two being concerned with the journeys to and from Russia.

B

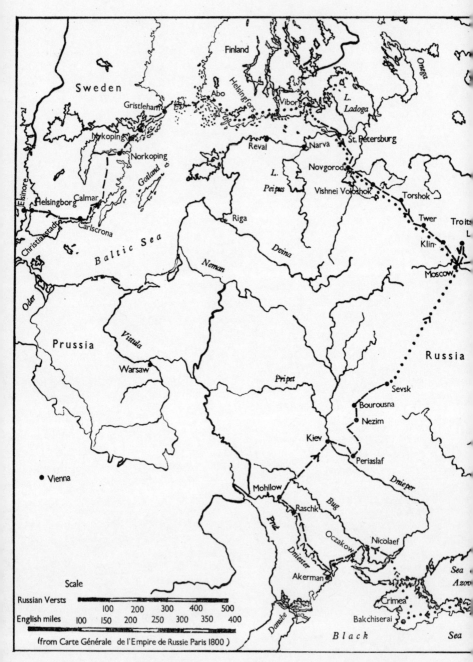

(from Carte Générale de l'Empire de Russie Paris 1800)

xviii

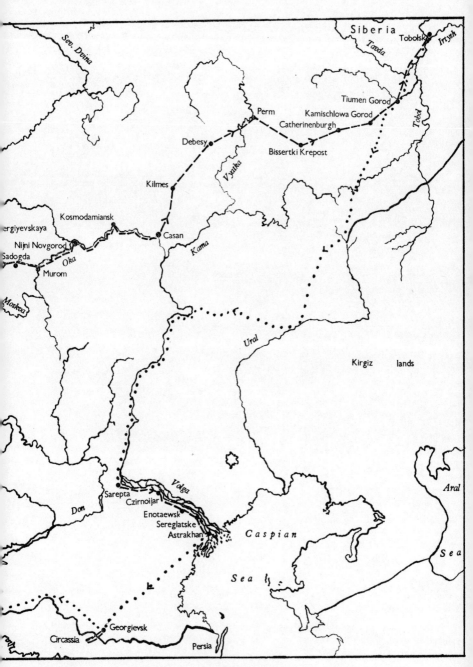

xix

1   Elsinore to Stockholm

*John Parkinson had set off in the early summer of 1792
on his northern Grand Tour. In company with Edward
Wilbraham-Bootle he stayed for a time in the civilized
atmosphere of Copenhagen. Their journey on through Sweden
gives a sense of venturing among a strange, rather primitive
people.*

Saturday, 30th June, 1792

The Sound is three English miles over. . . . Though we left
Elsinore at six and reached Helsingborg at a quarter after seven,
yet we were not able to get off till near eleven; we travelled however something more than nine Swedish miles to Wenneborg, within
one post of Christianstadt, where we slept. Our road lay through
the province of Scania, which is esteemed the most fertile of any
in Sweden, though without being told so we should scarcely I think
have suspected it, for the best part of it was an alternate succession,
nearly equal in proportion, of cultivated ground and open commons,
the land was strewed over with stones, in some places of a large
size, and the fourth stage to Tyringe consisted altogether of Heath
scattered over in this manner. What the face of the country was
during the last two stages I could not see, for it was one o'clock
when we reached the end of our day's journey.

At Helsingborg we found the floor scattered over with Pine
leaves; the first sight of this surprised us, but it is now become
familiar, for it is universally the custom in Sweden; and as the
scent of them is very agreeable, I like it extremely. The maid
servant, upon Bootle's giving her something for waiting on us, seized
his hand with an air of great thankfulness and kissed it; as well
she might, for by the advice of the French Consul's secretary we
had been instructed to give her twelve Schillinges, alias 12^d, which
in this country is a large sum. We had not been used to see People
without stockings, but in Sweden it is very generally the case; the
pretty girl who waited upon us here was if I remember right in
this predicament. Now and then they wear slippers on their bare
feet but very often not.

1

The way of travelling in this country is, after considering at what time you mean to set off and how far you mean to go, to send a peasant who is called the Forebote off three or four hours before you start to the next post, with a paper mentioning how many horses you want and at what time you mean to arrive. This notice is very necessary because the peasants furnish the horses in their turn and sometimes live at a great distance. Another peasant conveys the paper on to the next stage, for it contains instructions to all the Posthouses till you arrive at the place where you propose to stop. We had occasion including the Forebote's for six horses, for which we paid exactly a Rix-dollar = 48 Schillings or Pence a Swedish mile. This supposing a Swedish mile to equal seven English is at the rate of 8^d an English mile for the six horses, or something more than a penny farthing each horse. Cheap however as this seems to be, it is not long ago since the price was doubled. The Postillions as well as the Forebote think themselves handsomely recompensed with a Schillinge or penny, and on the road to Tornas I am told that they expect nothing. They wait an hour, but if the traveller does not arrive within that time they go away, but without expecting in general any recompense. The Patience likewise with which they suffer themselves to be kept in waiting is perfectly astonishing.

Our Postillions rode without stirrups, which we found out afterwards they generally do in Sweden. Having taken a man with us from Helsingborg, he acted as our Coachman and one of the Postillions always took his post on the trunk behind.

Sunday, 1st July

In the stage between Norje and Assuram . . . we quitted the Province of Scania and entered that of Blekinge. I then fancied that I perceived a material change in the face of the country, but till then it continued very much the same, except that the stones scattered about increased both in quantity and size and that large masses of rock seemed everywhere to be heaving their broad backs above the surface of the ground. We could not help exclaiming sometimes that the ground appeared to produce nothing but Granite. Even the Cornfields where the crop was really good were dotted frequently and generally with an immense number of these detached rocks, which raised their heads above the tallest blades and produced a very singular effect.

The women in this part of the country are well made and have good faces but are rather too masculine. They wear a jacket and a white shirt; a head-dress of white glazed linen, sometimes with two lappels behind and sometimes prettily tied in the way of a handker-chief before. Their arms are covered with nothing but their shift sleeves, and sometimes they wear no jacket over their shift, which is made to set close and exactly shew the form. The men seem to be strong, active, lively and civil, and dress often in a sort of short coat, which I look upon to be according to ancient costume and to have given rise to, not to be derived from, the present court and military fashion.

In the afternoon we lighted and walked several times up the hills. The evening was uncommonly fine. We made the last stage by moonlight between the hours of ten and twelve.

Monday, 2nd July

On our arrival at Carlscrona . . . we sent to enquire at what time Admiral Chapman and Admiral Modée,* for whom we had letters from Sir Sidney Smith,* would be able to receive us.

Admiral Chapman told us we could not have permission to see the Arsenal and the fleet, orders having been lately sent that they should not be shewn. We heard afterwards that two Danish gentlemen, of whom they had been a little suspicious, had been at Carlscrona a few days before.

Tuesday, 3rd July

Before we set off we determined to call again upon Admiral Modée, whom we found just coming to call upon us and who received us as the friends of Sir Sidney with the greatest possible civility, lamenting exceedingly that he had not seen us the day before. He shewed us four plans of the four principal Sea engage-ments between the Russian and Swedish fleets, in two of which he bore a principal part, he introduced his daughters to us and repeatedly pressed us to take raisins or figs. His youngest daughter he desired to sit down and play to us on the Harpsichord, having, he assured [us], an extraordinary natural turn for Music and drawing.

Sir Sidney Smith, upon one occasion when the King [of Sweden] asked him if there was anything which he could do for him, replied that there was not but begged that his Majesty would transfer the favour which he meant for him to Modée. This was truly English, said the Admiral. I did not overhear it myself, said he, but it was reported to me by one that did. In short his civilities to us quite won our hearts and we both felt the greatest regret at parting from him.

We travelled about seven miles and a half, i.e. five posts, this evening to Wassenclose, one post short of Calmar. Here we slept. The Postmaster at Padoda had consented for us to take on the horses though there was another Posthouse in the way. However when we came thither an attempt was made to stop us and it was by main force that we got the better of the Post Master, who followed us to the next stage to learn our names and lodge a complaint.

Wednesday, 4th July

We had but one Post to Calmar, where we breakfasted on Strawberries and clarified Coffee. The clarified Coffee, which we thought good, is made in a bottle corked up and boiled over a slow fire. A Physician was so obliging as to walk with us after breakfast to the Castle, on our way to which we passed by a large crop of the *Sambacus obalas*, known here by the name of Maneurte or Mannablood.* This plant bears a fruit which when pressed emits a red juice. The people of the country believe that it sprang from the blood of those who were killed in a battle on this spot, that the plant exists nowhere else, and that Linneus, who once saw it, pronounced it to be unique. What confirms these good people in their persuasion is the colour of the flowers. . . . The most remarkable thing of all, perhaps, was that our Aesculapius did not appear to entertain any doubts of the fact.

Thursday, 5th July

Between Forby and Tillenberg we bought some Strawberries on the road in a pretty Basket of Beech Bark, which they constantly make use of for this purpose. At Holmfred we each got a Mess of sourish milk, one of us in what I can conceive to serve occasionally for a chamberpot, and the other in a Washbasin.

Friday, 6th July

We set off this morning with a resolution not to stop till we had reached Stockholm, which we did not till the next day at two o'clock. . . . Thus we travelled fifteen posts without stopping.

2   Stockholm

Parkinson and Bootle arrived in the Swedish capital only a few months after the assassination of Gustavus III. Stockholm was still seething with talk about the late king and his enemies. The story is well known from Verdi's opera Ballo in Maschera, *which gave a bowdlerized version of events and characters calculated not to offend Victorian audiences. Parkinson pieces together a less romantic account which spares neither side and is probably a great deal nearer the truth. He learns about the different conspirators, about the character of Gustavus III* and about his methods of maintaining personal rule. For background there are scenes from diplomatic life and a sight of the extraordinary court of Gustavus IV.**

Sunday, 8th July, 1792

As soon as we had breakfasted we got a boat rowed by two women with naked feet and rowed down the gulph to call upon Mr. Liston* [*British envoy to Sweden*] at his country house. . . . Behind us we had the Quay with a considerable number of vessels lying along by the side of it, a line of lofty well-built houses stuccoed white beyond, and over them the palace rearing its magnificent wall higher and higher in proportion as we retired further from the Town. On our left the banks of the Gulph are shaded with trees, but on the right they almost wholly consist of high and naked rocks, near the town built upon all over and crowned with the church of St. Catherine, but lower down with houses only here and there at their foot. The outlet of the gulph below is not seen; therefore it has altogether the appearance of a Lake. Besides which, three or four rocky naked islands are one the site of a mill, another that of a battery and a third spread over with houses.

Monday, 9th July

Bootle and Westley* went this morning to see Ankestrom's head* and I was glad to stay at home . . . . Mr. Liston having invited us to dine with him again today, we went to him in the same con-

conveyance. . . . Mr. Liston talked without the least reserve about the late transactions and gave us a great insight into the Characters of all the principal people concerned in them.

I will endeavour to recollect what fell from Mr. Liston, concerning the late plot to assassinate the King, by relating first what he told us of the leading persons.

To begin with, Major Pechlin,* who though no legal proof of his guilt can be made out is supposed to have been at the bottom of the whole and to have set the rest on, he was one of the most strenuous opposers of the Revolution of 1772 [*establishing the power of Gustavus III*], and immediately upon its happening repaired to his regiment. He was followed by a Messenger from the King commanding his appearance at Stockholm, and in case of disobedience instructed to arrest him. When the Messenger acquainted him with the latter part of his instructions, Pechlin asked him for his orders; I have none in writing said he; then replied Pechlin, You are my prisoner, and took him into custody accordingly. For this he was brought for his trial and though he was acquitted, was ever after warm in opposition to the King and bore him the most implacable hatred. Mr. Liston knew him to be a person so exceedingly obnoxious to his Majesty that he had taken care to avoid his acquaintance.

As he [*Pechlin*] foresaw the very thing which has happened, he took the precaution to guard himself against it by never conferring with two of the conspirators at a time. He drew up the plan of operations, I think, in case the King had been killed. He talked over the project of the assassination separately with two or three of them somewhere where they dined together: yet when he came to be charged with these facts he had not the smallest recollection of any such thing; he recollected a conversation with regard to the Revolution in France but not one word in regard to the subject in question.

By the law of the land it has been the practice always in this country, when the presumptive proofs against a criminal are very strong and he cannot be brought to confess, in that case to keep him in confinement either till a sense of his guilt induces him to do so, or till other evidence arises to convict him. It was proposed some time ago in a Diet to repeal this law. Pechlin was the man to oppose the innovation; he did it with success; and is likely to become himself the victim of that success.

Though Torture has been abolished in Sweden, yet a species of it is still allowed under the name of strict confinement; by which they mean confinement where the Prisoner has not room to stand straight or where he stands up to the knees in mud, or where he is fixed with his back to a wall and thus prevented from lying down. A Torture somewhat of this kind was employed upon Pechlin; for two nights and days orders were given to waken him every 8 or ten minutes; in consequence of which a fever was brought on which they were afraid would put an end to his life; for which reason it was discontinued. All the other conspirators have concurred in accusing him, and are now very angry with him but without any good case; the whole world believes him to be guilty and yet he cannot be convicted. He passes the greatest part of his time, we are told, in smoking. We walked this morning to the house where he is kept confined in hopes of seeing him at the window but he was not visible. There is a guard here constantly of 200 men. This house belongs to the Court which takes cognisance of the crime, and here the other criminals are in durance as well as himself. The others of late have been suffered to dine together.

Ankestrom was originally a page and afterwards obtained a commission in the guards, which his wife[a] having prevailed upon him to part with, he became a farmer, and having heard of an estate in the isle of Gothland to be sold, he took a journey to look at it, at the time when the inhabitants, apprehending a visit from the Russians, had embodied themselves and were putting themselves in readiness to make the best resistance in their power. As they had no strong place he thought this very foolish and told them that the wisest thing for them would be in case of a visit to receive the Russians kindly and sell them whatever they had occasion for. For holding this kind of language he was taken up, tried and condemned to die. The King, however, set him at liberty; yet he did not revoke his sentence, which was still hanging over his head at the time when he committed the deed of assassination. Add to the above circumstance that he had, as he thought, unjustly lost a cause of considerable importance; which circumstance, together with the others preyed in such a manner on his mind that he professed to be weary of life and fell into a melancholy state of mind.

This may be supposed to have rendered him disaffected; at the same time he fell into the company of the other conspirators, who would lament their own situation and that of the Kingdom, which they spoke of as desperate, unless the King could be taken off, which was a thing out of the question. On some occasion of this kind, Ankestrom declared that he would undertake the deed, for which at first he was laughed at by Ribbing;* but when he persisted in his resolution, they listened more seriously to his proposal. Twice, however, he went with this intention, without putting it in execution, because Ribbing did not keep his appointment to meet him, which occasioned him to think that he was not properly supported. Upon these occasions he acknowledges that he returned home exceedingly out of spirits for not having been as good as his word.

Ribbing kept himself out of the way either because he did not believe that Ankestrom could do it, or rather because he did not want to involve himself in the consequences of being present. Finding however that Ankestrom would not do it without him, he met him there on the fatal night and being distinguished by the King through his mask was believed by him to be the assassin. The King said as much to his confidential friends and did not think himself justified in saying so publicly.

Ankestrom owns that he killed the King partly from a desire of ridding the country of a tyrant, but chiefly out of revenge. For that reason he had taken no trouble to acquaint himself with the names or views of his associates. He does not even accuse Pechlin and probably had no intercourse with him and knew nothing of him. As to the King, so far from suspecting Ankestrom, as he had [not] frequented the court for some time, he was entirely out of his mind, and perhaps not personally known to him. He [Ankestrom] had regular features, blue eyes, and long eyelids, and when a page was much in the favour of the ladies at Court.

Ribbing, having always been in opposition to the King, had not received any marks of royal favour and was mortified to see Ribbands conferred on others all around him and himself neglected.

The King finding himself impotent, or rather unable to get the Queen with child,* contrived to put Monk* into bed with the Queen without her knowledge. He made an appointment with her himself and under some pretence or other desired that not a word might be exchanged. The Queen however found it out and at first was exceedingly provoked, but she afterwards thought proper to renew her intercourse with Monk, till at last he was wearied and took a mistress whom he lived with publickly. The Queen was so provoked at his neglect that for a long time she would not speak to him. The present King and his brother who died are universally believed to be the fruit of this connexion. Every body talks of it, and nobody entertains a doubt about it. The King is even said strongly to resemble his father; and for this reason, as is supposed, they have sent him out of the way; he is residing at present at Hamburgh.

The late King is believed to have had no inclination for the fair sex. The ladies all affirm it, all talk of it, all detest him for his other propensity. His amusement was chiefly among the pages of the court. Rickhausen has the reputation of having been honoured with his affections. His last favourite was a great fat fellow; I think the Count de Taube.*

The King was suspected of being deficient in personal courage; indeed though he confessed that he possessed it not, yet he surmounted his feelings by the strength of his mind and in action never betrayed any want of coolness and intrepidity. That he was singularly possessed of what Mr. Liston called political courage appeared from several instances in the course of the last war: and particularly from his resolution to attack the enemy again immediately after the affair of Wyborg.

The Queen during the war is said to have been under great apprehension for her son, the legitimacy of whose birth, had the King and the Duke happened both to have been killed, might she conceived have been brought into question by the Duke of Ostrogothia,* who is still young enough to marry and have children. He has always been at the head of the party in opposition to the King. His residence is chiefly in the country, where he amuses himself with hunting and farming and lives with a pretty mistress, without troubling himself much about public affairs. In his person he was much superior to his brothers; but his talents are not extraordinary.

The King's Vanity was his ruling passion. It betrayed itself in all his words and actions. When he entered the Levee every step, every gesture, every speech was studied, and particularly so whenever he had occasion to address a stranger. He prided himself very much upon his eloquence; and indeed with reason, for if ever he could lay hold of any person belonging to the opposite [party] he generally succeeded in winning him over. He went with this confidence to the Court of Denmark, but old Birnsdorff,* who disliked him, was on his guard, and could not be worked upon by him in the least. This Minister, Mr. Liston told us, is a very proper man to manage the affairs of Denmark, being a man very unlikely to get into a scrape. He did not speak highly of his talents.

Tuesday, 10th July

We were under an engagement to dine again today with Mr. Liston, but the Spanish Minister M. Corral having desired Mr. L. to bring us with him to his house, we dined with him, although we are to be there by invitation again on Thursday.

The house is almost encompassed with water, being joined to the mainland only by a narrow causeway; so that the room in which we dined being very low it had very much the appearance of a cabin. Besides several pints of Claret placed round the table, there was a bottle of Port in ice at the bottom, and a bottle of wine de Graves at the top, which the Abbé and M. Corral invited the company from time to time to have. M. Corral distributed the Champagne afterwards in the same manner. This was followed by Malaga which the Abbé distributed and Malvoisier which was distributed by M. Corral. Before dinner a glass of liqueur was handed about, and the same again after our coffee. Our dinner commenced as at Mr. Liston's with Fish which was followed by soup.

As soon as the coolness of the evening would admit of it, we adjourned to the Chinese Summer house situated on a little eminence at a small distance from the house. From hence after staying for some time we went to Mr. Liston's and drank tea there. The Gulph, particularly the lower part, was diversified this evening with a great number of sails, the sky was clear, the weather calm, and the scene altogether perfectly delightful.

Mr. Liston knows most of the characters mentioned by Mirabeau, and though the picture is heightened and is indeed a caricature, yet it is always founded on truth. He is supposed to have sold them to a bookseller when in distress for money, and has been obliged to disown them when they appeared in public on account of the many harsh things which they contain. Chevalier pronounced Mirabeau to be an *ignorant*, a man who won the admiration of the world by the force of his style and the high colouring of his pictures in that famous work on Prussia.

The Eminence on which Ankastrom was executed was encompassed by a cordon of soldiers. When he was set down in this ring, with great fervour he first offered up a short prayer on his knees; he then embraced the two clergymen who accompanied him, one of them who appeared to be most in his confidence he embraced with particular affection. After which, lifting up his eyes to heaven, he seemed to be appealing in a silence but with the greatest earnestness to God Almighty. This he did twice with an ardour and solemnity which powerfully affected the minds of the spectators.

Upon asking Mr. Kean about this again to day, he represents him rather as stretching out his hands to heaven, as it were in order to embrace it, and as if he wished to beg pardon: and this with such an air of complacency as seemed to express an assurance of obtaining it. He then with great composure tied the handkerchief about his eyes, and was led up to the Scaffold by the two Clergymen. This consisted of a stand with an inclined plane rising from it upon which he laid himself down almost at full length, having adjusted first with great intrepidity the hand and the neck to receive the blow. The hand was cut off first, and the head immediately afterwards by two different executioners; the chief executioner per-

formed the latter service and his assistant the former, which was
ill done, for the cut was made but little short of the elbow. The
first stroke did not cause him to move in the least. All the heights
round about were crowded with spectators who observed during
the whole ceremony the most profound silence. This account I
received this evening from Mr. Kean, Mr. Liston's Secretary, who
saw the whole at no great distance, being placed in the first line
among the soldiers.

Wednesday, 11th July

We called this morning on Baron de Geddes and found him at
home. The Baron, I understood from Mr. Liston, was employed
during the struggle between the French and English parties here
in bribing on the side of the English. . . . The Baron told us at
the same time some good stories concerning Mr. Marshall's travels
in this country. Mr. Marshall has published travels through various
parts of Europe without having once crossed the channel. In his
travels through Sweden he calls the palace enclosed in a Castle
and talks of getting to dinner with some gentlemen near Lindkiop-
ing from Gothenburg, which is impossible to do in less than two
days.

Bootle went out with Westley in his chaise, I remained behind
with Mr. ———, an Englishman in the service of the Imperial
Legation. We took a walk together afterwards in the King's gardens.
He [i.e. the King] commenced the war with Russia in the hopes of
being able to take Petersburg, which most probably he would have
done, if his officers had not refused to act with him. By an article
of the Constitution, if Sweden is attacked, the Diet obliges itself
to furnish supplies for the defence of the country. In order to
justify therefore the hostilities which he meditated, he dressed a
number of Swedes like Russians and ordered them to commit
certain outrages on the Swedish territory. The taylor who made
the cloaths is still living.

The King is supposed to have introduced the national dress in
order to conceal his deformity. To the last he was as fond of a new
coat as a young man of eighteen and looked as much for admiration. The King used to say that every house in Stockholm was
a bawdy house but his own the largest.

Thursday, 12th July

Ankestrom's head and quarters are placed in the middle between
the place where he was beheaded and the public gallows, about

thirty yards perhaps from each. The head is fixed upon a post, I should think about five yards high, and the quarters laid upon frames like wheels, two on each side, but a little advanced and a yard or a yard and a half lower, the two legs on the outside, the other two quarters on the inside. His right hand is nailed on just below the head.

The place of execution cannot be less than two English miles from the centre of the Town; it is on the South side of it; and is almost encompassed by rocks which on this occasion were crowded with people who had thus an opportunity of seeing very distinctly every thing that passed. I set out this morning at six o'clock on foot with our valet de place to see this melancholy spectacle.

After breakfast we went with Mr. Westley to see the Opera House, where on the spot where the King was shot we saw the marks of his blood on the boards, as also on the sopha in a little room adjoining to the Theatre to which he was immediately carried and where all the foreign Ministers were admitted to his presence. Upon this occasion it was that he apologized to them for shutting the gates of the town, by which they would be prevented from sending Messengers to their courts.

He had just made a little circuit from one side of the Theatre to the other, and had not been come in more than ten minutes when the deed was done. The doors were immediately shut and the company were all confined till six in the morning, being required as they went out to give in their names. The report of the pistol was very small; and an attempt was made immediately afterwards by the conspirators to give an alarm of fire.

The King had a very handsome set of apartments in the Opera house where he had supped with a party this very evening. In the largest of these rooms I saw a painting said to be done at Rome, of which the subject is his meeting with the Emperor in St. Peter's. The Emperor makes but a pitiful figure by the side of the King, who is most ridiculously the hero of the piece. In a box provided for him and his suite are a large party of Swedes with three ladies behind them more conspicuous than the rest whom I could not help fancying that I recognized for Lady Warren and the Miss Berries.* The Pope is employed in saying Mass.

At the Spanish Minister's to day where we dined our party consisted exactly of twenty persons. The service of plate as well as the dinner was excessively handsome. We had no less than fifteen different sorts of Wine. Liqueurs were handed about before dinner and after coffee. When we took leave of M. Corral [*the Spanish Minister*] we went home with Mr. Liston, with whom we had two hours of charming conversation replete not less with information than candor.

He gave us a curious account of the way by which Sir Robert Ainslie* obtained his present situation at Constantinople. His Father was a Scotch Merchant at Bordeaux in whose absence the Son ran away with all the property he could lay his hands on and repaired to Paris. There by a connexion with the Duke of Choiseul's mistress he got intimate of a plan to attack our possessions in the East Indies; this he communicated to Lord Rochford, our Minister at Paris, by whom he was desired if possible to get some authentic proof. The Mistress bribed a frotteur (the man who at Paris polishes the floors with his feet) by means of a false key to get into the Duke's cabinet and steal the paper in question. A copy of it was taken; the English apprized of the plan sent out a fleet to remonstrate, and frustrated the scheme. In consideration Lord Rochford when Secretary of State, gave him the appointment which he has. He keeps a splendid house, he accommodates his friends in every way.

Constantinople is the only residence where a Minister may become rich. Public Ministers of foreign powers are indulged in the privilege of granting protections, which exempt the person who procures them from a great number of inconveniences and renders them not amenable to the laws of Turkey. The Price of a protection may be £500. Upon a Person's death it must be renewed. In a single year there is sometimes a demand for a great many. Thus the Minister becomes rich.

During the recent war with Russia [Mr. Elliott found] the King of Sweden, he told us, in a fit of distraction, tearing his hair and crying, for if Gothenburg was taken, he looked upon everything as lost. He would have been obliged to make an ignominious peace with Russia, to call a Diet and to restore the constitution to its ancient form. Rather than submit to all this, he had seriously conceived a design to abandon the kingdom and fly to Paris; with which view he and Armfeldt had been calculating whether with the jewels which he had with him, when sold, they should be able to maintain themselves with any degree of decency and comfort.

Mr. Liston says that our court had made no promise of succour to the Swedes. He in particular himself had been instructed to be discreet in what he said upon that head till the proper moment arrived. . . . What the King was chiefly in want of was Money. If we had privately supplied him with money, that would have enabled him to carry on the war and rendered our expensive armament in the year ensuing unnecessary. As it was he had nothing to pay his

c

troops with. The first campaign exhausted his treasury. He then borrowed as much as he was able. But at last he had neither money nor Credit.

Mr. Liston heard him reply once to a petition or address from the order of Peasants; he also heard him open the Diet, on both which occasions he acquitted himself extremely well, better indeed than any other person who spoke at the same time. His Voice was uncommonly distinct, his manner and his action dignified and impressive without being theatrical. Every discussion was before a committee from the several orders, at which he always presided. A great part of the members were overawed and prevented from speaking by the presence of the King, others dreaded his abilities, and those who were hardy enough to venture objections (and some there were who did it with great boldness) them he generally contrived to bring over, by his acuteness, by his accurate knowledge of the subject as well as of the history and laws of the Country, in which he was superior to all his opponents, but most of all by soothing words, by commending their frankness and admitting their objections to a certain degree, and by flattery under every form. Instead of being ashamed of these Arts, he piqued himself upon them and would relate with great openness to Mr. Liston the manner in which he managed and twisted these refractory members round his fingers, happy to have anybody with whom he could talk confidentially on the subject.

I had been told that he composed his speeches first in French and then translated them into Swedish. Mr. Liston seems rather to think that he composed them in Swedish and got some person to correct them afterwards; for he does not think that he correctly understood his own language. As French, however, was the language which he best understood and chiefly spoke, his speeches abounded very naturally with Gallicisms which he imagines gave rise to that idea.

Did Ribbing hold his hand over the pistol? Was the shot meant to be between the Shoulders instead of the loins? Ankestrom was the last person who left the Opera house. While Mr. Liston was present, soon after receiving the wound, the King enumerated the many attempts of the same kind which had lately been made; and in particular mentioned that of Margaret Nicholson.

Whipping for a person under sentence of death is a new thing in this country. One day when he was whipped, somebody asked Ankestrom, don't you feel yourself humbled by this punishment? He replied, until I saw the statue of Gustavus Vasa I did, but since then I am comforted by the consciousness of having been like him of some use to my country. The Family of the Assassin has been obliged to change their name, but the estate has been restored to his wife and children. Was it Horn* or Ankestrom who was spat at by Ribbing after he had made his confession? The other conspirators now under sentence of death have presented a petition to beg their lives, which the Duke is more disposed to comply with than the King. The Duke fancies that a compliance with it may serve to reconcile the nobility.

A Militia officer said to one of the conspirators: Consider that you have one foot on earth and the other in eternity. Pray Sir, answered Pechlin, what profession? A Taylor, Sir. Then be so good as to tell me, with one foot on earth and the other in eternity, how much it would take to make me a Pair of Breeches?

The War with Poland is entered into at the instigation of the present favourite of the Russian Empress. She sleeps with him in a bed separated by a partition, which whenever she chuses, is removed by means of a spring and serves as a signal to her lover.

Saturday, 14th July

A report prevailed today that the Conspirators who are condemned to death have attempted to make their escape last night.

Sunday, 15th July

We breakfasted this morning with Westley and Mr. Liston called upon us there with his coach and six and carried us to Dronningholm, the King's palace where he held a court today at the distance of about six miles from Stockholm.

Till the King made his appearance we wandered about and were introduced to several persons by Mr. Liston, especially to some of the gentlemen belonging to the court, whom etiquette required us to be made acquainted with.

Here follow notes on some of the courtiers:

M. Armfeldt.* How changed from what I remember him in Italy! His bulk is very much reduced; but his face is altered the most, being now sickly and fallen instead of flushed and rosy as it then was. He is reckoned to have been the King's greatest favourite, and the object of his greatest affections. No doubt seems to be entertained about the matter. Yet he is esteemed a man of talents and great openness insomuch that Mr. Liston said if he was asked about it and it was true he did not doubt but he would confess it. He is supposed to have been the author of all that the King did, of his expensive amusements as well as his wars. He is first Lord of the Bedchamber, Governor of Stockholm, and Colonel of a Regiment.

Madame Piper.* Is the daughter of the old Count Fersen who has always been at the head of opposition. The Duke of Ostrogothia wished to have married her but she would not have him. She is supposed to be very accessible, and to have sacrificed largely to Cupid notwithstanding her Madonna face.

When the King appeared we formed a ring round him; and he made the circuit paying his compliments and saying a few words first to one person and then another in order with all the preciseness and gravity of a hackneyed courtier, though he is but in his fourteenth year. He is small of his age but has a sensible, expressive countenance. When he came to where we stood Mr. Liston presented us; we bowed, and he in a very low voice, for which he is remarkable, addressing himself to Bootle said, combien de temps restez vous ici. Bootle did not hear what he said and therefore could not make him any answer, upon which he presently passed on.

A thing happened today which had hardly ever happened before. Dinner was not ready for some time after he had made all his speeches, the consequence of which was that he was obliged to speak again to several of the people by way of passing the time. We all adjourned afterwards to see him dine. The Duke of Sodermania* sat at one end of a long table and the Dutchess at the other, while the King sat in the middle on one side. The foreign Ministers and the strangers all stood together in one particular place. The rule is for him to call up the former one after another and to talk with them during the dinner.

One of the pages said a very short grace; the King then washed and left the room. When this ceremony was over we then, being as strangers to dine at the Marshall's table, repaired to the salle des etats, where we sat I think not less than eighty people to a very bad dinner. There was but one kind of wine and the meat was hardly sweet.

Mr. Liston had dined at another table as a public Minister with the ladies. When we met him again we were carried by him to the apartments of two or three ladies belonging to the court in order to be presented to them. In every one of these we found company. After this we went to the Duke of Sodermania's levee. From the Duke's drawing-room we adjourned to that of the Dutchess, who asked us where we came from, where we were going and so on. Bootle told her we were going to China. The Ladies when she came up either kissed her hand or her face, according to their rank; a Senator's wife alone has the right to do the latter.

A maid of honour who was never married, avowedly the mistress of Armfeldt, by whom she has two children, stood near us. Whenever her time approaches for being brought to bed, she goes into the country pretending illness.

The Dutchess of Sodermania was once they say very handsome and I can conceive it. She has a very odd way of bowing to the person whom she addresses. Her gait too is very remarkable. Like all the other ladies she was painted à la francaise.

The Dutchess was soon deserted by the Duke. She was afraid of having connections with him lest she should prove with child. She therefore had recourse to her own sex. Her first and greatest favourite is supposed to be a great fat Frenchwoman. What a Court!

With this presentation the ceremony of the day ended to my great joy, for I was most completely tired; I cannot indeed boast that I passed time pleasantly.

Monday, 16th July

As we returned last night from Dronningholm, we were shewn Count Horn's house at a small distance, the house where the conspirators formed their designs against the King's life.

An Edict has this day been published for allowing under certain restrictions the liberty of the Press. The late King it seems at the revolution had made a fine speech in praise of this liberty, which he afterwards, petit à petit, by little ordinances published from time to time, so completely destroyed that the editor of the Gazette was not permitted to insert the most ordinary article of foreign intelligence. He all the while exercised the privilege of saying whatever he pleased to the public. It was by this means that in 1789 he succeeded in persuading the great body of the people that the Russians had been the aggressors, although the Nobility were well acquainted with the trick which he had employed on that occasion. They even attempted by written papers to apprize the people of the truth. The authors, however, were found out and were actually lying in prison for this offence at the time of his death.

The Edict is much too long and too much in the form of a dissertation. The late King as is well known indulged in the liberty of sticking up pasquinades at the same time that he was so strict with regard to the press. One might fancy that the Edict has an allusion to that circumstance. We heard a translation of it read today after dinner at Mr. Ludolf's, by M. D'escars to a circle of French emigrés, or persons at least not likely to hear with pleasure so many strong expressions in favour of liberty. It was amusing to hear them reprobate and ridicule it.

With regard to the last Diet, he had been taking measures a long time beforehand. It was held at Gefle because he could not rely so much as formerly on the attachment of the inhabitants of Stockholm. At Gefle he carried the matter with a very high hand. He had a body of troops in the town provided with Cannon and all the other apparatus of war. No person was suffered to come without a pass; and if he was a person at all suspected, his actions were all watched. The Tyranny of these measures was insisted upon by Ankestrom in his confessions as one of the principal reasons for the desperate act which he committed.

An old woman at Stockholm, who passes for a prophetess,* about five years ago bad the King have a care of the first man whom he should meet with after leaving her house in red. He met immediately afterwards with Ribbing, just arrived from France, for he was in that service and actually dressed in red. The thing struck him so much that after the first salutation, the King said, Mais Monsieur, est-ce-que vous avez quelque chose contre nous? Oh! non, Sire, he replied with earnestness. Nous sommes donc de bons amis, said he. Oh! assurément, Sire, answered Ribbing. Fort bien, fort bien, said the King, and went. From this time he took an aversion to red coats. For which reason no person wore such a thing at Stockholm. Mr. Liston brought one with him but could never make use of it. Had he [the King] been alive, Westley could not on that account have gone to court in his uniform.

After this he frequently visited this old lady, and she repeatedly charged him to beware of the month of March. This dwelt upon his mind and made him exceedingly anxious to close the business of the Diet by the end of February. He was so urgent that his impatience became almost insufferable. On his return to Stockholm, he observed to somebody, 'cependant le mois de Mars s'avance'. The assassination however was committed in this month; and what is more remarkable only the day after the ides. It is remarkable also that Ribbing was at least the chief instigator of it. He it was who tapped the King on the shoulder and said, bon soir beau masque, by way of pointing the King out to Ankestrom; it was he also who, they say, laid his hand over the pan [of the pistol] to hide the flash.

The late King was fond of walking about the grounds at Haga gate alone; but he was so continually interrupted by people presenting petitions that he gave orders not to grant admittance to any one, and it became very difficult to get a sight of it. That difficulty still remains; we were therefore glad to accompany a party this evening thither who had got leave. Mr. Liston was so obliging as to carry us in his carriage. This favourite residence of the late King is situated about two miles from Stockholm on the Bransvick or Lake of Brans. The house consists of a centre and two wings with a single floor, forming altogether a long line. The principal apartments are an Anteroom and three others fitted up in a very shewy ostentatious way, not a little emblematical of their late owner. The first was hung with paintings copied from those found at Herculaneum. The last made up almost wholly of windows and looking glasses. They were all ornamented with a great deal of exquisite gilding, an Art which has been carried in this country to great perfection.

We saw his bedroom with particular sensibility because it was on the Sopha in this room that he was lying when Horn and Ankestrom reconnoitered the house in order to consider the practicability of carrying him off. They saw him through the window asleep, I think; and as his hair had been just dressed and the powder not wiped off, from the paleness of his face they concluded that he had fallen into an apoplexy.

His library is a charming little fantastic room; a gothic altar serves for the stove. Upon an eminence opposite to the house he has built a sort of chinese Temple and not far from it was at the time of his death erecting another temple in the Grecian style, but according to none of the five Orders.

Tuesday, 17th July

The King was a great Match Maker. There was a mutual effection between Ribbing and a great heiress. The King prevented the Match and effected one between her and Nielson (the person on whose arm he was supporting himself at the time when he was shot). A Duel between the two rivals was the consequence in which Ribbing was wounded. The lady died of a broken heart. This is supposed to have laid the foundation of Ribbing's antipathy to the King.

The Duke seems to be getting rid as fast as he can of all the King's friends. The deputy governor is sent away as well as Armfeldt.

3 St. Petersburg

Sunday, 4th November, 1792

By the assistance of Mr. Gould* and Colonel S., the governor of the Post, we crossed the Neva this morning, which we had gone to bed under the apprehension of not being able to do for some days. Col. S., under whose protection we had left our carriage and whom we called upon on our way to the river, had launched a large boat on purpose for us. We had first to worm our passage through a thick disjointed mass or crust of ice which was flowing down the river, of which in breadth it occupied perhaps a third part. After extricating ourselves from this, we came to a narrow channel which was entirely clear; and last of all to a large sheet of smooth ice covering near one half of the river, over which we walked supported by two men, for it was very slippery. I entertained no doubts of its being strong enough to bear us, because I observed that it was a good deal scated upon.

The Taurida,* i.e. the late Prince Potemkin's palace, alias the Horse Guards, alias the Queen's autumn palace (for it goes under all these names), this palace I say, and the Couvent des Demoiselles nobles* make a fine appearance from the water. Our entrée into Petersburg by accident was as imposing as it well could be. For the nearest way to Mr. Gould's house being through the Horse Guards, our entrée may be considered to have been by the superb hall and outer garden adjoining to that palace.

When we had eaten a second breakfast with our friend Mr. Gould we repaired to our lodgings at the Nobles' Club* . . . and were visited soon after there by Lord Granville Leveson* and Mr. Paget,* of whom the latter invited us to dinner with Mr. Whitworth* the English minister. We called, however, before we went to dine with him on Lord Borringdon.*

I cannot describe the impressions which were made this morning on my mind by the first sight of this magnificent town, which in grandeur very far exceeds every other that I have seen. But I am particularly struck in all the private as well as public edifices with such an uncommon display of Grecian Architecture, which might lead us to fancy ourselves under the genial atmosphere of Athens, instead of so northern a latitude.

Our party at Mr. Whitworth's except one Frenchman, the Abbé Girot, were all English, viz Lord Dalkeith,* Lord Borringdon, Lord Granville Leveson, Mr. Graham, Mr. Paget, Mr. Eaton the private secretary, Mr. Gould and ourselves. Mr. Whitworth being engaged, apologized for leaving us in the evening; we stayed a little time after him and then retired to our lodgings, highly pleased with the polite manners and uncommon civilities of our hospitable country- man. The rest of the company went to an Assembly at the Grand Chancellor's.

Monday, 5th November

Mr. Whitworth received us very kindly, made an offer to be of any service to us in his power, and begged whenever we should not be otherwise engaged, to dine at his house. Even when he dines from home himself a dinner is provided and the English frequent their usual ordinary. 'My inn,' he said to us with great good humour, 'is perhaps better than yours'.

Wednesday, 7th November

About seven we accompanied Mr. Whitworth and Mr. Paget to Count Osterman's,* the Prime Minister's, that being a preliminary to our presentation at Court, because it is by him that our names are announced to the Empress.* We found him with two other gentlemen and two ladies, to whom we made our bows as well as to him. The ladies immediately retired, and we sat down in a formal circle which was increased from time to time by the drop- ping in first of one person and another.

Count Osterman in person is said to resemble Lord Westcote;* being a tall, thin man with a protruding belly. He is not supposed to have much or indeed any weight in her Majesty's Councils; but is merely the organ for conveying to her the instructions of foreign Ministers and reporting to them in return her own good will and pleasure. Yet though possessing only the shadow of power, and endowed with very moderate talents, at these conversations in his own house he assumes the airs of the distracted Statesman and behaves with all the pride of a real authority, sitting sometimes entirely silent and sometimes addressing his whole conversation to a single person. He was said to be in a very tolerable good humour this evening. His house is open in this way every night; and the Ministers make a point of attending him in general on a Wednesday. The Count understands English. Paget and he are not friends; they had not spoke for the last twelvemonth, though before that they had been very courteous.

After discoursing about half an hour we withdrew, and by the invitation of Mr. Whitworth, who was going himself to Prince Gallitzin's,* we returned to his house, where I had a long and interesting conversation with Mr. Eaton.

Here follows notes of the conversation.

In the Greek church they are almost as superstitious as in the Roman Catholic and their houses are all furnished with holy pictures to which they pay great respect, never failing to bow and cross themselves when they enter the room where they are. Gould happened to have a print of Wilkes in his parlour. The Russians being in the habit of paying their devotion to pictures, when they came to him on business, first of all very often offered up their worship to what they perhaps imagined might be his favourite Saint. Mr. Sarbova, a friend of Gould's and a clergyman who had been in England and known John's character, was scandalized at this prostitution of divine honours and persuaded Gould to take down his saint and put him out of the way.

The whole religion of this country is said even among the common people to consist in the observance of these forms and of certain feasts and festivals. But as to Morality, that is wholly out of the question. The higher classes of people pay even no regard to the former. In low life the women are all whores, i.e. the married women. When the men find it out they beat them and there it ends. In high life the husbands, if they find out the infidelity of their wives, pass it over. The women, however, in high life observe some kind of decency and keep up appearances, though most of them have their private connections. There are some, however, who having married from affection are supposed to be faithful to their husbands.

The Empress attends very much to the education of her Grandsons and employs a great deal of her own time in instructing them and instilling into them her principles. The second Grandson Constantine* had Greek Nurses and has been taught the Greek language, evidently with a view to the crown of Constantinople. Eaton persuades himself that this is still the object and if the Empress lives ten years it will be accomplished.

It is believed that the Grand Duke* will never be Emperor. His mother does not pay the smallest deference to his opinions. Even if he does succeed, it is to be feared. For he is anxious to make

alterations and regulations which would render it more difficult to
commit abuses. The People in office live and fatten upon these,
this is what renders them well affected to the present Government;
this is what they will never suffer to be done away if they can
help it.

The Nobility at Petersburg are not the oldest and most respectable families. These reside at Moscow. Both Markoff* and
Besborodko* are what may be called upstarts. She [Catherine] does
everything in her power to keep the great people here attached to
her. They are left to do almost what they please with impunity.
The most severe punishment they have to fear is a dismissal from
their places and this is but rarely given. On their relations and
dependants all the good things in the gift of the Crown are
bestowed; and to this it is owing that the Army and Navy are so
ill officered.

Potemkin* is the only great Minister she ever had. Since his
death she has been her own. The absence of Besborodko for the
purpose of negotiating the peace has contributed to render her
more independent of him than she was before. Before that he had
been used to take down and digest her ideas. But upon his absence
she acquired a habit of doing it for herself. Markoff, who is about
thirty-six, is considered to have as much influence as any man.
It was he who drew up the public Papers relating to the Polish
Business.*

They open all the private letters, and copy all the dispatches.
There's a book containing all the dispatches of each Minister. The
Empress wrote once a letter in a feigned hand and containing some
obnoxious passages to see whether it would be opened and stopped,
and whether they observed her orders of examining all private
letters. Not receiving an account of it as soon as she expected,
she told what she had done and enquired why the obnoxious
passages in that letter had not been reported to her. The answer
was that it belonged to the department of Riga to examine it; and
accordingly soon after a copy of these parts of the letter was
received from thence.

The Empress certainly pays the Swedes a subsidy of £100,000.
A good part of it passed through Mr. Bayley's hands. In answer
to my question why it was done, they [Whitworth and Paget]
seemed to say, in order to keep the Swedes quiet and because they
were afraid of them. Yet Mr. Whitworth asked me whether the
Swedes appeared to be under any apprehensions from the Russians.

The Windows here are all double and never opened. They have
Thermometers both to show the external cold and to regulate the
internal heat. When the cold is down to 15° [below freezing point]

all the public places by order of the Empress are shut on account
of the danger incurred by waiting to coachmen and such people.
There are times when the intenseness of the cold keeps everybody
in the house. For instance when it is down to 32° or 33°, which
is the lowest point. At such a time not a soul is to be seen in
the street.

The grapes which they have at their tables here come from
Astracan, 1,500 miles by water. They pack them up with Canary
seed which fills the interstices and prevents them from foaming.

A carriage in this country is very cheap. No Person under the
rank of Brigadier General can run six horses. We with our horses
rank as Major Generals.

Thursday, 8th November

In the evening we called on Mr. H[ineham]. . . . I did not know
before that the Sister of the Princess D[ashkova]* was the mistress
of Peter III: the order which she wore was given after the revolution to the Princess.

Friday, 9th November

Lord Dalkeith, Gershore,* Sir Watkin Williams Wynn* and ourselves was the whole of our party today at Mr. Whitworth's. N. B.
Whitworth was in the Guards and served three years in America,
which he says was the most pleasant part of his life. On his return
he outran his income, went to Paris where he became acquainted
with the Duke of Dorset, to whom he is indebted for his present
appointment. He is supposed to be in the good graces here of the
favourite's sister.*

In the evening we went to the Russian play. I could almost have
fancied that the actors sometimes were speaking Italian. The name
of the piece was Tasa,* the subject a young Czar visiting different
courts and the author her Russian Majesty, who made a present
to the theatre of the dresses, of which a great variety is required
for the costumes of the several countries. Not having glasses with
me, I was deprived of the only pleasure which a person ignorant
of the language and not possessed of the finest ear for Music could
derive from such an entertainment.

Mr. Whitworth having procured us tickets from the theatre, we
repaired to the Noble's Club to an Assembly of Gentlemen and
Ladies who meet at the house where we lodge every Friday evening.
There was a room for dancing as well as for Cards. Their dances
were all either English or Polonese, especially a walking Polonese

dance said to be invented by the present King of Poland for the sake of talking with some lady who was agreeable to him. I could not help observing how universally the men's dresses were in our Fashion. As it was a ball the young men make a point of going in an undress. Though the several people of the first fashion subscribe to this meeting, it is considered, I find, a melange, where many persons of an inferior rank appear, and where the first rank of people in general do not shew themselves.

I saw the Prince and Princess Dolgorucki* enter. From the manner in which he went round paying his compliments I was ready to take him for a Sovereign in his own drawing room. The young Princess Galitzin* to whom the Prince of Wales was so partial was one of the company. Between eleven and twelve I stole away and went to bed, having declined Lord G. Leveson's invitation to partake of a great supper which would unavoidably have kept me up till three o'clock in the morning. . . . The Stars and Ribbands were so common that they could hardly be regarded as a distinction. The Countess Tolstoi* I thought the prettiest woman there.

Among the Russians while the Man kisses the Lady's hand, she will sometimes kiss his cheek. Ladies, I think, kiss each others' hands with great elegance and ease.

Saturday, 10th November

In walking through this fine Town one cannot help foreseeing that if ever it comes to be neglected it must necessarily become very forlorn and ragged, from the stucco dropping off, which will expose the shabby brickwork behind.

Zeuboff,* the present favourite, has held his present situation, to which he was recommended by a Saltikoff, about three years though he is still no more than twenty-two. His influence with the Empress in regard to public matters is very great; any person would be glad to treat through him, such is indeed the estimation in which he is held that his levées, if he held levées, would be as much crowded as those of the Empress; and as it is he is attended every morning by fifty persons or more who come to pay their court. His apartments are on the Ground floor under those of the Empress, with which they communicate by a private staircase. They do not stay together but their interviews are supposed to be after dinner.

His Predecessor (whose name I think was Manhoff*) had been appointed by Potemkin. The Empress had an affection for him. Yet he was tired and disgusted with his situation to such a degree that he opened his mind to Potemkin, who entreated him to support it till he returned from the war for a few months, promising to devise some method of extricating him from his situation with a good grace and wishing to have an opportunity of appointing a successor. In the meantime, however, his feelings being entirely overcome, he threw himself at her Majesty's feet and confessed himself unworthy of the favours which she was continually heaping upon him, for that it was not in his power to return her affection, being in love with another person.

The Empress, though thunderstruck at this avowal, for she was attached to the man, decided immediately on the line of conduct she would pursue; and having learnt that it was one of her own Maids of honour, sent for her directly; saw them aspoused with her own eyes; gave orders for them to be married that same night and of course to quit the palace, and afterwards commanded them to go and live at Moscow, having first conferred such presents or such settlement on her late lover as to enable him to live in good splendour. He is now, however, tired of his wife and regrets the life which he led at court. He was an ingenious character with talents that qualified him for business and if he could have supported the disgust of his situation would have taken a lead in public affairs and amassed as great a fortune as Orloff.*

As soon as this revolution happened, several people wished to appoint a successor. It was thought, however, that her Majesty would have waited the return of Prince Potemkin, if she had wished to shew herself unaffected by the desertion of M[amonov]. For that reason she very soon afterwards fixed her choice on Zeuboff.

Sunday, 11th November

We attended the English Minister between eleven and twelve to the Imperial Palace for the purpose of being presented to the Empress. In the Saloon where the ceremony is performed we found all the foreign ministers, to whom we were introduced, and a great number of strangers, nobility and officers assembled waiting for her Majesty to pass from the Chapel Royal [through] which we had come on our way. In this assembly half a dozen C[ossacks], dressed in furred cloaks and pointed caps, and the Poles with their black crowns of hair shaved round, made the most conspicuous figure.

The foreign Ministers formed a lane at the entrance of the room, and the line on her Majesty's left was continued by the foreigners who came to be presented. She was preceded by a large troop of Gentlemen in waiting, and as soon as she had entered stopped to receive the Homage of the foreign Ministers and all those foreigners, if there, who had already been presented. Each of them advanced from his place, kissed her hand, putting his gently under it, made a bow and retired. The only person among these to whom she spoke was the Austrian Ambassador, Count Cobenzl.*

She then came forwards, opposite to where we stood who came to be presented. Besides ourselves and Sir W. W. Wynn, a Polish nobleman was of the number and was placed first. The Vice-Chancellor Count Osterman presented us mentioning our names one after the other and we one after the other kissed her hand in the same manner as I have described before. The Empress is generally followed by the favourite M. Zeuboff, but having lost a particular friend Count Saltikoff the preceding evening he was under so much grief that he did not appear. She was followed, however, by a numerous train who passed curtsying along and afterwards sat down to receive the compliments of the men.

I forgot to mention that the lane formed by the foreign Ministers in the Saloon was continued without by a party of guards making a fine appearance.

From Court we returned to Mr. Whitworth's, where we remained until it was time to go to the Vice-Chancellor's Count Osterman, who had invited all the English to dinner. The . . . Count made a point of being exceedingly civil to us. . . . A round table was set out in the drawing room before dinner with bread, butter, cheeses and liqueurs of various kinds. They played at Cards both before dinner and after. Their game was Boston, an American game much in fashion here, being a mixture of Ombre and Whist. Philadelphia is another American game which is also in vogue at Petersburg. . . . The Count is much older than his lady and after the first unsuccessful night is said never to have slept with her.

Here follow notes on Potemkin.

He was a native of Russia and had his education in this country. The fine house now called the Horse Guards was too small for him, which alone Mr. Whitworth observed was sufficient to give an idea of the man. He had built a house at Bender as large as this at Petersburg and was building one at forty V[ersts]* from Petersburg much larger.

Till of late he did not like the company and never admitted them to his table. He could hardly be known for the same man when he was in good humour and when he was not. He had a custom when out of humour of biting his nails to such a degree that at one time he was very near bringing on some kind of a disorder by it. He was by no means, however, a revengful, malicious man. He treated his enemies with too much contempt for that. He

literally turned up his nose at them. His only support was the
Empress. For at heart every body else was his foe.

No Man possessing so much power ever did so little mischief.
The Empress is still supposed to go on with his plans. She shews
great respect to all his relations; among whom his fortune will be
divided, the Empress reserving only two Millions of roubles in
order to discharge his debts. Had he lived he certainly would have
gone on to Constantinople (Eaton). Gould says that he compre-
hended and understood everything. Yet Whitworth told me that
he looked upon his attainments to have been superficial.

He was 'willige' or great Hetman of the Cossacks.

At the Revolution in 1762 the Empress having no sword,* she
took one from Potemkin who happened to stand in the way. He
afterwards distinguished himself by affecting madness* out of his
love for her Majesty, and used to be walking perpetually under
her windows, mimicking all the airs and attitudes of insanity.

Potemkin was a strange mixture of things with regard to the
time of day. He would place [himself] under a Fountain and suffer
the water to come all over him without changing his cloaths. He
was uncommonly hardy; and used to sleep in a latticed sort of
Tent through which he could see all round him (Gould). G[ould]
does not hesitate to suspect that he was poisoned. He died having
ordered himself to be taken out of the carriage for that purpose.
The prospect of a peace, Gould thinks, hurt him. Pointing to a
ship which he had built, in that ship, he said to Gould, I shall
go to Constantinople.

Had Potemkin lived to return he would have removed the present
favourite. The Father of the present favourite, old Zeuboff,* was
probably accessory to his death. For the Empress, though not
afraid of him, was zealous [? jealous] of his reputation. Indeed
when he was there nobody, not even the Empress herself, was
thought of, the Prince was everything. When there were but two or
three carriages at court there would [be] a long string of carriages
at the door of the Prince. There was a decree empowering the
Prince to draw upon the treasury for any sums he pleased, without
being obliged to give an account of them.

He was for two years, from '75 to '77 inclusive, the favourite.
Foreseeing however, that he might [not] continue in favour always
as such, he contrived to make himself useful and necessary to her
Majesty as a man of Business. He contrived also to escape from
this situation in her good graces so highly that he was suffered to
appoint his successor.* And upon this successor's conceiving that
he might throw down the ladder by which he rose, he had interest
enough to remove him and put another person in his place.

About the year '79 he took very much to reading; and having an exceeding retentive memory, acquired in the course of two years a prodigious deal of Knowledge. About '81 or '82 he conceived a passion for travelling, and visited the southern parts of the Empire, where he conceived all the projects in regard to the Crimea, etc., which have been since put into execution.

It was but about four years before his death that he indulged in a passion for women. Such was the servility and depravity of the People here, that the last time he was at Petersburg women of the first rank made him the offer of their daughters. Old Nargekin was proud of the honour which he conferred on his daughters by debauching them.

At the time of Potemkin's death 40,000 men were actually on their march to take possession of the country belonging to the Chinese and lying on the north of the Amoy,* with a view to extend their conquests to Japan. This fact is not generally known. The Chinese themselves are not aware of this fact except by means of the English. The objects of the British Embassy to China are supposed to be in the first place a complaint in regard to the Monopoly at Canton and secondly to acquaint them with the views of the Russians. On which account they are exceedingly provoked at it.

When the news of the peace with Turkey arrived the fleets had actually set sail for Constantinople. Eaton saw the plan of attack and he thinks that it could not have failed of succeeding. Potemkin either had, or if he had lived, would certainly have broken the peace. The Turks had furnished excuses enough. In which case Constantinople would certainly have fallen. Potemkin was not aboard the fleet himself.

He and Markoff and another were deputed when young men by the University of which they were members to pay the Empress some compliment. She at that time remarked his physiognomy and ever after called him her 'eleve'.*

Having by some improper treatment brought on a cataract* at one time, he resolved to take his leave of society and appear no more disfigured after such a manner in company. The Empress in order to draw him out of his retreat, paid him a visit attended by all the people she could collect. He could not refuse himself. You are now, she said, as much seen as you can be; it is vain to shun the public eye any longer; quit now your retreat and come again into the world; for you have no longer the same reason as you had for remaining out of it.

Garing . . . told us, if he had lived, he very much believed that he would have turned Priest* at last: for that he sometimes took a fancy to hear Mass said while, in the adjoining room, he was lying on a couch and listening to the Music.

The whole Empire were his enemies; yet he kept his ground. Many a time when he came back to Petersburg and all the world expected him to be seized and imprisoned, contrary to their expectations he appeared as usual in all the plenitude of power. It is believed that he has often made the Empress herself tremble.

All his ideas were great. But as he had not a good education and had not acquired a just and true [discernment], he had [in] all the Arts, in Music, in Architecture and everything, a way of thinking peculiar to himself, sublime but fantastic and incorrect. I think that he was a composer in Music.*

Potocki* told me that Potemkin was a great Physiognomist, and that after regarding a Man from head to foot, as he had a custom of doing, he formed an idea of his character and was seldom mistaken.

Miss Betsy was at the fete given by Potemkin to the Empress either July twelvemonth or July two years [ago].* Two thousand persons were invited. The Empress arrived at seven, after which they walked about for a short time and then went to the theatre. In the meantime the Apartments were all lighted up and made a most splendid appearance. As soon as the play was over they sat down to supper. When the Empress went away, Miss Betsy saw the Prince kneel down before her and perceived him saying something to her, the purport of which was, as she afterwards understood, that he was obliged for everything he had to her bounty. That year there were balls every night because he had expressed a desire that these should [take place].

Every body rejoiced at his death. The Princess [Dashkova]* rejoices because she thinks that he was such an expence to the country.

He had promised to send Eaton* as Consul to Naples, from which he was to have proceeded with proper Artists to Athens in order to take casts of all the most valuable basso rilievos there which he would have deposited in his University at Catherinehoff,* a Town that he founded (I think a hundred and eighty Versts above Cherson, where he was also building a Cathedral).

While the Princess Dolgorucki was with the Army at Jassy he tried in vain to seduce [her]. He was equally unsuccessful with his niece Mad^me Potemkin,* who having [been] whipt by him when a child, had taken a violent aversion to him. Her virtue would not have stood in the way of his wishes. Another of his nieces was more complaisant. The last of his Mistresses is said to have been the Princess Michel Galitzin.* His influence was so great at Peters-

burg that Hineham did not doubt that he might have commanded
even the young Princesses Galitzin.

Here follow some remarks on Potemkin by the Princess Dashkova.

The Empress herself was afraid to contradict him. He was the
most extraordinary man during his life: and it is no less extraordinary that since his death his influence may be said to survive
him; for the Empress puts into execution all his plans.

The Princess Dashkoff used to tell him roundly that he was
no longer the same man, that she did not know him for the same
creature, that he was become a perfect child. How can you, she
would say, with so many affairs on your hands, how can you pass
whole days together in talking nonsense to a fond girl. When she
quarrelled with the Princess M. Galitzin, he came and interceded
for her in the most humble and insinuating terms. For a whole
week he continued those applications. He renewed them particularly at the Hermitage one day when he was sitting between her
and the Empress, at what time their conversation was so loud, that
her Majesty asked if they were quarrelling. The Princess in stating
the case told her Majesty that Potemkin was become a perfect
child; to which [he] replied with some acrimony 'Si je suis enfant,
dieu merci que je ne suis pas tombé dans l'enfance'.

At the same time that she allows his great talents, his insinuating
manners, she calls him the flea of Russia and thinks his death a
good thing for the country.

Monday, 12th November

We called this morning on Dr. Pallas,* who lives two Versts out
of Town; we did not, however, find him at home; he was with the
little Grand Duke giving him a lecture at the Hermitage; but we
met with Mrs. Pallas and sat with her for some time. She told us
a good story of a Mrs. Camarode, who, being wife to her Majesty's
Gardener, expected to be received and noticed in the best company
as everybody belonging to the Empress is here, her Gardeners, her
Valet de Chambre and her Grooms. But not finding that the case,
she took at much dudgeon and came away much dissatisfied.

Mrs. Pallas' Grandfather or Grandmother was English. She also
is a native of Hanover, for which reasons she considers herself
as almost an Englishwoman. I have observed that the Hanoverians
are always very fond of claiming their connexion with us.

Mr. Pallas sets off in the beginning of the year for Astracan, from
whence he proposes to make a tour into Persia. They intend after-

wards to visit England and Italy. He pretends that the number of foreigners who are recommended to him and whom he is obliged to entertain compel him to leave Petersburg. But I suspect by what fell from Mr. Whitworth today that the place itself is disagreeable to him.

In the evening we went to see Democrite* at the wooden Theatre and afterwards accompanied Mr. Whitworth to Count Saltikoff's* and Prince Galitzin's; but got admittance at neither place.

It seems to be thought that they did not understand the effect and extent of the Armed Neutrality in this country when they proposed it: that the French contrived to make it appear as her Majesty's own measure; and having done so, there was a certainty of her abiding by it; for that is one of the leading features of her character not to recede from an opinion or a resolution.

Tuesday, 13th November

Dr. Rogerson,* a Scotchman and Physician to the Empress, was of our party to dinner at Mr. Whitworth's. Dr. Rogers [*sic*] told me that the deaths within a certain time were become two in a hundred fewer than they were in the year: and that Putrid Fevers are now very uncommon. He does not think that the Dysentery which People are liable to be seized with on their arrival here is owing to the water so much as to the Air. He reasoning from the Analyses of the water and from the case of several people who have been seized with it without drinking the water.

About half after five Bootle [and I] paid another visit to the Princess Dashkoff, who though in deshabille was so good as to receive us. We sat with her for a considerable time. Her conversation evidently savoured of disaffection to the Empress; she regretted a constitution like ours, she spoke of their abode in Petersburg as a sort of exile, she seemed unwilling to allow the present Sovereign the smallest merit for what she had done towards the embellishment of the Town.

Our conversation turned upon the Duke of Sodermania,* whom she had known at Spa, and who then discovered a want of affection for his relations, and as his brother had no children, the hopes of succeeding to the throne.

Between eight and nine, Mr. Whitworth conducted Sir W. W. Wynn and us to the Duke of Sierra Capriola's,* the Neapolitan Minister, where there was a ball and a supper to which we had been invited. Here we were presented by Mr. Whitworth to several gentlemen and to ladies without end, whose names, however, he did not think it necessary to mention. We went round a whole circle bowing in order, first to one and then to another. I neither knew their names nor should I know them again by sight. They, however, recollect who have been introduced to them better than we to whom we have been introduced. Besides, it is a form necessary to be observed.

From this time to about twelve they continued dancing à la polonaise, which is literally no more than a walk, and à l'anglaise alternately. When a polonaise dance begins, any gentleman standing near to a lady offers her his hand and joins the procession: when the tune is done you bow to the lady, another tune commences and you offer your hand to another lady. You [are] given an opportunity of talking by turns to all the ladies in the room and [this] makes an agreeable change.

At about twelve the greatest part of the company sat down to supper. A few stood and got helped to what they liked behind the chairs of those who sat. Most of the People except the dancers stole away as soon as supper was over. Lord Borringdon was so obliging as to sit me down: 'Qu'avec vous M. l'Ambassadeur de Suede'. A great deal of the best company in Petersburg were present on this occasion; especially the Nariskin, the Saltikoff and Galitzin families.

Wednesday, 14th November

Before dinner yesterday the Vice Chancellor Count Osterman desired Mr. Whitworth to send the names of all the English who had been presented. This was the prelude to an invitation which we received from her Majesty this morning to a play at the Hermitage. There is the great Hermitage, the little Hermitage and the private Hermitage. The first is what we were at this evening and the only one to which strangers are admitted.

The Polish deputies made their acknowledgements to day to the Empress for her interference in their affairs. We repaired to Court in hopes of seeing this ceremony between eleven and twelve. As none but the four first classes of Nobility (Field Marshals, Generals in Chief, Lieutenant Generals and Major Generals) were admitted into the audience Chamber, it was doubtful at first whether strangers would be allowed this honour. . . . By the interposition of Dr. Rogerson (Dr. Rogerson has the rank of Major General) with the Master of Ceremonies we got admission however.

From the windows we saw the procession of the deputies, which consisted of six or seven coaches and six. The Empress took her seat on a throne placed under a Canopy of red velvet; the Crown and Globe and Sceptre lay on a table by her side. There were six

in all but not more than two or three of them were in the Polish
habit. They entered by a door opposite to the throne accompanied
by the proper Officers, bowing very low to her Majesty all together,
first at the door and afterwards two or three other times till they
reached the middle of the room. One of them, Branicki,* addressed
the Empress in a Polish speech which he delivered in a very
audible, manly tone of voice. He is or was Crown General. He
married Potemkin's niece and therefore is entirely in the Russian
Interests. He is even suspected of aspiring to the throne of Poland.
Her Majesty sat with a very dignified and imperious air; supporting
her right hand with her fan. She wore a star and I think a red
ribband. We can think of nobody whom she reminds us of more
than Mr. Leycester of Toft. Her manner was much more Majestic
than it was on Monday. On Sunday she appeared very gracious and
condescending. Count Osterman replied in the Russian language on
the part of the Empress, but in so low a tone that if his speech
had been in English, I could not have understood him. The
speech of the Pole might last about ten minutes and that of the
Russian about five. Count Osterman not venturing to depend on
his memory held a copy of his oration in his hat, to which he was
continually turning his eyes like the Dean of a College presenting
a young man to his degree for the first time. Bootle says that while
he was speaking the Empress smiled at her Minister's embarrass-
ment and spoke to some person behind her. As soon as the reply
was finished the Polish deputies, preceded by Branicki, advanced
towards the throne bowing to present the public letter of thanks
with which they were charged and to kiss the Empress's hand:
after which they retired the same way they had come, walking
backwards and repeatedly bowing. The Empress then withdrew,
handed from the throne as she had been handed to it by the grand
Ecuyer, Nariskin.* Several ladies were present at the ceremony; and
they took their places all together on her Majesty's right hand.

While we were waiting in what I believe they call the presence
Chamber, the four eldest Princesses* passed through the crowd on
their way to the Empress's apartments to pay their respects: and
afterwards the two grand Dukes. They also returned through the
same room, receiving as they went along every possible [mark] of
attention and reverence. The two eldest Princesses seem to be about
seven, eight or nine, the two youngest are quite children. There
is a fifth, an infant. These Princesses are the daughters of a Princess
who came to Petersburg along with the first Grand Duchess,* to
be fixed upon as a wife for the Grand Duke. They say that the
Empress considers it as an act of justice to her to choose one of
her daughters on this occasion. The first Grand Duchess was a

clever woman; but having shown a disposition to gallantry and intrigue, she is supposed to have been taken off. She died at least a year after her marriage. Rasomovsky* is still in exile for having been one of her lovers. The present Grand Dutchess* is a very good kind of woman; but not supposed to have great talents. The eldest [of the Grand Dukes], Alexander,* is a stout young man, with his hair undressed, setting up his shoulders rather like an unformed Youth. His temper is said to be very amiable. Better than that of his brother, who is said in this respect to resemble the Grand Duke.

M. Zeuboff the favourite stood somewhere near the Empress but I did not get a sight of him. The variety of dresses in the Presence Chamber was very striking. There was a Turk, or rather a person in a Turkish dress, the Mufti of her Majesty's Mahometan Subjects (the Greek, who acts as an interpreter, is remarkable for repeating Homer according to the modern Greek Pronunciation and a little crazy withal). The Cossacks however were the most remarkable in this respect. One of these Cossacks in a white Uniform looked like a Butcher's boy more than an officer. Those in black might almost pass for Chimney sweepers. The greatest part of them however were in red turned up with yellow like the Staffordshire Uniform.

We dined with Mr. Yeams. . . . As unfortunately we did not sit down till past four, and we were obliged to be at the Hermitage a quarter before six, I did not [have] much time for enjoying our excellent dinner.

Our carriages not arriving in time we borrowed Dr. Rogerson's and instead of the Theatre were set down at the Grand Duke's apartments; from whence we were obliged to walk a long way to the Hermitage. In our way to the theatre we passed through a Suite of twelve apartments all crowded with paintings. Before we entered the theatre we were required to deliver our Swords. The Theatre* resembles the ancient theatres in the arrangement of the Seats, which are of a semicircular form and rise one above the other. This has a very agreeable effect and it must particularly from the stage.

The Grand Duke, the Grand Dutchess, and the young Princesses of Baden who arrived on Sunday Night, entered before the Empress and took their seats on one of the Benches. On their entering the company all stood up. The Grand Duke makes rather an insignificant appearance. The Grand Dutchess is a large woman and seemed to behave with great decorum and good humour. The eldest of the two Princesses is said to be pretty and though only 13 might very well pass for two or three Years more. The other who is only 11 seemed to me the more lively of the two. M. Zeuboff accompanied and sat near the Empress, but I did not get [a] sight of him, or of the two Grand Dukes till they were going out. The Company all stood when the Empress came in and continued standing till she sat down. The Grand Duke then set the example of doing the same. As everybody was very much dressed, particularly the men, the appearance was very brilliant. The play was Partie de chasse d'Henri IV,* and it was followed by a ballet in which le Pique* danced. It is the fashion to cry up very much the Scenes and the decorations, but I own that I was not particularly struck with them.

When the play was over Mr. Whitworth conducted us to . . . Prince Gallitzin's, where we supped. Their house is open in this manner every Wednesday; and here one meets with the best company. After supper we adjourned for a short time to where they were playing at Cards and then came away. I had a great deal of conversation with a Russian Gentleman of considerable rank, M. Anikoff,* who speaks English very well.

N.B. Doctor Rogers [sic] accompanied Prince Repnin's Embassy* in 1775. They rendezvoused at Kieff and marched from thence pitching their tents every Night, a thousand strong. In Bulgaria the leader of Banditti, who they knew wished to attack them, rode with them for several days. I think the presents filled no less than sixteen wagons. The Embassy took up a year and a half. The Turks paid so little regard to any of the presents that the Prince did not think it worth his while to give the whole.

N.B. There are a great Number of wild dogs in Petersburg, especially near the Admiralty, where they have their abode under some trees. The Empress will not suffer them to be destroyed, perhaps in opposition, somebody observed, to the humour of her Husband in this respect who sent people out to every part of the Town with Clubs for that purpose. These Dogs bear a mortal antipathy to all strange dogs. They would be a greater nuisance, however, if they were liable to go mad, which I understand they are not, either in this country or anywhere else, at least in the same proportion as with us. At Constantinople even, when you are obliged to go stepping over them in the streets, canine Madness is very uncommon. At that place a certain number of them form themselves into a sort of fraternity,* occupy two or three streets, and suffer no strangers to appear in their little domain. There are people at Constantinople who make it their business to beg for these dogs.

N.B. Mr. Whitworth said today that the Count d'Artois* was expected here and that the Empress had publickly expressed her determination to give the Emigrés an Asylum.

It is believed that the Emigrés employed the good offices of a lady to whom the King of Prussia was attached, to prevail upon him to push forwards the operations as he did [*i.e. the war against the French Revolutionaries*].

Friday, 16th November

Near the Hermitage on our way to the English line after having called on Mr. Yeams, our carriage broke down and was left with a single wheel, for the hind wheel came off and the horses ran away with the two fore ones.

Saturday, 17th November

At twelve o'clock we had appointed to go with Gould to the Taurida Palace, which was built by the late Prince Potemkin and is now the autumn residence of her imperial Majesty. We were met there by Paget with three Poles and a Polish lady. Unfortunately the young Grand Duke happened to visit the palace this morning; which obliged us, as we were seeing it in some measure by stealth, to hide ourselves for half an hour in a gallery.

This noble edifice was created in twelve months about seven or eight years ago after a design of the Prince himself. The most remarkable thing in it, however, is the great hall. This room is 60 feet broad and 250 long, terminating at each end in a bow raised a step above the floor and separated from the winter garden on one side and the salle du dome on the other by a double colonnade of eighteen Ionic Columns. Simplicity, grandeur and good taste reigns throughout, especially in the architectural decorations. In the bow at one End the Prince used to dine and has often entertained the Empress. In the bow at the other a band of Music was stationed which always played during dinner. The Empress dines in the middle of the room. The Galleries in the Colonnade were intended for Spectators. The Empress resided here about a week only this year, but she intends to make a longer residence the next.

The dome in the room which I call the 'Salle du dome' is a decagon, which as well as some other is exceedingly well managed. A temple stands in the middle of the winter garden wherein is placed a marble statue of the Empress by Shubin* with this very chaste and elegant inscription in Russian, 'To the Mother of her country and more than Mother to me'. There are two vases one at each end of the great hall, copies from the antique at Rome, adorned with bas reliefs representing a Bacchanalian procession and the sacrifice of Iphigenia, the price of which was ten thousand ducats. The garden, which consists of a number of walks winding among groves of winter plants, is embellished with marble Statues, Urns and vases. Artificial palms support the roof. The festoon and various decorations of that kind which were put up three or four years ago on occasion of a great illumination made here by the Prince still remain. On that occasion the wax alone was an expense to him of fourteen thousand roubles, [which] equals near eighteen hundred pounds. He had given orders, which orders I suppose were countermanded, for an organ to cost fifty thousand roubles.

The young duke's business this morning was to see a curious piece of Mechanism made by Cox in which a tune is played with balls; a golden peacock unfolds his plumage and a golden Cock crows. A tree with gilded leaves embellishes the work. The Peasant who gave the model of a bridge with a single arch for the Neva, distinguished by an order, acts as the showman.

We had to dress for the Imperial Minister's ball when we returned from dinner. The Ball was exceedingly brilliant. About one o'clock or half after twelve the company sat down to supper; the ladies according to what I understand is the Russian fashion, entirely separate from the men. We did not get away till near two after holding a long conversation with the Princess Dashkoff who was excessively civil. Though she blames us for some things, upon the whole she is a great admirer of the English Nation, envies us our constitution and regards a well-educated English Gentleman as the glory and perfection of his species. What renders her dissatisfied with the Government and the Court [is] among other things the *éloignement* of her son* from Petersburg. As I am told, they dread his abilities and choose therefore to keep him at a distance. She superintended his education and travelled with him herself.

Sunday, 18th November

In the evening we paid a visit at Count Osterman's where we found a formal circle, and the conversation entirely general. The Count came in soon after us, bowed very formally to the company and then sat down immediately to Cards. In entering we were almost poisoned with the Stench of the necessary. Though in fact there is no such thing in any Russian house; in the whole Palace there is said to be not one. They have however I suppose some common receptacle, from which the odours in question issued. In winter, from being froze, the inconvenience is not conceived: but in Spring, particularly when it begins to thaw, the Nuisance is insufferable.

Notes on the Empress.

They are by no means well affected to the Empress in Moscow. Two persons of some consequence, Swedenborgians by profession, have been lately sent from that place to Schlusselburg—all societies have of late been discountenanced here. The Free Masons* have not met for some time.

The Empress had expressed her surprise to hear that Lord Gower danced with his Chin in his bosom. The Princess Dashkoff advised him and Lord Borringdon, and especially Sir Watkin, to take a Dancing Master.

Monday, 19th November

. . . Bootle and I paid a visit to the Princess Dashkoff, whom we found at cards with two Cavaliers, one of the order of St. Vladimir and the other of St. Anne of Holstein. She received us with great civility and was addressing her conversation to one or other of us continually whenever her game left her at liberty. She advised us to purchase the Russian costume, i.e. the different habits of the several people who compose the Russian Empire, which are to be had here at the China Manufactory. She recommended, Extracts in five volumes quarto, from the Byzantine Historians, which consist of two hundred volumes folio; the Cryptomereous plants, an essay by a person of Vienna which got the piece issued by the Academy of Sciences here; and the Medallic History of this country, or rather engravings of all the medals since the time of Peter the Great, with comments upon them containing in fact the history of the country. She had subscribed some years ago for a print of the death of Lord Chatham and seemed to take it very well that we offered to make inquiries about it.

Tuesday, 20th November

Lord G. Leveson told us of a General S[uvorov]* who is supposed to have destroyed in the Crimea etc. not less than a million of the human species. It was this Savage that commanded at Ismail: who having orders to transplant the remainder of its inhabitants from the Crimea to the banks of the Bog or some such place, to the amount of 50,000 people, was the cause or permittor of them to perish from hunger; till at last enraged at the treachery which was used towards them, unarmed as they were, they fell on the three thousand troops who conducted them, and were cut to pieces instead of dying by famine. On setting out on this long expedition through a desert country they took no more than three days' provisions with an assurance of meeting with Magazines on the road when there was no such thing. This assurance continued to be held out till there was no possibility left of retreating.

Potemkin boasted that not more than two persons escaped from Ismail; and they he believed were starved to death.

An English Officer told Mr. Whitworth that while he was serving in the Black Sea he observed a very beautiful girl in a village near which he was stationed to whom he made love in dumb Shew and seemed to [be] not unkindly regarded. Soon after this the village was set upon by the Russians and he hastened thither as soon as he was aware of it to look after the safety of his Mistress: whom, led to the spot by the cries of female distress, he had the horror to find in the hands of three or four ruffians who were piercing this beautiful creature as she lay on the ground with repeated wounds. One of them was an officer and is now a Major General; but Mr. Whitworth would not tell his name.

Golofkin,* an officer in the Guards here, gave Bootle and Leveson the following description of a woman's life in this place. They lie in bed till very late and take what he calls a little *cochonerie* before they get up. They then dine, afterwards dress for the play, and conclude the day at some rout or ball in dancing or cards.

Wednesday, 21st November

We were so late to dinner at Dr. Pallas's that though they had not risen from table everybody had dined. He however received us with great kindness and seemed only to be sorry on our account. Dr. Pallas was born in '41. He is rather above the middle size, stoutly made, and not at all corpulent. His manners are obliging and unaffected; his conversation unassuming, judicious, deliberate and simple, but rather cold. There is something peculiar in his sight. His dress was very plain and almost negligent; viz. a dark coloured coat, a spotted waist-coat, black breeches, mixed stockings and half-boots. The waist-coat and the breeches were not new. I hope [there] is no harm in recording these particularities. Nothing but my veneration for the man should have induced me to do it. If Dr. Pallas had only been distinguished by a title or ribband I should certainly not have done it. The Order of St. Vladimir is honoured by having him in the number of its knights.

Pallas observed that though everything has gone on successfully in this country, the Ministers appear to mind nothing but their pleasure. Besborodko is said to be the greatest follower of women that ever was: yet though he never sleeps without a bedfellow, he is constantly obliged to be with the Empress between six and seven in the morning. I was surprised to hear after we came away that Mrs. Pallas was taken from the Town and was his mistress before she became his wife. She is a tall handsome woman. He has only a daughter and she, I believe, was by his former marriage.

We saw the young Grand Duke going out to take an airing in a sledge, which we particularly remarked, because over his horses there hung a white cloth which the air puffed out and swelled like a sail. This it seems is very much in use among genteel people in order to prevent the horses from throwing up the snow into the face of the riders.

Thursday, 22nd November

They furnished us with a sledge this morning for two persons with a pair of horses in it, one of which kicked and the other, if he once got the bit in his mouth, was hardly to be held in by my worst efforts. We therefore presently dismissed this equipage, and got into two hackney sledges in which [we] accompanied the whole party of English to the Yekaterinehof* to see a bear belonging to the Empress baited. Her Majesty keeps several wild beasts here and several different kinds of dogs. This identical bear undergoes a baiting of the same kind every Sunday morning for the amusement of the populace. But I thought it a very poor amusement and never paid five roubles more reluctantly for a spectacle. For as soon as ever a dog had seized poor Bruin and he in his defence attempted to hug his adversary, a number of fellows interposed with staves and prevented it. It was no wonder therefore to see the dogs fall upon it with great courage and fury because they knew by experience that they had nothing to fear. One of these animals was obliged to be conducted and held by two or three men. It was quite a sledge race to where we saw this exhibition; we went at a prodigious rate. . . .

We dined with Mr. Raikes* today, where we met Count Romanzoff* the son of the Marshal who resides at Moscow discontented with the Court, as the generality of the people at Moscow are. This gentleman, who seems to be a very sensible man, had been in England and appeared to have acquired very just ideas of our character, government and political situation. . . . He imagined that we should have much to fear, if the French Revolution was successfully established, for our tranquillity. He seemed perfectly aware of the antipathy which our common people bears to strangers. He brought a charge of inconsistency against our Constitution for giving to our Kings the power of putting their negative on bills and at the same time not permitting them to use that power. By way of parallel to the Massacres here he quoted the Massacre in Ireland. He seemed to imagine that the new French Government was likely to make a conquest of all the surrounding nations and last for three hundred years, on which I did not at all agree with him.

Till three years ago there was an Italian Opera here, but the Empress then put a stop to it, observing that they might translate the Italian operas into Russian, which would do quite as well. While the Italian opera was kept up they had the best performers that Italy could furnish.

The Empress used formerly to give a Masquerade every Sunday to the world; but when they came at last to be neglected, she ordered them to be discontinued.

The Russian Peasants are remarkable for singing in parts. They often carry on even their conversation in a kind of recitative. It was observed today that they are well made about the chest upwards but not so well below.

We went to dinner at three. Our horses, Coachmen and Postillions waited for us at the door till eight. We then went to Mr. Bayley's and they waited for us till [ten], the boys all the while on their horses and probably asleep. I have never yet observed, I think, what a Turkish appearance our Postillions make, owing particularly to the lower part of their dress.

Friday, 23rd November

We called at last this morning on Quarenghi* the Italian architect in the service of the Empress, to whom we brought compliments from Sergel. He was excessively communicative and friendly and we sat with him in his shop for a considerable time.

Quarenghi has no mercy on the Russians, whom he represents from first to last as a set of rascals. 'Des gueux, des voleurs de grand chemin', was the appellation which he bestowed most abundantly on those, particularly the generals or Lieutenant Generals, who are placed at the head of each department. He gave us a very droll account of the conversation between himself and the person with whom he was obliged to communicate at the head of a certain department, when he built the theatre at the Hermitage. This Gentleman's objection to the form of the theatre was that he knew of none like it. The sturdy architect told him that he should not alter one tittle of his plan, and that the only concern which he had with it was to furnish him with brick and mortar.

One of these gentlemen, when Falconet* was going to cast the statue of Peter the Great, said to him one day, as if he had been a brother Artist, 'Let us consider how we are to manage about the casting of this horse'. Falconet proudly spurned at his interference.

Quarenghi is going to leave the country. He has sent away already all his books and papers. The principal buildings he has erected here are the Exchange, the Bank, the Academy of Sciences, the theatre at the Hermitage and the Raphael's Gallery, besides three houses at Peterhof. He disapproves entirely of introducing without distinction such a quantity of Architecture, as everyone must remark at Petersburg. It gives him a surfeit, he says, of the Grecian column to see it prostituted in such a manner.

We dined at Mr. Whitworth's where in addition to the usual English Party, we met with the Abbé Girot and Prince Sapieha, one of the Polish Deputies whom his father, the Crown General, has obliged to come on this errand contrary to his own sentiments and inclinations.

At Laff's this evening,* where we paid a visit before we went to the Ball in our own house, we met with a great variety of Characters, though the company was but small: for instance, the old Greek Dragoman, a Pole in his proper dress, the Son of the Turkish Basha, the Tartar Sultan, Baron Vergara etc.

Saturday, 24th November

The glass has fallen and it snows. I have taken my first lesson this morning in German.

Three of the Poles, Brotocki, Potocki* and Ogenski,* dined with us today at Mr. Whitworth's. Potocki has considerable demands on the Russian Government for supplies furnished. . . . In his heart he is supposed to dislike the Russians but this consideration keeps him in awe. We stayed here till it was time to go to M. Bezborodko's where we were invited to a ball.

The Count Bezborodko seldom gives balls and this was supposed to be in compliment to the Polish and English strangers. The company was estimated at three hundred, including several persons of inferior fashion, all the most genteel people in Petersburg. The very spacious apartment was set apart for dancing; the rest, consisting of a numerous suite, handsomely furnished and finely lighted up, were for the accommodation of those who chose

to play at cards. Another suite was reserved for the supper, a very
splendid one to which we sat down about twelve o'clock and at
which we had a great variety of dishes, all sorts of wine and all
sorts of fruit. The imperial minister invited Bootle to taste of a
water melon, telling him by way of inducement that they
came from Bukovina. Two of the Tables were particularly
magnificent.

The Count Bezborodko is a tall, lusty man with swelled legs, the
effect I believe of intemperance and debauchery, in which however
it is said he is no longer able now to indulge. To his balls in the
country he invites all the prostitutes in Petersburg. I was shown one
of his secretaries, a smart man whose fortune is to be made for having married a cast off mistress of his Excellency's. He is reported to
do the public business in the most careless manner. In order to
avoid the importunities of suitors, his house is provided with
abundant means for escaping from them whenever he thinks proper.
I am told likewise that he has a stated set of phrases with which
in going the round of his levée he puts the people off who have any
business with him, such as 'Will you be so obliging as to call again
another time, Sir'; 'Sir, I have not forgot'; 'Sir, your affair has been
mentioned to her Majesty'. These forms of speech are so regularly
and invariably repeated that a person may be favoured with any
one of them which he likes, by placing himself in the proper situation. Besides presents from the Empress, his appointments and
estate amount to 70,000 roubles a year.

Ice Lemonade, Orgeat and Ratafia* were handed about before
supper. Both the men and women seemed to be particularly well
dressed.

Sunday, 25th November

The Empress having graciously permitted all the foreigners in
Petersburg to see the Hermitage* this morning, we repaired thither
between the hours of ten and eleven. Our party was Lord Borringdon, Lord Dalkeith, Mr. Garshore, Sir W. W. Wynn, the Marquis
V——, the Marquis Tiana, the Count Stackleberg,* another gentleman and ourselves. We were not permitted to enter with swords or
sticks; but they were required to be delivered up before we went
in. Quarenghi joined us there and was of great service to us in
pointing out what particularly deserved our attention. In so short
a time, however, and in such a crowd, it was impossible
to see such a profusion to any good purpose or with any
satisfaction.

We first saw the Royal apartments, which occupy that side of the building which fronts towards the river, we then passed through the picture Galleries which [form] the three other sides of a square. Afterwards we went by Raphael's Gallery to the Cabinets of Medals, Mineralogy and what I must call for want of a better word 'bijouterie': and we concluded with the Theatre, which as well as Raphael's Gallery, copied after that at the Vatican, were the work of our friend Quarenghi. This last, he said, had given him immense trouble.

The Apartments as well as the Galleries are crowded with paintings, good and bad placed promiscuously together: composed on the whole I think of no less than ten collections. There are several valuable pieces in this number from the Italian School, but the finest are from the Dutch and Flemish. I shall only mention, the Adoration and the Bacchus by Rubens, the Wounded Adonis by Vandyke, three pieces by Teniers—two landscapes, and a third affair, the largest picture he ever painted. At least if there is a duplicate of this or one more as large that is all. Three or four admirable pieces by Wouvermans. The prodigal returning by Rembrandt. The pictures by Teniers are all hung up in one room, those by Wouvermans in another, those by Vandyke in a third, those by Nic. Poussin in a fourth, and those by Luca Giordano all together in a particular part of the gallery. This is almost the only order observable. In the galleries copies were making of some pictures, particularly of Scipio's continence by Sir Joshua Reynolds and of Guido's Doctors consulting on the immaculate purity of the Virgin Mary (this is reckoned one of the finest pictures Guido ever painted). Sir Watkin recognized here the Perseus and Andromeda by Mengs which having been ordered by his father at Rome, was taken on its way to England by a Spanish vessel and sold to the Empress.

At the back of the long room where the Empress usually sits is a winter Garden composed of several little groves of evergreen trees, encircled by gravel walks and inhabited by a great variety of foreign birds. It is a curious circumstance that the arrangement of this garden is altered every fortnight. In point of size and beauty it is not to be compared with that at the Horse Guards. The Empress, we were [told], takes no delight in it and seldom goes into it, as one might conclude indeed from the forlorn state, particularly of the gilding.

In one of the apartments we were shown the trap doors through which her Majesty can have her dinners sent up when she chuses to dine without any attendants. A portrait of Zeuboff's brother,* a young officer in the army, of the French Princes and that of a favourite (who died, as Q[uarenghi] expressed it *en sa place,** a

E

very worthy young man, *qui convenoit parfaitement à l'Imperatrice*) appear in the Gallery. I was very much struck with a portrait of the Empress in the uniform of the Guards and on horseback as she was habited on the day she mounted the throne.

In one of the apartments we were particularly desired to remark two models by Falconet, one of a female sitting, the other of Pygmalion with the statue which he made before him. They were greatly commended by Quarenghi. The Hercules of Sir Joshua Reynolds, which was ordered by the Empress, but for which it is doubtful whether she ever paid, is in the Cabinet of Medals. Quarenghi's opinion of Sir Joshua is that his excellence was confined to portraits, in which department he allows him all possible merit, as he does for his admirable discourses.

They manufacture larger mirrors at Petersburg than anywhere else in Europe. These apartments are embellished with a profusion of them and they often produce an agreeable effect. In the *Cabinet des Mineraux* etc. we saw several specimens of the Marbles in the neighbourhood of Petersburg, of which we were assured, both by Quarenghi and the Princess Dashkoff that there is a great variety, but almost totally unknown to the Russians themselves. In what I call the Toy Cabinet over each of the Cases there was a model of some ruin in Rome and Quarenghi told me that they have somewhere in the palace models like these of all the Roman Ruins.

Princess Dashkoff having desired us to call on her as soon as we could after dinner, because she was engaged to go to the Hermitage at six, we hurried thither almost as soon as we rose from table, but were still too late. The Princess, having heard from Hineham that we talked of going to China, advised us at Count Bezborodko's ball in the first place not to think of any such thing because it was impossible and in the second place not to talk of it because it would render us suspected, at this time particularly when England was endeavouring to cheat Russia out of her Chinese trade.

Monday, 26th November

About twelve we received a visit from Quarenghi. . . . Speaking of the Favourites, he told us that there had been fourteen *en titre*;* that several had been dismissed for bad behaviour, especially for their infidelity. The Empress's hour of dining is one, after dinner she retires to the Hermitage where she passes about two hours with the favourite; as she is now old she varies her hours according to his inclination and finds it necessary to pay her court. His levée

is attended every morning before the Empress's by all the People
of the first Quality while he is dressing; during which time they
all stand and he keeps his seat. His father himself pays court to
the son. The Empress Elizabeth* had her lovers but they were
amongst her Ministers etc.

She is generous from ostentation. Her Valet de Chambre,* the
most honest man living and exceedingly attached, has never
received anything above his wages.

Quarenghi's father has been dead six years. His property is
enough to support him. His pension from the Empress is, I understand, 3,000 crowns, which has been punctually paid. *A later note:*
Quarenghi's Pension is 4,000 roubles a year.

Tuesday, 27th November

We called upon Bayley this morning to look at some Pelisses,
and Bootle fixed upon a Bearskin the price of which was 325
roubles.

We . . . concluded the evening at Nariskin's, supping there as
usual. Among other company we had the Sultan, a Cossack Colonel
and his wife. After supper they danced a Scotch reel. . . .

I saw this afternoon the copy of a memorial presented by
Esterhazy* to the Empress the 15th of this month the purpose of
which was at the requisition of the Spanish court to intimate what
her Imperial Majesty might have done, and to enquire what she
was willing to do, for the Emigrant Princes. It was written in a
high strain of flattery as all the memorials to her are. The alliance
which was at one time in agitation between Prussia and France is
alluded to. Though the faction in France is said to have been
encouraged by hopes of assistance from England, the sentiments
of the British court are reasoned upon as unfavourable to their
views. The Empress is particularly solicited to furnish a body of
Cossacks for the support of the Swiss.

Wednesday, 28th November

Eaton went with me to the Russian shops and assisted me this
morning in buying a Bearskin Pelisse, which I got for 150 roubles,
though I was asked for it three hundred.

The only addition to our usual party at Mr. Whitworth's today
was the Prince Sapieha* . . . Prince Sapieha generally found from
six to twelve persons at Z[euboff]'s in an afternoon. He received

him always with great preciseness and was exceedingly particular
in his enquiries concerning Poland; his questions implying that he
made the country and its affairs his study, and at the same time
discovering a considerable degree of penetration. His countenance,
he fancies, does also the same. But he describes his manner as
uncommonly haughty.

At six o'clock he constantly attends the Empress. Ostermann and
the other Ministers he represents likewise as excessively inquisitive
and almost impertinent in their enquiries. They ask [him] from
what Province and what district he comes, and a variety of such
particulars. They ask the Prince particularly what company his
father had with him, how they amused themselves, whether the
confederation was popular, and whether the Country was united in
their political sentiments.

Thursday, 29th November

Quarenghi represents the Empress's manner in conversation as
uncommonly generous and insinuating. He declares that he does
not feel himself under the smallest restraint with her. He has now
been here thirteen years yet he never went to her when he did
not find her employed in reading or writing. From two to four is
the Time of Mystery. She seldom speaks German; Quarenghi had
never heard her speak [it] but once; it seems as if she studiously
avoided it. He spoke of her with great candour, acknowledging
that with all her faults she was possessed of very splendid and
noble qualities.

Zeuboff had the management of Polish Affairs. During the
absence of Besborodko he transacted the business which belongs
to his department and wishing to continue it, was very near driving
him out of administration. This Zeuboff has the Character of being
an active little man, who however behaves with no small degree
of hauteur, which in a person from the dust as he is gives no small
offence.

Saturday, 1st December

In the evening we called on Hineman with whose sensible and
intelligent conversation I was exceedingly pleased. . . .

The Russians are totally destitute of principle. A man of rank
is capable of pilfering anything that comes in his way and is not
ashamed of doing so. A Nobleman went into a shop and pilfered a
watch. The wife of the watchmaker perceived him do it, but as he
wore a star was afraid to say anything. She told her husband how-

ever of what she had seen and he recovered the watch. This dirty action, instead of causing the man to be banished out of company, rather excited admiration and only caused people to enquire of the wag an account of the way in which he was able before the face of several persons to effect his purpose.

As to truth among the men or chastity among the women, they are entirely out of the question. Are we to impute the want of the latter virtue to their practice of permitting their daughters to bathe till the age I think of fourteen in company with their father, mother and brothers?

The late Emperor is said to have been strangled.* This piece of intelligence was communicated to a M. Peterhoff [?] I think by Prince Potemkin at a time when he thought himself at the point of death.

Orloff, Potemkin, Lanskoy, Mamonoff and Zeuboff are five out of fourteen. Coxe is said to have procured an account of the expense which these gentlemen have occasioned to the country. A party was considering which of the Canals had cost the most money; when one of them archly observed there was not a doubt about the matter; Catherine's Canal (this is the name of one of them) had unquestionably been the most expensive.

Here follows a note on Grigory Orlov.

He as well as his brother was a man of great strength. He went at last out of his senses. After he was in this state, however, H. has seen him play at billiards with the Empress. He is supposed to have been strangled in his house at Moscow. The Empress had a son by him who is now living either at Nerva or Reval. Alexei is still living at Moscow.* They were five brothers all living together, who though born gentlemen were a lot of desperate fellows, who owed their elevation altogether to the revolution.

A Note on Lanskoy:

It was he who died 'en place', and whose portrait we saw at the Hermitage. He had obtained such an influence over the Empress that it was thought he would have ruined Potemkin. It is certain that after his death his legs dropped off. The Stench was also insufferable. The boy who gave him his coffee disappeared or died I believe the day after. All these circumstances lead [one] to suppose that he was poisoned. The Empress was inconsolable for his loss. No Person but her faithful Valet de Chambre was suffered to approach her. Grief and the loss of sleep occasioned some spots to appear on her breasts which led her to fancy that she had caught the putrid fever of which they made her believe that L[anskoy] died. For four months afterwards she kept herself shut up at Peterhoff. Her first reappearance was on occasion of the Polish Deputies; which gave Nariskin occasion to say 'A plague on these Polish Deputies, I have not sat down to one of these murderous dinners before for an age; nor should, I believe, but for them'. His speech made the Empress laugh for the first time after the death of her favourite. He was a very strong man, though ill made below, and without the appearance of being a muscular man. Lanskoi died nine years ago.

The Secretary of the French Embassy at the time of the revolution [of 1762] had an opportunity of acquainting himself with many curious particulars, and composed a history of it, which he meant to have given the world, if he had not been bribed to suppress it. The agent employed on the business was Diderot. It was in contemplation to take the author off, but this idea was given up, because there were two other copies known to be existing besides that in his own possession, one given by him to the King and the other to the Archbishop of Paris. He is now lately dead and the work is expected to appear.

Though great sobriety prevails in the houses of the Russian Nobles, the old manners still survive in those of the lower class of people. If you drink with a Russian Merchant it is hardly possible to get away without becoming intoxicated. It is a part of hospitality to press the wine upon their guests.

Semelatoff has 100,000 Peasants. He furnished a whole regiment when the Nobility were required to give one in a hundred of all their slaves, to recruit the Army. Mary Luffofna told me that her father has an estate near Kieff of 5,000 Peasants: for this is the way of estimating their estates.

The Princess Dashkoff says that during the extinction of the Arts in every part of the world for some time, when nobody could say what was become of them, at that time they took their abode in Russia.

Sunday, 2nd December

We went again a small party consisting of the Marquis del Vaglio, the Marquis his companion, the Venetian Count and ourselves along with Quarenghi to see the Hermitage. . . .

Notes on the rooms at the Hermitage:

10   A very small room. Two busts of Potemkin.

12   In this room there were no less than four parroquets.

13   Cabinet. Bust of Alexis Orloff. Bust of Tchernichef.

14   Billiard Room. The Empress is fond of billiards and plays every day.

15   The library. Two little paintings here by the Grand Dutchess.

19   Gallery. Portraits of the Royal family, among which that of the Empress in *habit de voyage* is the best portrait of her existing. A full length of Prince Orloff on horseback. He was a fine character and truly attached to the Empress: *vraiment attaché, bon homme*. Alexy Orloff on horseback, habited as a Turk.

The Portrait of Landskoi, the favourite who died *en place*.

N.B. The Empress makes the tour of all these apartments every day.

Being the anniversary of the Regiment of Ismailof, and also that of her Majesty's inoculation,* it was considered as a Gala day. . . . About eleven in the evening we went to a Masquerade at Leoni's after having supped at Sir Watkin's. There were not less than ten or twelve rooms open, of which those where they danced, another much larger at the back of it, and a third with an Orchestra for a band of Music were the largest. In several of the other rooms there were Card tables, in one or two a sort of bar where lemonade, orgeat and such things were sold, and [in] other little apartments rather more retired a few of the Company were at supper. Some people were in characters, some entirely concealed, others without either mask or domino, and the crowd in consequence of the price being only one rouble and a half was immense. I was very much amused with a Cossack dance which I happened to see. Bootle was present at a Russian one. We were all dressed *à la Venetienne* in a Domino and Biretta, as we understood that genteel people generally are. I came away about three and could [not] help being struck with the long lane of servants holding the pelisses of their masters and mistresses and sitting on the stairs from top to bottom. One of the masks was a London Tippy Bob* with all the extravagances in his dress of the fashion last spring. The number of the company is said to have been 1,400–2,000.

Orloff was the Empress's first favourite after her accession. As Q[uarenghi] represented him as being extremely attached to the Empress, so E[aton] represented her as being exceedingly attached to him. His command over her was so complete that he is even supposed to have beat her. He was supplanted at last by Potemkin, the only man capable of succeeding in such an attempt; after which he, Orloff, married his own niece. If now Potemkin did not come into place till 1775, and Orloff was taken into favour from the time of the Accession, his reign must have been of thirteen years' duration. Potemkin retained this situation only for two years but he went out with such influence that he appointed all his successors except the last. . . . Landskoi died nine years ago, that is in 1783. He was succeeded by Mamonoff, who retired in disgust. His successor the present favourite has held his place three years. Mamonoff must therefore have had it six. And as the number has been fourteen in all, there must have been a very quick succession between the years 1777 and 1783, there must have been no less than eight in the space of six years.*

Monday, 3rd December

Bootle and I took a long ramble this morning. . . . It was pleasant walking in the middle of the streets, where the snow was beat by the perpetual attrition of sledges and carriages to the fineness of Dust, the colour of which was nearly the same as that of brown salt. Though these were continually passing and repassing, the stillness of the streets reminded one of that with which at a race carriages bowl over the turf: or with which they run over sand. I could have fancied myself likewise sometimes in a riding school where one hears nothing but a dull heavy kind of sound. The cleanness of the streets and their freedom from dust, for this snow does not fly, is no small advantage which they have over ours. By the bye, these circumstances render pavements such as ours in London much less necessary than they are there. I saw one carriage today, and one only, on sledges.

The Grand Duke's parties in the country consist of about 150 persons. They go at six o'clock and pass the first two hours at the theatre where they are warm and comfortably seated and where they see a French piece well acted. When the play is over they amuse with dancing polonaises and country dances till ten, at which hour they sit down to supper. After supper they dance again till twelve and then go away.

It is usual here to pay a visit of condolence to [an] acquaintance upon the death of a friend immediately after, that is the day after the death of a friend, before the deceased is buried. The mourner is found surrounded by a circle of friends and relations come on the same business; the visitor makes a pathetic bow and is answered with a tender and significant gesture; this is all that passes. The company sits in silence like a Quaker meeting, and after having stopped as long as decency requires, retire to make room for others. The room is so dimly lighted that you must be there a couple of minutes before you can distinguish the objects around you. The party to whom the visit is made is in deep [mourning] and so are all the attendants. Mr. Whitworth paid a visit of this sort to the Countess Suvorov upon the death of her husband. I forget whether this was the visit which he was obliged to pay four days after his arrival, before he was acquainted with the lady.

Our party at Mr. Whitworth's was entirely English. He was uncommonly cheerful and entertaining. Witness his story of his reception at a University on his way to Kieff when the King of Poland, Stanislas Poniatowski, went to meet the Empress. The King, who had passed through before him and had run the same gauntlet, put the learned body upon giving him all this trouble. When he arrived he had fasted 48 hours. His dinner was on the table. Yet the speeches of the several professors and other cere-monies detained him full two hours; all the while in sight of the dinner which he was longing to begin upon.

Tuesday, 4th December

It struck me as we were walking about the Town this morning that at Petersburg one looks at two or even four horses with the same indifference as on a hackney chaise or a hackney coach in England. I saw a hussar riding after Volkonski's sledge this morning and understood that none but persons of a certain rank are entitled to that distinction.

Besides the English party, the Abbé Girot and M. Masson,* a French surgeon, dined at Mr. Whitworth's. The Abbé had an abbey worth 700 a year. He came here under the Protection of Nassau,* that Knight Errant, who at present is the Lord knows where. Masson was the man who opened Potemkin, and who under pre-tence of long arrears due to him, received a gratuity of 20,000 roubles.

The Duke de Richelieu,* whom I remember by the name of Duke de Chinon in Italy, arrived at Petersburg yesterday. He is said to be a moderate man. His estate was 400,000 livres or 20,000 a year. Out of this they have allowed the Dutchess, who has never left France, no more than 800 livres a year. The Duke de Noailles, who is a very prudent man, and Montmorency have continued in France.

We called on the Princess Dashkoff in the afternoon but she was gone to Court. We returned therefore to Mr. Whitworth's and came in for the conclusion of Robespierre's speech. [*A report from Paris?*]

N.B. Did the Empress Elizabeth use to call in a soldier from off guard when she had occasion for him and give him ten roubles for his trouble?

The following is the list of favourites according to the order of succession. *This page has been torn out but some notes remain:* He [Grigori Orlov] was father of a Prince* and Princess. The Prince has forfeited the Empress's favour and is living as an exile at Narva or Reval. The Princess is living and married.

He [*Zorich*] happened to be at Tsarskoe Selo the day he had been dismissed by Potemkin and suspected what had happened from finding nobody but an old Major in his apartment. Potemkin ordered him in a very cavalier style to take himself off and find another Empress* if he could that would pay him so well for etc. He has large landed estates in Pskow where he lives upon them with all the magnificence of a Sovereign.

Wednesday, 5th December

A ceremony at the palace: We found the Audience chamber very full and glittering with gay dresses embroidered in silk, silver and gold, most of them new on the occasion. The Empress did not enter till about one. She came as usual preceded by a long train of gentlemen and followed by a long train of ladies, who were all as fine as they could make themselves. We all, that is all the foreign ministers and strangers, kissed her Majesty's hand; she appeared very gracious, and while this ceremony was performing, addressed her conversation to the Persons standing near her. As she passed along Brotocky was presented to her as going away, to whom I fancied she wished to put on an air of hauteur and defiance.

Some time afterwards the Grand Duke and Grand Dutchess passed through the crowd, having been to pay their compliments, and we followed them, for the purpose of being introduced, into the adjoining room. We only bowed to the Duke but kissed the Dutchess's hand. They both seemed to receive us with great civility and good humour. The Duke asked Sir Watkin, who stood first and acted the part of foreman, how long he had been here and the Dutchess observed that there was a great number of our countrymen at present in Petersburg. After this we retired into the Audience chamber, where they presently passed arm in arm, the Duke strutting like the Baron in the haunted Tower* with the most ridiculous air of dignity and importance as if he was aping or burlesquing it. The Duke is a spare man with a very vulgar, insignificant, disagreeable countenance. He is in point of majestic and real dignity what the City or The Hague or the Hambourg Militia are in point of discipline and a military appearance. The Dutchess gives the idea of what I believe she is, a good mother and a well disposed, agreeable woman.

All the strangers and foreign ministers were invited to dine at Count Osterman's, the Vice Chancellor's, and as the hour of dining was two we had barely time to go home from court before it was time to wait on his excellence. The stench on the staircase of Count Osterman's is insufferable. I shall not soon forget his velvet black boots and the cane with which he walks about, calling to one's mind the figure of Belisarius.* All the company . . . was not assembled till near three. In the meantime we wetted our appetites with the liqueurs and savoury things on the side table in the corner and amused ourselves with walking about and conversing. Though we could not be fewer than seventy, we all sat down at the same long table (this table had a pretty colonnade in open work in an Arabesque style in the middle). A Band of Music or an Orchestra was playing all the while. Of a sudden towards the latter end of the dinner the Clarinets and kettle drums struck up, as a signal, I thought, of rising from table. But it proved to be a signal for drinking her Majesty's health. [We] all got up to drink it. I sat between Count Stallingberd and Lord Dalkeith and the day passed very agreeably.

At six we repaired to the ball at Court. The Empress followed by all the ladies in procession entered very soon after we got there. The Ladies were very richly dressed; Madame Potemkin particularly had not fewer diamonds than the Queen of England, in Whitworth's opinion. I understand that her dress in some places was entirely studded with them. Scarcely had the Empress taken her seat than the Ball began. It even seemed to begin as soon as she made her appearance. There was something very fine in the sudden opening. The Minuets with which it began might last about half an hour. A circle was made for them and the ladies seemed to stand round. The two young Grand Dukes, the two Princesses of Baden and the three young Grand Dutchesses were in the number of the dancers. The eldest Grand Duke is a very handsome young man with a fine open countenance. He is the Empress's favourite and is spoken of by everybody. His brother's countenance is quite the reverse of his, exceedingly disagreeable and unpromising. His character and temper likewise are not well spoken of. They [the Princesses of Baden] are both fine girls, but particularly the eldest. The two eldest Grand Dutchesses are very fine girls : the third is quite a child.

The crowd . . . was so great and they stood so many deep that I was able to see but very little of the minuets. Polonese dances succeeded and were continued until the ball broke up about eight. None but persons of a certain rank and officers in the Guards were permitted to dance; even foreigners were not allowed. Or at least the two Ambassadors were I believe the only exception. It was curious to see old Cobenzl and Hading leading about the little Grand Dutchesses. The circle was broke and new ones formed from time to time which gave more people an opportunity of seeing. A Gallery encompasses the Ball room; this also was full of spectators. The whole company is said to have been not less than two thousand, a motley crew, in which however Uniforms predominated in such a manner that it seemed rather to be a Camp than a court. The Cossacks, Kirghese and Tartars intermingled contributed very much to the oddity of the appearance. While Vergara and Sir Watkin's dancing master could gain admittance, this implied that the company was very mixed. A fine courtier glittering with embroidery and Diamonds was a curious contrast to a dirty Cossack with his long beard and his coarse, plain cloaths.

N.B. Madame Potemkin's muff valued at 5,000 roubles. Was it the same that the Empress gave him? The man who poisoned Potemkin about here now (G[ould]). The Empress when she received the news of his death shut herself up in her room for some days. But if her grief was real, it has been said, why enjoy herself presently as she did at the Horse Guards? Michel Galitzin when Potemkin attached himself to his wife triumphed in the thing and said that he should now come in for something good. Gould has seen the Prince [Potemkin] with nothing on but a pair of Breeches with his Nieces, dangling them on his Knee. Potemkin was appointed favourite a second time and kissed hands upon the appointment. I think Gould saw it.

About ten we went to the Ball at the Countess Saltikoff's, where the company was very elegant and everything conducted in the best style possible. Instead of all sitting down to a table, we were separated into a number of distinct parties, each at a round table. Bootle and I were at the table with the Countess and the Princess Dashkoff. We were introduced also to the Princess Michel Galitzin, who is said to be one of the most clever women in Petersburg, as she is one of the prettiest. She is not liked, however, because she is supposed to have written the characters of all the principal women here, though she has not communicated it to more than two or three persons.

It was so late when we left this ball that though I had got a ticket and had my dress in the carriage I did not chuse to go to the Masquerade at Leoni's, where however I set down Bootle and Lord Leveson Gower.

A note on Russian baths.

Often when they appear red hot the people here in 20 degrees of cold come out of the baths and roll themselves in the snow. On the eve of Holidays the Common People are bathing all the day long. The charge is 5 copecs each. For a room to yourself a rouble. Gould compares the throwing of cold water in that case to the receiving of a great knock on the pate. Private Families have baths of their own in which they all bath together. Of late in the public baths the men and the women have been separated.

Thursday, 6th December

In our walk this morning we stumbled upon Mr. Whitworth, from whose conversation I learnt that in consequence of the hostile appearances on the side of Turkey, Suvorov as commander of the army and Ribas* as commander of the fleet in the Black Sea had received orders to repair without delay to their respective stations: that Russia was in a bad plight and not a little alarmed; that she might repent now of not having entered into an alliance with us; that for some years past she had evidently leant towards France, but that it had always been and might still be an object perhaps for the Northern Powers to form a union and balance the scale against the house of Bourbon. The armed Neutrality, he told us, had certainly originated in M. Vergenne's Cabinet, though it was so artfully suggested to her that she was led to consider herself as the contriver of it.

I find that Mollendorf* is marched at the head of fifteen thousand men towards Poland, where another dismemberment is apprehended.

At 5 o'clock we went by appointment to the Princess Dashkoff's who received us very obligingly. She has made a collection of curious books for us; she has chalked out several routes for us to chuse; and when we have made our choice, she has promsed us letters both for that route and for Moscow.

When we left her we went to the theatre to see Oleg, a sort of ballet composed four years ago by the Empress herself and intended to represent the old Russian Costume, which she has enabled them to do by making them a present of all the rich Garments which were preserved in the Imperial Wardrobe. The Empress has composed herself several other dramatic pieces. As she proposed to make a present of these dresses to the theatre, the Oleg might be intended to bring them into use. . . . What pleased me most of all in it was the Russian Dance, which seemed to be executed with a great deal of grace and animation. The Scene is sometimes at

Kieff and sometimes at Constantinople. Many of the tunes are Russian. The ceremony of the Espousal and the marriage is I imagine borrowed from the manners of the country. In the last act the Greek Emperor entertains the Russian General with a theatrical exhibition in imitation of the ancients. Not less than two hundred persons are present at this spectacle.

Friday, 7th December

This being St. George's Day the Knights of that order dined with the Empress. About 12 o'clock we repaired to the palace to see this ceremony. The Knights according to their respective classes preceded her Majesty from the Chapel where they had been to Mass and passed through the Audience Chamber. She stopped as usual to receive the compliments of the foreign Ministers and strangers. It was remarked that she appeared upon this occasion to be agitated in a very unusual manner, seeming to discover, behind the foreign Ministers, something or some person which surprised [her]. What was very extraordinary in consequence of it, she advanced two or three steps forward, still keeping her eye as I understand fixed on that side. The *Corps diplomatique* were in doubt what it could be, whether she only saw one of the Knights out of his place, or the face of some person who alarmed her.

About eight months ago it was known for certain that three men set off from Paris with a determination and after having bound themselves to assassinate her. They were stopped, however, on the frontiers. Yet Gould says that one of them has escaped all the vigilance of the police.

A French confectioner to the Empress some time ago being infected with the Democratic Principles, though in good plight here, desired a passport to leave the country, which being refused him from time to time, he made his escape without any, [being] anxious to revisit his native country and enjoy the liberty of the new constitution. He lately, however, presented himself at Riga, expressing a desire to come back, to make his peace with his royal Mistress and to be reinstated in his former employ. They arrested him and he is now in prison. Another Frenchman, who could give no account of himself and pretended to be connected with some French Subpreceptor of the young Grand Dukes, has been taken lately into custody here.

The Grand Dukes and Grand Dutchesses were in the procession; and came presently afterwards through the Audience Chamber to that in which they held a sort of Levée, which we attended. A circle was formed and they addressed their conversation to three or four persons in it and then retired.

We hurried now to the great hall where the Knights dine. The tables seemed to be placed lengthways and breadthways as they are represented by the dotted lines [*here a diagram shows the tables ranged round the hall*], and contained covers enough I was told for a hundred persons but I should think for a great many more. We took our station in the spot . . . directly opposite to where the Empress sat along with the foreign Ministers. The procession entered in the same order as it had passed in through the Audience Chamber, which likewise was preserved in regard to their places. On the Empress's right sat the Comte de Suvorow-Rymniski, and on her left the old Admiral M. de Tchitchagow.* She helped the soup herself and gave it to the Admiral first. A Band of Music accompanied the dinner. What likewise enlivened the scene exceedingly was the Galleries that ran round the room and were full of spectators. At the end of about five minutes the Empress made a bow to the foreign Ministers, the meaning of which was that she would not give them the trouble of waiting any longer and we all retired. This is the constant etiquette, because the foreign Ministers attend out of form and civility. In the course of the dinner afterwards the Empress's health was drunk by all the Knights standing up; and their's again in return by her.

He [*Admiral Tchitchagow*] repulsed the Swedes at Reval and commanded at Viborg; though as he failed to avail himself of the advantages which he had there,—for until Creuz cut his cables no order of that kind was given,—it is imagined that he would not have been loaded with such honours and favours if it had not been according to orders. I was told, I think, that he has realized an estate of 300,000 roubles a year. Besides which he has the orders of St. Andrew and St. George. One reason of heaping all these favours on him was the reflexions which were cast in the Public papers, particularly the English, on the Russian Navy; as if they had no good officers and were obliged for all their successes to foreigners. The Empress by this conduct to Tchitchagow meant to show to the world and to the Russian Nation that she thought otherwise. He is a tall, thin old man.

When the Empress was shown a plan of the battle of Viborg by the person who brought the news of it, she asked why Creuz had cut his cables. The person remained silent. 'I will tell you,' she said, 'because they did not feel the same anxiety to serve us.' Yet Creuz has not been much reprimanded.

Trevannion* was killed in the affair at Viborg; Marshall* and Denniston* in that of Svensk Sound. The same ball which proved mortal to Trevannion took off Aiken's leg.* Marshall was a brave young fellow of 24: he commanded a 40-Gun frigate [with] 230 men: he fought till the crew was reduced to 30; when observing a man going to strike the colours, he shot him and then taking them himself threw himself into the sea and was drowned.

From Court Sir Watkin and I went to the French Comedy where the play was 'le jaloux'.* From the play Bootle and I went to Luff's where I was introduced to Golofkin. I left him, came home, put off my sword and went for half an hour to the Club des Nobles. The day was concluded with a supper in our apartment at which besides the English we had the company of Golofkin and Anikof. I did not get to bed till a quarter before four, nor Bootle till half after five.

Rogerson said that we might have the pressed caviare in England but that the fresh would not keep. They have it even at Petersburg only in the winter; because it is brought from the Volga; the best I think from as far as Astracan. The coldness of the weather enables them to transport it so far without spoiling. I think they said that it would not keep more than about a fortnight. They spread it on dried toast, putting pepper to it first. Need I mention that it is the roe of the sterlet [*i.e. small sturgeon*]. The black Caviare which comes from the Volga and from Astracan is the best. It is a fortnight coming. In winter it will keep a month. The Yellow Caviare comes from the Crimea.

Monday, 10th December

This last year out of 850 ships that came to Petersburg 600 were English; and in point of freight generally speaking an English ship bears the proportion of three to one compared with a foreign ship. In consequence of not having a treaty our merchants are obliged to pay the whole or part of the duties either in Dutch ducats, in Spanish dollars or in bars; in consequence of which they pay 40 per cent more than the favoured nations, i.e. more than the French, the Portuguese or the Dutch. Had any English fleet made its appearance only, they believe that a commercial treaty would certainly have taken place on our terms. . . . While the treaty of commerce subsisted the house of every English Merchant was a sort of Asylum to anyone who chose to take refuge there. . . . Port wine has been drunk here for not more than three years. Three years ago a single Vessel from Portugal supplied the demand but now they require three or four. . . . The English keep themselves very distinct and hold the Russians in great contempt, particularly for their want of principle and good faith. . . .

Madame Protassov* is supposed to be a taster [*i.e. of prospective favourites for the Empress*]. It was only on Saturday that a notion or report prevailed of Mamonoff's being put under confinement at Schlusselburg, together with two or three other nobles of Moscow for having let their estates on leases, requiring an annual payment from the tenants and leaving the other profits to them. About two years and a half ago the wife of Mamonoff having suffered herself to report certain anecdotes of the court, the public inquisitor, whose name I forget, was sent to Moscow to give her a flogging, which he did.

Potemkin was a perfect Charlatan, and if he was going to be in company with any one very conversant with some particular subject, he would contrive beforehand to set two people conversant with the same, disputing upon it: from whose conversation he would collect enough to appear very learned to that person in the absence of the others. Rogers had this I think from a man who was employed to write the memoirs of Potemkin.

We saw the Academy this morning to which we went in sledges. Our party was Lord Borringdon, Ld. Leveson Gower, Sir W. W. Wynn, Bootle and myself. It contains a great many curiosities. . . . Several of the Articles in the second room are of gold and have been found in Siberia in the repositories of the dead. . . . In the Cabinet of Natural History, a large handsome room, we saw an Elephant of immense size. . . . In another room we saw a full-length figure of Peter [the Great] in wax of his natural size. He is sitting on a sort of throne; the clothes are of blue silk and the same as he wore at his marriage to Catherine; his face is from a model taken of him after his death. He appears to have been a very tall man; he was at least four or five inches taller than Lord Borringdon, as we perceived, upon his Lordship's standing under the mark of his height. In this same room they shew several things made with his own hands such as Pairs of shoes. . . . A pair of Stockings mended by himself is in the number of the curiosities.

The present Empress had deposited in the Academy her own Manuscript of the Code of Laws which she composed. It is in the French language; and a great part like a dispatch, occupies only half of the Page. The whole is not in her own handwriting. They shewed us a passage in which the following expression occurs: '*Comme les filles sont assez portée au marriage, il faut encorager les garçons*', etc.

They shewed us some very indelicate mechanical curiosities from China. And also a padlock to secure the chastity of their women in the same country.

F

Tuesday. 11th December

At twelve o'clock we repaired to court in order to be present at the ceremony of the Empress dining with the Knights of St. Andrew. [*a similar ceremony to that on St. George's day*]. . . . We then attended the levée of the Grand Duke and the Grand Dutchess . . . N.B. The Grand [Duke] and Dutchess had a quarrel about some ugly little girl* that the Duke had thought proper to attach himself to. Some person, I know not who, remonstrated to him about it. He at first took it in dudgeon and said don't talk to me, you are all under petticoat government. However a few days ago they appeared to be reconciled. The Empress and her son were likewise not long ago on bad terms. Can anybody have promoted the misunderstanding between the Duke and the Dutchess by throwing this little girl in the way of the former?

Though the whole number [of the Knights of St. Andrew] is more than sixty there were not more than twelve present. They were dressed in the proper habit of their order, which consists of a green manteau, a hat *à la étui** with a plume in it, a coat and breeches of silver brocade, the waistcoat of gold stuff, white stockings, white roses to the shoes and the hair flowing down the shoulders. Branicki the Pole wears his hair *à la Polonaise*, i.e. short and shaved round. He was obliged therefore to use false locks. A concert of vocal and instrumental music accompanied the whole dinner from an Orchestra at the extremity of this large room. The Platoon composed of rocks etc. represented something at Peterhof. The greatest part of the service appeared to be of massive gold. The Knights being so few in number sat at a great distance from one another. On the Empress's right hand sat the Grand Duke, on the left the young Grand Duke. Her Majesty appeared to be in good spirits and good humour and conversed very much with her son, who appears to me to carry on his countenance a very melancholy air, an air of chagrin and discontent.

We dined with Quarenghi and had an Italian entertainment as well as an Italian party, composed chiefly of Artists.

From him we went to the Princess Dashkoff's whose conversation was uncommonly amusing this afternoon. The Orloffs she says were always her enemies. Some time ago when she was on bad terms with the Empress, Potemkin waited upon her, I don't know for what purpose. She told him that being left a widow at the age of twenty she had submitted to live in a very economical retired manner for the sake of her children. 'What then,' she said, 'do you think I am not capable of doing at the age of forty-two? Let the Empress take my pittance from me. I have still resourses, I will go to England: there I will publish the Empress's letters to me which will bring in 10,000; I will afterwards publish the memoirs of my own life: they will not fail to bring me 20,000 more.' Her salary as President of the Academy is 3,000 roubles. Potemkin's soup,* she said, every day I think for three months before he gave his great fete, while the rehearsals were going on, cost as much. For during all that time he kept a sort of open house. (Mr. Whitworth contradicted this in regard to the soup. He gave one of Occa which might cost 1,000.)

She travelled in western Europe under an assumed name. At Paris they wished to have paid her great honours, i.e. the Duke of Choiseul,* out of pique I think to the Empress: but she would not accept of them.

She has a house and estate 140 Versts from Moscow: her steward is an Englishman and she offers to give us letters to him; and let us reside there if we have a desire to make ourselves acquainted with the manners of the people.

We staid with her so long that the Ball at court was almost over when we arrived there. The Empress was so fatigued with the morning's business that she did not make her appearance. It was curious to see the Knights of St. Andrew; they had laid aside their robes and had their hats off. Still they were sufficiently distinguished by their red stockings, their coats of silver cloth and their flowing hair.

Wednesday, 12th December

There was a little frost in the morning but the glass is still from one to three degrees only below the freezing point. Borringdon and Gower defer their journey on this account till Sunday, the roads at present being so bad.

I had hardly time to get a walk before dinner, for we dined with the Duke of Sierra Capriola, the Neapolitan Minister, at half past two. Lord Carysfort* was in love with the late Dutchess of Sierra Capriola and caused himself to be put into the papers so often as on the point of going that the Dutchess told him at last that he would be taken for a diligence. Whitbread* was likewise violently in love and returned after having set off.

When a marriage takes place in Russia the eldest female relation of the bride on the father's side attends in order, as soon as the consummation is over, she may carry the bridal shift bearing the honourable marks of Virginity to the friends either of one party or the other, but I believe the lady's. The person who told Gould this is a man of rank and was married at Court and he acknowledged that this custom had been observed in his own case. He represented it indeed as still universally prevailing in the country. After this it was curious to hear Golofkin speaking of the French Barbarians for suffering till this revolution earlier Segneurial rights to continue.

Friday, 14th December

The present Grand Signior* is about seven and twenty. He is supposed to be addicted to an unnatural practice which though common in Turkey, is very unpopular in the Sultan, the not having children being a sufficient reason for deposing him, none but children after his accession being capable of succeeding to the throne. He was cruel in the beginning of his reign, but seems likely to relent and tread in the steps of his father, who was a very wise prince. . . . The present sovereign is fond of spirituous liquors and is generally intoxicated in the evening.

Whitworth does not believe that Potemkin was poisoned. Eaton says that the symptoms implied it to have been done with the Aqua Tofana,* a slow poison.

Lord Borringdon and Lord Granville Leveson set out this morning at seven o'clock to go over the ice to Cronstadt and got back about half past four, having run no small risk from the holes and cracks in the ice, over which they went all the way in sledges.

Count Stallingberg by means of a certain air can burn a diamond which consumes without leaving a *caput mortuum*. He keeps the air a secret because when first he made the experiment those before whom he performed it pretended that it was an old discovery.

Saturday, 15th December

Baratinski* was one of the persons concerned in the murder of Peter 3[d]. Orloff was another. A third was struck dead with lightning. Baratinski though apparently so gentle, is a great *fourbi*.

Has Siberia* been depopulated by the small pox and particularly the Venereal disease?

We breakfasted this morning with Quarenghi, Sir Watkin, Bootle and myself: and we saw all his plans. That part of the Hermitage in which the theatre is, the Bank, the *hôtel pour les affaires étrangères*, the Academy of Sciences, the Palisade towards the river belonging to the summer palace, the palace at Peterhof and a burying place for the royal family are his principal works. They are all in excellent taste and far superior to all the other buildings. He has made some plans which have not been executed, especially one of a theatre and another of Shops, both very beautiful.

Sunday, 16th December

We paid a visit in the evening at Count Osterman's, who came up and conversed with us. . . . I talked with Count Stallingberg concerning his experiment for burning diamonds. It is by putting it into a certain kind of air, which he supposes to be the Element of Fire. The Diamond takes fire of itself and consumes without leaving a *caput mortuum*. He burnt a diamond in the presence of the late Emperor Leopold which weighed twelve Carat and a half and was worth two hundred roubles.

Young Baratinski* gave all the English an invitation to the Ball at the Princess's of the same name née Holstenbeck,* the mother of the Countess Tolstoi. . . . The Gentlemen supped above stairs and the ladies below. They did not break up till a very late hour. The men, having done supper first, they began to dance without the ladies.

Monday, 17th December

We dined as usual at Mr. Whitworth's and staid there till eight o'clock waiting to see Lord Borringdon and Lord Granville Leveson set off for Moscow, which they did . . . in two Kibitkis, one for themselves and the other for their servants. Their soldier rode in front of their own.

Tuesday, 18th December

We called this morning on Dr. Pallas and sat with him a considerable time. He proposes to set off about the 12th of January on his intended tour, for which reason we found his house in some confusion. We understood from him, though it was kept a secret, that a proposal had been made by the Prince de Condé to establish a colony of 5,000 French Emigrants somewhere on the coast of the Black [Sea]. Not more than a thousand of this number are Nobles.

He advised us to make use of bells in travelling as a safeguard both against robbers and wolves, both being overawed by them. The Journey from Astracan to Moscow would take up, he said, with gentle travelling about twenty days. At Catherinbourgh and Orenburgh he seemed to say that the snow is all gone in the beginning of April. Robbers are chiefly to be apprehended in this country in Autumn. If he had not a family he should not be afraid of venturing into Persia notwithstanding the unsettled state of the country. His present intention seemed not to go beyond Mount Caucasus or some part of it.

Thursday, 20th December

In the evening we were at a little ball of the Countess Golofkin's, where we found a party who had been on a sledge excursion in the morning. They had dined at a house a few versts out of the Town, employing all the time they had both before and after dinner in dancing. We had the pleasure of seeing both a Cossack and a Russian dance here in great perfection. They are full of animation and spirit; but they savour, especially the latter, exceedingly of the savage and barbarous. . . . The Countess Golofkin challenged me to dance a Polonaise with her, which I did here for the first time. The ladies were so questionable in point of chastity that there were not above three or four whom, as they passed in review before us, Bootle did not condemn with a squeeze of my arm which he was holding. It was after three I believe before we took our leave. Upon the whole this was one of the most agreeable parties I have been at.

Friday, 21st December

Peter the 3^d is said to have made a declaration, at the time when he made known his intention of imprisoning the Empress and marrying E[lizabeth] W[orontsov] that the Grand Duke was not his son. His father's name was Saltikoff.*

The Empress Elizabeth's death is supposed to have been hastened. Two days after her Physician, a man exceedingly attached to her, had dropped down dead immediately after drinking a cup of coffee, her issue which she had in her leg dried up and she was gone in an instant.

Zeuboff transacts now the greatest part of the public business. The affairs of Poland and France are wholly in his hands. The family is low and the father has lately been ordered to Moscow on a charge of embezzlement. He had formerly been very near going into Siberia for a Malversation of the same kind. Z[euboff]'s appointment took place at Tsarskoe Zelo about three years ago, at the time of the war. The first public token of it was her going out in a carriage seated between him and his brother. The people were ready almost to exclaim aloud at the indecency of their conduct.

After Landskoi's death she remained a widow for eight months. The name of his successor was Yermonhoff* or something like it. He remained only a year in office.

Sir James Harris* put into Potemkin's hands the plan of a treaty between Russia and England. He, having been considering it in bed, left it under his pillow. Mad^{selle} Gabel his niece's femme de chambre stole from there and procured Count Panin* a sight of it, for which she was richly rewarded. Upon this, the armed Neutrality was set on foot to counteract the Prince's project; and when the matter came before Council, he found himself in a minority. Mad^{selle} Gabel married a Swiss who is now a Lieutenant or Major General in this service. The armed Neutrality put an end also to the Prince's proposal for the cession of Minorca on condition of Russia entering into a strict alliance with us and furnishing 20,000 men to be sent into America. Sir James Harris was sounded on this subject.

Besborodko, though indolent and debauched in the highest degree, is a man of uncommon abilities. Marcoff has more application without the same talents.

St Priest* a great rogue. He made a fortune by receiving Money from both parties. Had he so little to do in the arrangement of the affair between the Turks and Russians? Did he write an excellent dispatch on that occasion?

Sunday, 23rd December

This being the name day of the eldest young Grand Duke we made a point of going to Court. On this same [day] we had the honour of kissing his Mother the Grand Dutchess's hand and there was a ball in the evening. Before we went into the Audience Chamber we halted for some time in the Chapel Royal, where the Music was very fine. The Empress seemed this morning to be uncommonly cheerful; and so she did I thought at the ball in the evening where she stood in the front of the circle and talked very affably with several people. For the first time I got a view this morning of Zeuboff: he is of the middle size, a genteel figure but not handsome. The Court was crowded as usual with a motley crew: a Persian, a Georgian and an officer from white Russia particularly attracted my attention.

Friday, 28th December

. . . the Empress had composed four plays, viz Oleg, Tavey and two others, one of which was composed after the commencement of the Swedish war with an intention to ridicule the King. But on his appearing to be such a formidable enemy, the copies were called in and she particularly put one into the fire which was in her possession. In Oleg two Eagles fly towards Constantinople as guides to the Russian Arms. I believe that all these pieces were designed originally for her own theatre only and to that I think they ought to have been confined.

The Rouble in 1788 was worth 4/0^d; now it is only worth 2/7½^d, And Copper which had only an arbitrary value and served only for convenience, determines now the price of the rouble.

Saturday, 29th December

After leaving my German master, I called upon Quarenghi and took a walk along the Quay. It is curious to see the river intersected at present by paths and roads in such manner that one can only force the imagination to look upon it as anything else than a plain.

In the evening we called upon the Princess Dashkoff who very obligingly invited us to sup. The supper consisted partly of things entirely Russian, particularly the cold Soup, the Caviare and the Postilla. Postilla is a sort of Apple Cheese made chiefly of apples and sugar, an excellent sweetmeat and peculiar to this country; peculiar indeed almost the Princess told us to the provinces of Psov and Kostroma. It is scarcely to be bought in Petersburg; where it is met with, it is usually made in the house. They often mixed it with Cranberries or Currant Berries; but that part is kept distinct from the Apples. Cold soup is composed of Quass*, bits of fowl, onion and cucumber; with the addition of Horse radish which they put into it as the Italians do Cheese, according to their taste. Though exceedingly nauseous to a foreigner the Russians are exceedingly fond of this soup, which they say is particularly refreshing and pleasant in summer.

After supper the Princess made us drink some Quass: they put a little mint into it. It certainly is a very quenchy draught. The Princess could not help exclaiming how much is this superior to lemonade. As the Russians live so much on salt meat and are very subject on that account to the Scurvy, acids of every kind are necessary to counteract the scorbutic habit of their bodies. Thence perhaps the frequent use of them and their great fondness for them.

Upon my asking the Princess whether the population of the Governments of Olonetz and Arch Angel were considerable she answered in the negative and attributed it to the great number of Sectaries in these parts, a sort of fanatics, who make it a principle to abstain from marriage.

She played us several Russian tunes, two of which particularly pleased me, one a peasants' tune, the other made by the inhabitants of the Volga, in the time of Peter the 1$^{st's}$ grandfather, on some memorable occasion.

My enquiries concerning the comparative number of Peasants subject to the crown led her to remark that all those who had belonged formerly to the church and Religious houses and had been in this reign annexed to the Crown, were in a much worse plight than they had been previous to that regulation.

Pss D[ashkova] : St Priest, if he would have consented to stay here, might have made his own stipend, so high was the Opinion, which they entertained of his talents. The Empress had been so lucky he said, that he did not doubt, but that Potemkin, whom he regarded as the evil genius of her Reign, would soon die. Which happened in the ensuing campaign.

Sunday, 30th December

They perform the ceremony of blessing the waters three or four times in the year. The waters so blessed are I imagine for the service of the churches. The next ceremony of this kind will take place on the 16th of January near the Canal at the end of the Imperial palace. It is a very solemn function; the concourse of people great; and a strong guard always attends.

The Empress has never confided in the Princess Dashkov since she threatened to publish her letters. The Princess's income is about 30,000 a year. Yet, said W. [*Whitworth*], she is always complaining of poverty. Bayley when he called on her in the morning found her in a sheep skin, without stockings and with her shoes down at the heels. Indeed I understood that this is her common way of dressing.

The Consul* has in all £1,000 a year as such, 300 from the Russian Company and about 700 at 10 roubles each from the ships. He is not permitted to be in trade. Mr. Bayley has been [here] forty years and perhaps worth 30,000. They would sooner take the word of an English Merchant, than the Bond of any other, especially a Russian (Bayley).

Count Orloff drinks off a bottle of Champagne at a draught. He has a very large stud of horses, which he takes a pleasure in shewing; as he does in gratifying the curiosity of a stranger in every respect. He resides constantly at Moscow. (Bayley).

The Russians fight with their elbows stiff and their arms outstretched. There was to be a battle between fifty on a side this morning a verst or two from Petersburg. Count Orloff keeps a great number of these boxers.

Letters have been sent sometimes to our Minister under cover to Bayley's house. In that case they make a practice of carrying them to the Post Office. Upon carrying one in particular, the Director said 'You have done very right: we know very well what that packet contains'.

As many of the peasants are rich, and their property lies entirely at the mercy of their Lord, for this reason they make a practice of burying their wealth in the ground. In this manner they account partly for the disappearance of the silver and gold Coin. They would naturally be very apt to do this, when the gold and silver rouble became so much more in value than the nominal. Owing to the same cause the Copper is continually decreasing. Now for this decrease no other cause can be assigned. For being intrinsically less in value than the rouble, it cannot be exported. Notwithstanding the fall in the value of the rouble, the taxes have not been raised in proportion, nor the payments to the Nobles. So that the Crown and the Nobles are losers and the Peasants gainers by that fall. Sherematof* only takes four roubles a head from his peasants when he might just as well take ten. This likewise is the case with many others. Yet it seemed to be allowed that the Capitation Tax had been raised.

Their way of preserving Furs. They keep them very close from the air in the first place. Then they put up with them little bits of raw skin; and strew pepper, camphor and something else. But in general they send their skins to the Furrier and give a rouble for having [them] taken care of.

The white sheet in the sledges used to be confined to the Royal family. But now Mr. Bayley thinks that the three first ranks have the right to use [it]. And the two last coloured or striped sheets and that any person may make use of nets.

Wednesday, 2nd January, 1793

Mr. Whitworth had a great diplomatic dinner, at which besides the foreign minister, Markoff, Korkassof* who is going to Constantinople, Platta, the confidential friend of Potocki, and the Prince Dolgorucki were present. In the evening we were invited to a private Opera by the Count and Countess Golofkin. They two, Varvara and Mary Luffofna* were the performers and they acquitted themselves very well. The latter in particular discovered considerable theatrical talents. La Baronne Stroganoff:* she pressed us exceedingly to go to their house again. I like her exceedingly. Princess Lobomirski: she is niece of Potocki's confidential friend who has the character of being a great rascal. From the opera we adjourned to the Count's house where there was a ball and afterwards a very handsome supper. I joined in the Polonese dances and upon the whole passed my time very agreeably. Having now a considerable number of acquaintance among the ladies, the Society is become

now much more agreeable to me than it was at first. It struck
three o'clock as I got into bed.

Dr. Pallas told us that though the climate of the spot on the sea
of Azoff allotted to the French Colonists is good and the soil rich
and dry, yet there is no wood and a scarcity of good water. I
asked why they had given them a settlement in the Crimea. He
said that the late Prince [Potemkin] had given away to private
persons all the best situations in that country. He spoke of the newly
ceded territory between the Bug and the Niester in high terms,
and supposed that it had [not] been chosen because they might
be afraid to trust a body of Frenchmen on the Frontier. Yet
young Nariskin told me that this country also is in want of wood
and water.

There lies a desert Dr. Pallas told us today of three hundred
versts between the Calmuc* and Kirghese Tartars.* The hordes
of the former may be visited without any danger. A stranger fixes
his tent with them, and gets supplied by them for money with
whatever he wants. They are very much attached to this roving
way of life, which in his opinion is a very happy one. According
to the season of the year they go first towards the South and then
towards the North.

Thursday, 3rd January

Bootle went to the Tennis Court and I to the Newfski market,
called so from being held in a spot not far from the convent of
Alexander Newfski. It takes place always a few days before Xmas.
The peasants from all the neighbouring districts bring beef,
mutton, veal, pork, fowl, game, butter and even hay, all except the
last in a frozen state and from hence the people of Petersburg
supply themselves with these articles for the winter. They have at
the same time an opportunity of doing it with almost every thing
else, but particularly as I was a witness with leather, meal and
corn. . . . I even passed by two or three Premises full of sledges
to be sold. The Perspective was crowded with sledges belonging
to persons who were going to purchase or returning with their bar-
gains. It was curious to see whole pigs in several of these sledges
as stiff and upright as if they were stuffed. The Market itself which
occupies a very large space, was entirely filled with the sledges of
the peasants, in which the frozen meat either remained or was
piled up against them. The pigs in particular were for the most
part fixed upright round about the sledges. . . . I can never look at
these poor people without reflecting with horror on the degrading
circumstances of their servile condition.

The Princess Dashkoff whom we visited after dinner treated us with some (what I must call for want of the true name) Cranberry Postilla.* She told us that they make great use of the berries of the mountain Ash in this country. They make a liquor of them, they make a Postilla of them, and I think that they eat them without any preparation, but [not] till after the frost has touched them. Miss Bates described their taste as partaking of a very agreeable bitterness.

She [*Princess Dashkova*] said that the sovereigns having been for a long time all women who had come to the throne by a kind of usurpation, they had all been under a little awe and had carried on a very mild government. She gave it as her opinion if the Grand Duke listened to the counsels of those who would be disposed to suggest severe principles to him and a very different line of conduct, that a revolution would probably be the consequence. She represented the Golitzin family* to be very numerous, very stupid and very proud. . . . The palace of Ice which was erected on the Neva in the reign of the Empress Ann, was created she told us on occasion of the marriage of a Prince Golitzin who served as a buffoon at court and with a view to humble that aspiring family.

She has a painting by Sir Joshua of his own niece, which she regards as his masterpiece because she did not suffer him to lay on his perishing colours.*

We were engaged to Baron Stroganoff's or we should have supped again with the Princess D. who very obligingly invited us. At the Baron's we found them employed in the first rehearsal of a play. The Princess Alexis Golitzin, Baron Stroganoff, the eldest Mad^{selle} Constantinoff and three other gentlemen were the performers. . . . They had one of the French Players to give them directions. Plays in private houses are much *à la mode* at present in Petersburg. Last year Balls were the rage. I was told this evening that there [are] no less than six plays at present on the *Tapis*. There are no less than eight *theatres de societé*, for instance at I. Saltikoff's, Dolgorucki's, Stroganoff's, Somoilow's, Golofkin's, Moushkin-Poushkin's.*

After supper the young men amused themselves with wrestling, taking up a candle out of water with the mouth, and with other such gambols. It might put one in mind of the amusements in an English country gentleman's house. Upon the whole the evening was very agreeable.

Friday, 4th January

As it was the eve of their Xmas Day, we had a ball at the Club, but I understand that we ought to have visited all our acquaintance in order to pay them the compliments of the season. We ought likewise to have gone and heard the midnight mass, which was performed as well in the Greek as in the Roman Catholic Churches.

Saturday, 5th January

There was a court this morning but we did not go to it. Zeuboff made his first appearance in his new order of the black Eagle, which had been sent to the Empress by the King of Prussia to dispose of as she thought proper. His Brother Valerian who is honoured with the white Eagle brought it the night before last. . . . Being the Xmas day of this country, it was celebrated in the evening at court by a variety of Gambols, in which the Empress takes a part. She is said indeed to be so fond of such pastimes, that not a week passes, but she amuses herself with something of that kind.

N.B. Women of all ranks paint here. But what is remarkable is, that as I understand, all the lower classes of women do this.

N.B. Prince Wiazemskoi,* had till lately the management of the Finances. But of late the Empress has taken them into her own hands employing Somoilow as an assistant only. Old W. though three score and ten is said to be never a day without a girl.

Sunday, 6th January

We went this morning to the English Church.* The men and women sit apart. In the sentences after the belief they pray for her Imperial Majesty along with the King, and in the Litany along with the Queen. I was very much pleased with their organ which was not too large for the place. Mr. Percival's income as Minister of this Church is I am told seven hundred pounds a year.

Baron Torby . . . told us today that the Piemontese Count Alfieri* thinking himself not sufficiently perfect in the Italian language went and resided eight years at Florence in order to improve himself in it, before he ventured to become an author and to write his tragedies. The *Pretendante* fell violently in love with him and they were living together not long ago at Paris. He was a prodigious admirer of our Constitution. He was likewise I think a great Democrat till he became witness to the enormities committed in Paris. His mind since then is changed.

Monday, 7th January

Count Starenberg* came in before we were risen from table. He told me that certain persons belonging to the two clubs which had

been discovered in Vienna, had been endeavouring to prevail on
the Emperor to raise recruits and levy new taxes in order to render
the people discontented and lay the foundation of a revolution. We
stayed for about half an hour at Madame Zagraski's* and afterwards went to Baron Stroganoff's where we supped. . . . Madame S.
would be more agreeable if she did not spit so much.

Tuesday, 8th January

It [was] curious to see the beards of the Russians frosted by the
freezing of their breath. The fur of my Pelisse near my mouth
looked as if it was powdered owing to the same cause. Mr. Bayley
compared the sensation in this weather of walking on the snow to
that of pressing the paper enclosing a quantity of hair powder: I
was struck today with the justness of the comparison. . . . Bootle
complained of the difficulty of breathing, from the great degree
of cold. I cannot say that I was sensible of the same myself; but
I felt the cold in the carriage very sensibly about my head. Though
the day was perfectly clear, yet the cold condensed the smoke in
such a manner that all around Petersburg it seemed to be thick and
heavy.

Wednesday, 9th January

Somoilow* gave a dinner and Bezborodko a ball today in honour
of the treaty signed on the same day last year with the Swedes.
The number of cards delivered out for the ball was said to have
been eight hundred. . . . The Company were expected to come in
Masquerade dresses without masks. Men wore Dominos with
Birettas, the women some dominos, and some only a piece of fine
lawn streaming from the head behind. It was observed that many
of the ladies' dresses were extremely elegant. The tunes to the
Polonese dances were composed on the occasion and what was very
extraordinary, were accompanied with voices. I was very much
pleased with them. The dancers were confined to one large room
where however it was insufferably hot; but there were not less
than eleven or twelve rooms open besides where they were playing
at cards. The coolness and comparative tranquillity of the latter
was an agreeable change from the heat, confusion and din of the
ballroom. I was told that in all there were as many as fourteen
tables for supper, three of which were below stairs. I reconnoitred
them all, by doing which I was very near losing the opportunity
of getting a seat. The attention of the Count to his company was
very striking. He wore a blue Domino which made him a con-

spicuous object in an assembly where almost all the men were in
black and brown.

Friday, 11th January

At Count Golofkin's they were casting lead for the purpose of
telling fortunes, a piece of superstition constantly practised on the
eve on the new year. They also make use of wax for the
same purpose. On this night they have also several other
superstitious practices which among us are abserved on St. Mark's
Eve.

We saw the Marble Palace* this morning. . . . The furniture is
all of silk; yet there was also velvet and cloth of gold. The Drawing
[room] is excessively handsome. In this room nothing is wood but
the floor: the doors cost 15,000 roubles, being veneered with silver,
not to mention ornaments of brass and gilding. The walls are
covered with marble and ornamented with marble pilasters, basso
rilievos etc. Yet I cannot [say] that it appeared overcharged. The
wall at the end is three yards thick. N.B. In building this palace
they forgot the offices.

The Presence Chamber is a very beautiful apartment. The hang-
ings and chairs are of flowered velvet made at Lyons. . . . The
Stove was forgot, which made the Empress very angry. They have
contrived it in what seems to be [a] door. . . . The Russian Sweating
bath. The Ball room fifteen fathoms long, which was intended
originally for a Riding house. So many ill-natured Criticisms were
made on this palace that the Empress forbad it to be shewn. We
saw it by stealth.

Saturday, 12th January

This being new year's day according to the old stile, it is kept
as a great festival in this country: For which reason the Court
was more crowded than I had ever seen it before, and we had the
honour to kiss not only the Empress's hand but the grand Dutchess's
also. The Duc de Montmorenci Laval* along with two other Gentlemen were presented to her Majesty this morning. The Duke seemed
not to be aware of kissing the Empress's hand, but when he did do
it, he did it with a loud smack. . . . In wishing one another a new
year there was more kissing than usual among the men. . . .

We then [went] for a short time to the Countess Saltikoff's where
there was a select and agreeable ball. . . . I danced polonaises with
the Countess Golofkin, Mad[selle] Schatz, Madame Somoilow and the
little crooked widow.

Sunday, 13th January

I got up this morning with a confounded rheumatism in the shoulders, which went off soon afterwards, but was brought on again by my going out into the air in order to breakfast with Garshore—for not having observed the glass, I did not know that there were so many degrees of cold.

N.B. Potemkin at one time, such was the influence of his enemies, received orders to repair to the Army. Some friend of his however interposed and having stated to the Empress how necessary [were] his services, prevailed on her to send a courier and recall him. His enemies finding this out persuaded [her] to dispatch countermanding that order. He suspecting the business of the second, did not open the letter but returned immediately. When he arrived, his enemies were thrown into the greatest confusion. In his travelling dress he flew immediately to the Empress. They told him that the Empress had given orders not to admit any person, and particularly by name not to admit him. This was said to him, G[arshore] believes, by Zavadovski.* Potemkin immediately seized him by the Collar and pushing him forced his way never the less to the Empress's presence. A violent altercation is said to have happened between them; in course of which Potemkin threw a candlestick at her head. The issue was however a reconciliation and the reinstatement of Potemkin in all his power.

N.B. Upon some occasion Potemkin is said to have —— Princess Michel Galitzin's —— in the presence of her mother the Countess Souvalow and her aunt the Countess Soltikoff. Soltikoff himself is said to have carried Potemkin's letters to the Princess Michel Galitzin.

Woronzoff* is going to Moscow and Besborodko also it is believed. In short it is thought that a Storm is brewing against Zeuboff. Esterhazy is in the Empress's *societé* and passes the greatest part of his time in Zeuboff's apartments.

Besborodko at a masquerade is not ashamed to go leering about at all common girls there.

Monday, 14th January

In the afternoon we called on the Princess Dashkoff's, where we did not stay long, because we were engaged to a ball at Count Stroganoff's,* given to a select and very genteel party, on occasion as was imagined of the young Princess Golitzin having formally accepted the proposals of the young Count. Count Stroganoff's house is reckoned the finest, the best furnished, of any in Petersburg. . . . The Empress introduced the Count to [the] King of

Poland at Kief, as a man who had done his utmost endeavours to ruin himself but had not been able to succeed. . . . N.B. The Count is in the Empress's private society.

Excursus on monarchy in the notes.

Milton, Harrington and Sydney have treated expressly of the danger and inutility of Monarchy; but the subject has been much more profoundly as well as popularly discussed within these two years. Those who will take the trouble of perusing the 'Essai sur les Privileges' and the sequel to it 'Qu'est-ce que le Tiers Etat' of the Abbe Sieyés, Paine's Rights of Man, parts 1 and 2, Barlow's Advice to the Privileged Orders, and Oswald's review of the Constitution of Great Britain, will find almost every thing that the subject affords on one side of the question.

The King's income equal to the labour of 60,000 men. By an act of Parliament 22 George 3 c. 22, in the distribution of the civil list income 32,955£ is appropriated to pay the salaries of the Lord Chancellor, the Speaker of the House of Commons and all the judges of England and Wales; and 89,799£ to pay the menial Servants of his Majesty's household.

Is it true, as Cooper asserts, in his pamphlet somewhere that sixty persons command a Majority in the house of Commons?

Tuesday, 15th January

We saw the Marble Palace a second time today. A survey of it has been taken lately; which gives rise to a persuasion that it [is] going to be inhabited. Mr. Y[eames] imagines that the Empress's son* by Prince Orloff who is at present residing at Reval is the person. A Notion it seems has long prevailed that the Empress has bequeathed it to him by will. The Empress's son by Orloff when at the Academy was a very promising young man. His allowance is 150,000 roubles a year; but having incurred great debts, it has been reduced to 12, and the rest is kept back for the use of his creditors. The Empress has other Children in the palace. The two Mad^{selles} Protassoff are supposed to be her daughters.

In one of the rooms there is a bust of Prince Orloff, and Busts of his four brothers. His death was caused by grief for the death of his wife which drove him out of his senses. His madness was most outrageous. . . . Orloff's ghost is believed to haunt the palace.

Count Orloff never comes to Petersburg but on business or without being sent for. It is imagined that they wish to place him at the head of the Admiralty in the place of Koutousoff,* who is

G

very unequal to the situation. The Grand Duke is nominally at the head of this department. Zeuboff, somebody observed, looked very small in the company of the Count. He [*Orloff*] bears the character of an honest [man] with good plain strong sense. The People adore him. He is said to have the interests of his country much at heart. He is likewise very much attached to their ancient customs. Somebody told me that his house is a perfect image of that of an old Russian nobleman.

The Palace cost five or six millions of Roubles. Many of those who were employed got Fortunes.

Hineham told them [*Bootle and Sir Watkin*] that the Empress in conversation with the Princess Dashkoff on the subject of Mr. Fox's late behaviour, after condemning it had said that she would throw a veil over his bust,* which she sent for, if it would not look like an imitation of the French, and that she would even sell it but that it was not worth while, for that she could not get thirty roubles for it.

Thursday, 17th January

We were present this morning at the blessing of the waters, a ceremony held in great veneration all over Russia, and performed on this day in every part of the Empire professing the Greek religion. Mass being first said in the Chapel Royal, a numerous procession consisting of several Bishops and priests intermixed with a variety of other persons and brought up by little parties of soldiers conveying the colours of their respective regiments, set off from the Chapel, passed through the palace, and advanced along a scaffolding erected for the purpose to an octagon pavilion erected on the Canal which encompasses the Admiralty. The Archbishop, after the proper service had been performed descended by a ladder, dipped a cross into the water down to which a hole had been cut through the ice, baptised a child, and sprinkled with holy [water] the colours which had been carried in procession. A number of canons were fired to announce either the commencement or the completion of the ceremony, during [which] I observed that the people by crossing themselves expressed a great deal of devotion. They did the same particularly as the cross passed by and indeed kept their heads uncovered almost the whole time of [the] procession, both as [it] went and as it returned. For after the ceremony they returned in the same order. The Crowd of people was immense; the area before the Canal was almost entirely filled; there were likewise a great many spectators on the top of the palace as well as on a low building adjoining to Count Bruce's. In general they make a point of conscience not to be absent on this occasion. The soldiers who had been on duty near the Pavilion made almost the circuit of the Area after this and passed in review under the Empress's windows.

To day the weather was not very severe; when it happens to be so it is exceeding hard service to those poor fellows, who remain on their posts from eight in the morning without any extraordinary cloathing. There have been instances of [a] great many lives being lost. For which reason, if the cold is very severe, the Empress now defers the ceremony. I had the curiosity to go up to the Pavilion about half an hour after the water had been blessed and was much amused to see the anxiety with which the people were procuring it in Jugs and bottles; some were drinking, others washing their faces, and one man had dipped his whole head in and drenched his locks most completely. As the procession returned several persons were employed in sprinkling the holy water over the crowd on each side. Sir Watkin as a stranger by his own account was particularly favoured.

The Bishops, or at least those whom I took for them, wore a sort of Crown. The other priests, as well as the rest of the procession, were bareheaded. The priests wore gaudy vestments by which they were distinguishable as well as by their beards and their hair floating at a great length down their shoulders.

Friday, 18th January

We dined the usual party with the addition of Dr. Guthrie,* Akin and the Abbé at Mr. Whitworth's, where the arrival of Brooks the messenger did not fail to interest us all very much. Somebody asked him how long it was since he had been in bed. Not, said he, since I went to fetch Mr. Dundas from Scotland. He set out the 29th December. He had been fifteen days coming from The Hague : but he had been detained forty-eight hours.

Notes of a conversation with Akin. Admiral Grieg* commanded in fact under Orloff in the Mediterranean at the battle Tchesmin. The Empress wished Orloff to take the command again in the Baltic against the Swedes, telling him that he should as before have Grieg under him. But he declined it, telling her Majesty frankly that he [knew] nothing about sea affairs; that even at Tchesmin he had done nothing himself; that Grieg had done everything; and that he was determined not to rob him a second time of the honour to which he was entitled. Grieg died of a broken heart for not having succeeded better though it was owing to the cowardice of his officers, three of whom he broke.

Sunday, 20th January

We dined at Mr. Whitworth's without him. He was engaged at Bezborodko's. The object is to prevail upon Repnin not to supply France with naval stores: in which there is a prospect of succeeding.

Tuesday, 22nd January

From the Princess's [*Dashkova*] we paid a visit at Count Golofkin's, where I had a great deal of very agreeable conversation with the Count. . . . The Noblesse generally bathe he says once a month and the common people twice a week on Wednesdays and Saturdays. . . . Bootle and Sir Watkin went then [to] the ——— and I came home.

Thursday, 24th January

Having had the Rheumatism for some time, I resolved this evening to try a Russian Bath. I had ordered it to be prepared in good time. This is necessary because two hours are required for that purpose. As I entered I met with two or three men entirely naked; whether they were persons employed in the baths or persons bathing I do not know. I undressed myself in a small room close by the bath, with a stove and surrounded by a bench. The bath itself might be about five yards in length and four in breadth. The heat was very considerable when I went in, I remained for some time on the lowest bench, until indeed I began to be in a perspiration. The bathing man then, who was as naked as myself except that he had a pocket to hold his Sponge hanging down sometimes before and sometimes behind, the bathing man I say began then with lathering and scrubbing my head. No groom ever took half so much pains with a horse's head. After he had done it enough he poured little buckets of warm water repeatedly upon it in order to clean it and wash away the soap. I then took my place on the lowest of the two elevated Benches, where when the heat was increased by throwing water on the hot stones, it almost took away my respiration. Here I underwent another lathering and scrubbing, from head to foot first lying on my belly and afterwards lying on my back. This done, the man poured several buckets of warm water on my head as I sat, the first of which excited a very acute pain between the shoulders where he had rubbed off the skin a little. He repeated the operation of pouring buckets of warm water on my head. . . . I found the sensation exceedingly agreeable, I felt like a River God;

or like the statue of Moses with water flowing down a long beard
and long locks.

I reposed for a while after this on the lower bench, and then
ascended to the higher again in order to undergo the process of
being lathered a second time with a bunch of Twigs. It had been
performed before with a handful of hemp. I sat for a while on
the lower bench after having passed through this second course of
discipline. Having then been three quarters of an hour in the bath
I retired into the adjoining room, was rubbed down well with a
sheet, dressed myself and drank a bason of strong punch. As I was
exceedingly afraid of taking [cold] I staid in this room till I was
thoroughly cool, indeed almost as long as I had been in the bath.

One thing was omitted, which I was not aware of till it was too
late. They dip the Bunch of Twigs in water, put it into the stove,
and then dash [it] over the naked man, whose sensation from it
I am told is very acute and singular. So likewise is I am told that
from the pouring of cold water upon the head.

N.B. The price of heating a bath is a rouble. Besides which I
gave the man who rubbed me 80 copecs and the man who brought
me the water for my Punch 20. In the public bath the price is only
4 copecs.

In this Bath there were four other separate baths like that in
which I bathed. Besides the public ones, one for the men and the
other for the women, Dominico told me that he knew of ten such
in Petersburgh. Formerly the men and women had one common
bath: but by a late regulation they have been separated. By the
frequent use of warm baths the women relax themselves exceedingly, as appears particularly by the hanging down of the breasts.
Men make a practice of coming to bathe with their wives or with
their whores. Besides these great baths, every gentleman has one
in his house.

Count Orloff is come here to procure the divorce of a woman, to
whom he is attached and whom he wishes to marry, from her
husband, who has no inclination to part with her (Whitworth).

Sunday, 27th January

. . . When I came back I found Bootle gone out and was soon
after prevailed upon by Sir Watkin to accompany him to see the
Empress's jewels along with Hineham. It turned out however to be
the Hermitage, which I now walked through for the third time.

We dined at Baron Stroganoff's where the company was very
numerous. . . . After dinner M. Somoilow sent for two Moldavians
who had been brought to Petersburg by Potemkin, to play for our

amusement, which they did, one on a fiddle and the other on a sort of Guittar several tunes, Russian and Turkish as well as of their own country. Their heads were shaved like those of the Poles, their complexions were dark, and their dress between the Polish and the Asiatic. This day's visit was calculated, I take it, to give one a just idea of the hospitality, the confusion and uncomfortableness of a true Russian house.

On our return we staid at home a couple of hours and then betook ourselves to the Countess Saltikoff's where everything is so different in style that one might fancy oneself transported in a few hours to a polite assembly in Paris or London. The Duke de Laval:* Dumourier,* always esteemed a great Projector, employed as a secret Emissary of the Minister; though he served in the Seven Years War, he never had any credit for military Talents. Custine* a strange mixture of Avarice, Devotion and debauchery. Valence* in no repute whatever as an officer. Montesquieu* the author of several publications, a clever man.

Wednesday, 30th January

The Baron Sternberg* dined with us at Mr. Whitworth's. Dalkeith's speech, the dispute about the word 'respectable' and the spilling of the coffee made this day rather remarkable. . . .

Thursday, 31st January

Sir Watkin, Bootle, old Gould and myself made a party today to go and see the palace of Tsarskoe Zelo,* Bootle and I in one Kibitki, Gould and Sir W. in another. . . . We saw first the apartments of the Grand Duke and Grand Dutchess, afterwards those of their family the young grand Duke and Grand Dutchesses, and lastly those of the Empress. We asked to see the Favourite's but they would not grant us permission. They open either into the Chinese or the Cupola room. The division of the apartments belonging to the young grand Dutchesses is singular. A Gothic Screen divides the room into two unequal parts; at the back of this the attendants wait. Behind the bed is a Divan where their woman sleeps; and in front of it also is another where another person always sits up. The Curtains enclose the spaces in which this stands as well as the bed; round which white dimitty curtains are drawn; but at the top is open. . . .

The baths consist of two floors on the upper of which there are three apartments, and on the lower the baths. In the largest room there is a large bath lined with tin. I believe, into which either hot or cold water can be let in: in the next a large tub with two cisterns [?] above it by means of which the water can be made of any temperature; there is also a Russian Bath. The Empress's dressing room is adjoining to the second. The apartment in the middle is of a considerable size, but those at each end rather small. One of these is cased with Jasper and the other with Agate. That which is lined with Jasper is ornamented with columns of agate. I think we were told that this building cost 500,000 roubles: not including the Agate and the Jasper, which comes from the mines of Kolgwan. When it was finished the Empress walked over it holding Cameron by the Arm and said, It is indeed very handsome 'mais ça coûte'. She frequently dines in the Baths when her party is small. She also sits there a great deal in hot weather on account of their great coolness.

But her usual dining room is in the Gallery. This is a long room encompassed by a broad walk, on one side protected from the South by the building in the middle and on the other from the North. She walks on one side or the other according to the circumstances of the weather. On the Balustrade round this walk she has placed a great number of Bronze busts: and here we saw that of Fox between the busts of Cicero and Demosthenes. In order to arrive at the Gallery we descended from the hanging Garden I think by a stair, on which I remarked the statue of Junius Brutus.

After seeing the palace we passed on our return to Mr. Bush's* by the *Chambre de matin*, which serves as a repository for all the statues both antique and modern which the Empress has bought. The marble Bust of Fox is here with the rest; but the door being nailed up, we could not gain admittance. All the statues and sculptures are to be placed in a Museum, which she has it [in] contemplation to build.

Bush showed us a superb plan which she had conceived for this Purpose. It would consist of a Colonnade, commencing from the Empress's apartments, making an oblique angle with the end of the palace and leading to the Museum, round which the Colonnade would also run, and the outer apartment of which would be a semicircle of the dimensions of the Rotunda. The Museum he told me would itself be between two and three thousand feet either long or round; and the whole walk half a mile. It would cost with cream [?] columns a million and a half roubles. At one time the Empress was determined to have all the columns of the Verde antique from Kolgwan. But being calculated that the expense would be £200 each, that idea was dropped. The principal charge arises from the Carriage. Afterwards there was an idea to have them of cast iron. At present the plan is given [back] and Cameron is desired to give another. Is that a modification of this, or something in the way of what Quarenghi showed me? There was to have been a walk on the top of this Colonnade, as well as below.

The garden altogether is six miles in circumference, and in the French style, as it was laid out at first in the reign of the late Empress, partly in the English. A walk in the latter as I understood runs round the water and is at least four miles in length. Several buildings* for different purposes and in honour of several illustrious characters are scattered up and down: for instance the Theatre, the *Chambre de Musique*, the *Chambre de Matin*, the *Amirauté*, the *Temple Turc*, the *Temple Chinois*, the *Arc Chinois*, the *Obelisque de Comte Romanzoff*, the *Colonne de memoire de comte Frederic Orloff, la colonne Rastrelli, l'Arc Triomphal de Prince Orloff, la Pyramide Egyptienne* (a burial place for dogs), *le pont de marbre, les Bains* and a *Ruine*. Some of these we saw at a distance but as the Ground was covered with snow we did not go up to them. We should I believe have gone to see the Granite Columns in the Church of Sophia, if old Gould had [not] been impatient to go to dinner.

The Empress passes the months of April, May, June, July and August at Tsarskoe Zelo, except that for about a month of this time in the month of May she goes to Peterhoff. She rises at six; she takes a short walk before breakfast and breakfasts at eight; she then employs about two hours with her Ministers; after which she walks out again and dines at one. After dinner she sits down to cards till five: she then goes out again with the whole royal family to walk. Sometimes they have Music and three times a week a play. She retires to her apartments at eight never supping. Zeuboff leaves her at ten and then gives a great supper to all the generals and courtiers at the Court. He always dines with her, her family very seldom, only indeed on great days. One thing struck me as very remarkable, even when the Grand Duke and Grand Dutchess reside at either of their own country houses, their Children always remain with the Empress. He [*Bush*] spoke well of Zeuboff. He never was known to do any harm to anybody and whenever it is in his power he is glad to do a service. He told me that before Mamonoff and after Landskoi there was a favourite for about two months who was turned off for *incapacity.** He is living now at Moscow.

Besides the hay in the bottom of our Kibitki, we had a feather-bed and a wolfskin, so that we lay perfectly soft. Over my velvet boots I put on my Kirghis; and over my great coat lined with squirrel skin, my Bearskin Pelisse and Sir Watkin lent me a fur Cap: so that except a little in the face I did not suffer from the cold in the least. The road was so uneven in some places that our Ishworshick was obliged to lean from his seat twice to prevent us from going over. Not far from Petersburg we passed by a very large Crescent called Yagerhoff, now building, for the Dogs, horses and people who belong to the Imperial chase. The walls are not yet stuccoed. We also passed by an Imperial Villa called Tchesme* built in a Gothic style. . . . We also passed near the Chinese Town* which the Empress had built after the model of that at Kiachta.* The houses seem intended for habitations but it is not yet known to what use she means to put them. There is or is to be moreover a place of worship in the same style.

Sunday, 3rd February

Hynam: Some people suspected that the Empress was married to Potemkin.* Peter Luff would say that there was even a stronger tie. It is difficult to say what that could be, unless there was a plot between them to take off the Grand Duke. N.B. The Grand Duke has no friend because he cannot be trusted. N.B. Ramzoff a natural son of the Princess Dashkoff's father was at [one] time expected to have been taken into favour and was courted by all the world with that view. The Empress had given rise to the notion by observing one day pointing to his lodging that R. lived there. Hearing however of the attentions paid and of some indiscreet expressions which he had used, she changed her mind.

Potemkin was a Sergeant in the Guards and was placed in July [1762] at the door when the Emperor Peter IIIrd was murdered. Being at one time as he thought on the point of death, he revealed the following circumstances to Peterhof [*sic*]. Two Corporals were employed to put him between two feather beds and in which they succeeded and Baratinski and another person were actually upon the bed for the purpose of smothering him. But being though not a strong man very active he disengaged himself. Alexi Orloff then went in, seized him exhausted as he was by the throat, squeezed it with all his extraordinary force, and the unhappy Prince dropped down dead* as if he had been shot. The two Corporals did not survive that day. For Poison had been administered to them before they undertook the business.

About five o'clock we went to the ball at the *Corps des Cadets*. This ball recurs once a month on a Sunday beginning at four and lasting till six. It begins with a number of speeches made by the boys of one such class. Then they dance for about an hour. They then walk about and have an opportunity of breaking [away] to their friends if they have any in the company present. The last thing is to arrange themselves accordingly to their classes and exercise a march. A very numerous company forms a circle round the room.

The whole number of boys and young men is about 800, though the establishment is only for 6. The Count D'Anhalt* or the Empress adds and supports the rest. They are divided into five Classes: of these the two first are dressed in Uniform, the other three in stone colour, light blue and dark brown. Each class has their own dormitories and their dining rooms. They are admitted from the age of five to that of eight. An Election takes place but once in three years. The Mothers come with their children whose pedigrees are examined; the Children themselves undergo a Scrutiny; and then out of the number declared eligible they fill the vacancies by lot; as they pretend, yet it is believed that they find the means of shewing favour. The distress of the Mothers whose children are rejected is excessive.

Monday, 4th February

Sir Watkin set off this evening for Moscow. . . .

Tuesday, 5th February

We saw Peterhoff and Oranienbaum to-day. . . . We visited the celebrated and favourite retreat of Peter the 1st, as also a small house adjoining where we understood that the Empress herself resides when she comes to Peterhoff. They both go under the name of Mon Plaisir and are delightfully situated on the shore of the gulph almost close to the water. N.B. When any woman of rank or indeed any woman in low life is reproached with her gallantries, her answer is that our mother does the same. (Gould). . . . In coming back my driver amused himself for a good part of the time with singing. When the wolfs appeared, he made a prodigious outcry and was highly delighted to oblige some poor people to quit the road and with overturning a sledge.

Saturday, 9th February

We dined at Mr. Whitworth's, where Paget asked me first who were the best w—— in Petersburg, and soon afterwards whether I was in orders. . . . We supped at Madame Watkofski's. There was but a young man belonging to the Corps de Cadets, M. Fermier and ourselves. M. Watkofski accompanied the Grand Duke in his travels. She sings and plays delightfully on the Harpsichord. She favoured us with several charming tunes. I particularly admired one or two of her hymns. Her father forbad her to read the *Liaisons Dangereuses* and the Confessions of Rousseau.

Monday, 11th February

Mr. W[hitworth] gave it as his opinion today that had the advice of St. Priest been followed instead of Necker's* timid counsels, the King of France might have been still on his throne. St. Priest's advice was for the King to retire to some safe place, and to trust the defence of his cause to his friends at the head of his troops. The D. de Richelieu when he was at Petersburg maintained that the estates of the *Emigrés* would enable the French to carry on the war for the next ten years to come. Not finding the Princess Dashkoff at home in [the] afternoon we went and sat with Hynam, who as usual gave us a great deal of curious information. During his illness Potemkin caused four persons, one in each corner of the room, to syringe him with cold water. He was then in a high fever and died four days after. He also caused bottles of Seltzer water one after another to be poured on his head in order to assuage the pain. . . . The Empress disliked Madame Souvalow, yet finding from Potemkin's Papers that he had given his promise to obtain for her the appointment of fetching the Princesses of Baden, on that account she was sent.

Wednesday, 13th February

The Empress in her orders for going into mourning expresses herself to the Russians in such manner as this 'For the death of the King of France who has been cruelly murdered by his rebellious subjects'. There was no ball at the Princess Golitzin's this evening on account of the late melancholy news.

Saturday, 16th February

The King of France's will, the sending away of Mr. Chauvelin* and the circumstances of the execution make the subject of every conversation.

Sunday, 17th February

We went . . . to the Countess Saltikoff's where we found a crowded and splendid ball. They supped as usual at a number of separate round tables. Several people endeavoured to dissuade us from our intended tour into Siberia.

Monday, 18th February

The road over the gulph was so bad and so deep in snow that we were three hours in going to Cronstadt this morning . . . the hard beaten path being very narrow, we could [not] conveniently go with three horses abreast, for the near horse was continually plunging up to his belly in the soft snow. They mark the road one half of the way with trees and the other half with sticks made conspicuous by a dark rag. The first thing we did after our arrival was to call upon Admiral Creuse,* a fine old man of sixty who speaks English very well and looks upon himself as an Englishman. . . . Captain Thesiger dropped in at the Admiral's at the same time with us, and though engaged to dine out, undertook to conduct us round the Harbour and Docks. Thesiger is supposed to be a natural son of the Duke of Portland. He was with Rodney on the 12th of April: he has also been no less than three Voyages to China.

The old Admiral gave us an excellent dinner, for which after walking six, seven or eight Versts we were very ready. He is as fat as Bootle with a fine countenance, easy unaffected manners, and apparently a very solid understanding. As we had found the road over the ice so bad, we determined to return by Oranienbaum and Peterhoff, though it was full twice as far.

Tuesday, 19th February

We went to the public baths this morning out of curiosity. In one of them a number of women were entirely naked without seeming to regard us: some sitting on the elevated floor and others coming out into the cold air; and others again dressing themselves under a shed out of doors. They did some of them take hold [of] the bundle of Twigs so as to hide their nakedness but apparently with great indifference about the matter. Nothing could be more disgusting than most of the figures, their breasts hanging down in a most hideous manner. . . . We concluded the evening at Nariskin's, where I had the honour of having a very curious question put to me by the Countess Golofkin and Madame Somoilow. I ought to have mentioned that before our going to Nariskin's we paid a second visit to the Baths. The heat was excessive but that did not prevent us from entering. Most of the women appeared to be entirely unconcerned at our presence, but one at last took offence and we thought [it] advisable to make good our retreat for fear of having a pail of hot water thrown in our faces.

Saturday, 23rd February

We went very early without any occasion for it to Baron Stroganoff's, where we dined today, and where we met with a multitude of people who came to dine officially with M. Somoilow. I counted I think thirty at table. M. Nariskin, a Chamberlain who married a sister of Stroganoff's, was there with his wife. Also an unmarried sister of Stroganoff's, who having never yet come into company, as his sister-in-law told me, seemed alarmed about taking my arm when we walked in to dinner. She seemed I must confess to be a very complete hoyden. Orloff, a general of the Cossacs* who distinguished himself by attacking Hassan Pasha's cavalry, was likewise of this party. When Somoilow entered he was received with as much deference as if he had been the Empress. After dinner we talked for some time with M. Marmot, a Frenchman, and we were then invited into a forlorn apartment where we found Madame Somoilow with a Miniature painter who took a sketch of Bootle and her, which they exchanged. Her foolish husband immediately after his marriage had read to this good Woman the *nouvelle Eloise*, the *Liaisons Dangereuses* and *Farblas*, of all which books she talked with the greatest possible *sang froid*. We called after this . . . upon Hynam with whom we staid till eleven o'clock, though we went with a determination to come away in an hour. Hyman says the Empress is acquainted with the conduct and character of every Englishman in Petersburg. The Grand Duke is supposed to have an intrigue at present with Mad^selle Poljanski,* the young lady whom we met with at the Princess Dashkoff's, the daughter of the Countess Elizabeth. His other mistress* is excessively plain.

Sunday, 24th February

From Court we went for a while to Mr. Whitworth's and then to Count Osterman's where we dined. Our party was about twenty six. We had Music during dinner, and the performers were his own peasants bought for that purpose. I asked Marchese how many dependants of this kind the Count might have in his house and he said about a hundred; he told me at the same [time] that Wjamzemski who died lately had 160: whom he cloathed and fed. General Kakhouski* who commanded in Poland and General Koutousow* who is going as Ambassador to the Porte were in the company. Marchese told me that Koutoussow's suite would consist of 1,000 persons. . . .

From Osterman's we went and sat down to the bottle again at Whitworth's. About nine o'clock we made our appearance for about half an hour at Luff's. The Mufti of the Tartars, the Pasha of three tails and a Kirghese being sitting together made a good group in this diversified picture. [The Pasha's] brother and two children were beheaded and he would have had the same fate if he had returned to Turky. He enjoyed formerly an income Luff told me of two millions; the Empress allows him at present twelve thousand roubles and a house.

Monday, 25th February

We went to the Princess Dashkoff's this morning in sledges and drove fast through the dirty uneven streets, being afraid that she would think us late. She gave us an account of her Manouvre to prevent the Countess Esterhazy from being presented otherwise than in the common way. She told us that the Grand Duke by insinuating that it would be agreeable had introduced the Custom among the Russians when they paid their respects to him of kneeling, which is not observed to the Empress.

We had only the English party to dinner at Mr. Whitworth's. Bootle and I were left by ourselves with him; he was very communicative and told us that Russia had not consented to break their treaty of commerce with France, but had engaged to send twelve ships of the Line to cooperate with the English fleet and withdrawn herself from the armed Neutrality.* The Thursday after this business was settled, he found out that they meant to sign the Treaty of Partition. He therefore waited on Besborodko, Osterman and Zeuboff to remonstrate against the propriety of such a Measure; and especially at the present juncture, which gives it the appearance of being done with the concurrence of England. His remonstrance has he believes suspended the business. The Share of Poland which falls to Russia contains 2 Million 600,000 inhabitants, the line marking it passes through Polotsk, Minsk, Lusk and Kaminiec. Prussia gets Thorn and Dantzic and a district running quite up to Warsaw, making the Vistula the boundary, and extending as far as Cracow. Cracow is to be the Emperor's whose allotment being not in proportion to that of the others, he has been very indifferent about the transaction. The Empress likewise was not anxious in the matter. The King of Prussia has been the principal mover.* This affair has been settled ever since last January. Whitworth had procured a sight of the letter which the Empress wrote to Besborodko on the subject.

Tuesday, 26th February

We concluded our evening at Luff's, which we left however before supper. Here we heard of the French having declared war against England and Holland. . . . I forgot to mention that on our way to Weitbrecht's we stepped into the Catholic Church, where the French were this day taking the Oath. The Oath was read to a large circle: who proceeded afterwards to kiss the Gospel and the Cross presented to them by two Priests; and when that was done went up to the Altar and put down their names. As we came out, being taken for Frenchmen, Bootle heard some of the common people abusing us as such. There was a considerable concourse of people and carriages.

Wednesday, 27th February

Baron Stroganoff having caused two ice-hills to be erected at a Villa six Versts from Petersburg on the way to Peterhoff, he gave a dinner there today to which we were to have gone in sledges. But the badness of the roads obliged them to go in carriages. We breakfasted about twelve at Baron de la Turbie's:* like an Italian he gave us Macaroni for one thing. When we arrived at the place of our destination, though the wind was high and the ground at the foot of the hills very slippy, it did not prevent the company from going down. Even Madame Somoilow ventured before dinner, as several of the ladies did after. I went once under the escort of Golofkin. The other English, Lord Dalkeith, Bootle and Garshore did repeatedly. You ascend by a stair to a platform; from whence an inclined plane floored with long oblong masses of ice descends to the ground. The adventurer places himself either alone or with another person before him on a little low sledge, and slides down the inclined plane with a degree of force which causes him to continue his course for a considerable time after he reaches the level. He then takes up his sledge and ascends with it by a stair to another hill of the same kind which is situated in such a manner, as to enable him to slide back to the stair of the other, in a line parallel to his former flight but at the sufficient distance not to interfere with it. They have also besides sledges a large mat couve, for it is in the form of a couve [? *cuve*, tub], on which they go down without the smallest danger; four or five Persons one behind the other descend in this.

These hills were not more than two *toises** high, but they are sometimes, and particularly on the Neva when the strength of the ice allowed it, of three times that height, with a declivity most alarmingly rapid. There is no Comparison we were assured between the Velocity of the Motion down one of these and that which we experienced. Yet these Russians make a practice of skating down these frightful descents, and that not infrequently with a child in their arms or on their head. We had a very cheerful and excellent dinner: after which the company, ladies as well as gentlemen, returned to the Amusement of the day.

Thursday, 28th February

The Chevalier de Mirmond did us the honour of a visit this morning, and gave us a good deal of information in regard to our route between Astrakan and Asoph.

The Abbé [Girot] not chusing to take the Oath intends to leave Russia and go to Hamburgh. Indeed Petersburg can no longer be an agreeable residence to the French who are all detested here, the emigrés by no means excepted. The most insolent things were said the other night to the Prince Dolgorucki for having invited Laval.

On our way to the Princess Dashkoff's, whom we went to this morning by appointment an hour later than we had fixed, the streets in consequence of the thaw were inconceivably rough. . . . This thaw begins to make us hesitate about our tour; which I would relinquish for my own part without the smallest regret; especially since I have discovered that Dresden and Vienna are to be sacrificed for it.

Friday, 1st March

In the evening we paid two visits, one at Baron Stroganoff's in order chiefly to thank M. Somoilow for his letters, the other at the Princess Dashkoff's whom we found with a face swelled by crying for the departure of her brother. As usual we found a crowd of the people at Stroganoff's. The Princess D. told us that his debt amounted to 400,000 roubles. Speaking of Count Stroganoff [she said] that he had 'infiniment de connoissance', but that he was 'foible de charactère'. Speaking of our friend La Baronne S. [Somoilow] she did not hesitate to call her an idiot. Speaking of Count Romanzoff, she said that he was a great deal too caustic, a man who prided himself on his scholarship, a man very likely to set the two countries by the ears together. Speaking of Stakelberg, she said that he was not perhaps a man to be relied upon in very great matters; but that yet he [had] done nothing in the present instance deserving of censure; that he understood the world perfectly, and had a surprising way of assuming a superiority. Speaking of Count Tchernichev,* she allowed him to [be] a man of Talents but at the same time remarked that he was the greatest courtier living. It is extraordinary that neither Besborodko nor Osterman were acquainted with the appointment of Romanzov to the Swedish Embassy.

We heard today of a murder committed on an Englishman by two Ishworshicks in coming from Cronstadt. They strangled him. An Ishworshick has confessed to have murdered no less than nine persons this winter. His way was after laying open their bowels with a large knife, to rifle their pockets and throw them into the river.

Saturday, 2nd March

I called this morning upon Mr. Yeames to see the Print of Gholtzius,* from which he fancied that our altarpiece at Magdalen College had been borrowed. It proved to be a Print from a picture by Rubens, in which the group in the background bears such a strong resemblance to that in ours, as makes it certain that Rubens must have had our picture in his eye.

I heard today from the Abbé Girot that there are about 1,000 French in Petersburg. The number of English is supposed to be 15,000. When Wroot first came here there were not more than 300. Every Englishman at that time was known.

Sunday, 3rd March

When the frost is certainly over, they cut away the snow in order to level the roads, but as they expect a return of frost, they have not done that in the present instance. It was so very rainy and dirty that I staid at home all the morning, Baron de la Tourbie, Baron Hoggner, M. Doyen, M. Dupuis, M. Lambert a young Frenchman in this service, the Abbé Girot, the Abbé Lautrech dined with us today at Mr. Whitworth's. We went from thence to the Countess Saltikoff's ball, where the company was fashionable but not so numerous as usual. After staying a while there, I went home and changed my dress in order to pay my compliments at Luff's, this being his Birthday. For as I was in mourning, if I had not changed my dress, my presence would have been regarded rather as an ill omen than a compliment. Paget, by having black breeches and stockings on, lost the pleasure of a salute. On my return I sent up to Bootle, who having however sat down to supper after he received the message, and kept me waiting in the carriage

H

a full hour, the consequence was that when we arrived, we found the company all gone.

Monday, 4th March

A Polish Officer who had come courrier from Warsaw in five days, a distance of 200 German miles, dined with us at Mr. Whitworth's. After dinner we made a very long visit to the Princess Dashkoff where we were joined by Lord Dalkeith and M. le Chevalier Garshore. She was very civil to my Lord but seemed to take very little notice of the Chevalier.

Tuesday, 5th March

The day was concluded at Luff's, where I sat during supper by the side of Mary Luffofna, whom the father asked me whether I did not think pretty. Stedingk the Ambassador's brother* was at Luff's and joined in persecuting poor Madame Lewoff, who was almost too foolish to laugh at and too lousy to be approached.

Wednesday, 6th March

. . . the day was excessively fine, and we walked along the Quay to the end almost of the English line. We met the two young Grand Dukes in their carriage, the Saltikoffs on foot and the Princesses of Baden also on foot. We dined at Mr. Weglin's where I met for the first time with Mr. Percival and Mr. Hill. Hill says there is a fine road from Tobolsk to Ufa. He supposes we shall be obliged to stay a fortnight at Tobolsk until the snow is melted. Bentham* penetrated 1,500 miles into Tartary and would have been cut off on his return if he had not changed his route.

Imagining that there would be a German Ball, I did not put on a dressed coat, which prevented me from going to the Princess Golitzin's. Bootle knew of it though he did [not] mention it to me, and prepared himself accordingly.

Thursday, 7th March

I took a long solitary walk this morning on the river. . . . While I was afterwards at the Shops with John I had the curiosity to take a glass of gluckwa for which I paid two sous; I would also have taken one of Tisane but I had no more Copper. The syrup of the Gluckwa is the berry that grows under snow, mixed with water. Men are continually hawking these liquors about. The former is cold and the latter warm.

We dined at Mr. Whitworth's where Bootle did not fail to remind us of his birthday. The dinner was not pleasant. In the evening we ... concluded the day at the Imperial Ambassador's who gave a supper in compliment to the Countess Potocki who is come here to thank the Empress for the order which she has conferred on her. She loudly declares, I understand, against the partition of Poland and that her husband knew nothing [of] it. He is said upon hearing of the entry of the Prussian Troops to have taken to his bed and to have been for two days very ill.

Friday, 8th March

In the afternoon we called first on the Princess Dashkoff, then on Madame la Generale Somoilow at her new house. . . . Madame Somoilow led us all over her house, which is exceedingly handsome. N.B. Gould says that Somoilow's share of Potemkin's fortune will be a million and a half of roubles = £180,000.

Radiskef* who married a Volkonski was banished to Tobolsk two years ago for writing a satire on the Court entitled a Tour to Moscow. His wife would have been permitted by the Empress to marry another man. But she chose rather to accompany her disgraced husband.

4 St. Petersburg to Moscow

Monday, 11th March–Saturday, 16th March

We proposed to have left Petersburg this morning at 7 o'clock but owing to several delays and particularly the non-appearance of our soldier, we did not get away till four in the afternoon, so that it was dark before we reached Sophia, and we passed through Itchora, Tosna and Luban in the night. Having been advised to take Ishworshic's horses for the first 116 Versts in preference to post, we changed only once namely at Tosna. The night was remarkably clear and fine, I made a trial of every possible posture in my Kibitka, and except as it was interrupted by the joltings of my vehicle, I enjoyed a very sound and comfortable sleep. The fur of my Taloup as well as my pelisse were wetted and hung with icicles by the freezing of my breath. Even at this first setting out I was struck with what afterwards struck me much more, that the road from Petersburg to Moscow does not appear to be so literally cut in a straight line through a forest as it had been represented.

We arrived at Tchadowa just at Sunrise; here we breakfasted and took leave of our Ishworshic's horses. In the stage to Sparskoe Polise Bootle paid me a visit in my Kibitka. The Postillions take a great pride in going at full speed through all the villages. I was as much struck as Coxe, though apprised of it by him, with the desolation of Novogorod. We crossed the great Volkoff by a bridge and the little river of the same name at two places on a raft. In this country as among the Roman Catholics little chapels are frequently erected by the side of the roads, particularly in the villages. Our drivers in general shewed no want of respect either to them or the Churches. Whether drunk or sober, whether in bad humour or good, whether decent or beggarly in their appearance they hardly ever failed to pull off their hats and cross themselves most devoutly on these occasions. It was dusky when we arrived at Bronitza; we passed the Mesta over the ice without being aware; and here we ate our dinner. From thence to Krestzi Gorod our journey was in the night, during which I slept tolerably well, as well as could be expected in such a jolting vehicle, with the usual squabblings at the

Posthouses and the usual melodiousness of the Russian drivers. The sun rose while we were changing horses at Krestzi Gorod, where I observed a Church and several handsome houses of brick stuccoed white. The Empress seems to have made a point on this road of embellishing as many places as possible in this manner, particularly with shewy Churches. The contrast between the wooden huts of the Russians and these gay specimens of Grecian Architecture is very striking and almost ridiculous.

I was witness at Kholilof by the light of a deal slip to the manner of determining by lot with a rope who were to furnish us with horses. By trying the weight of the Kibitkas they obtain a right [to] chuse likewise which of them each man prefers to take. . . . During the stage from [Savidof] the frost was so sharp that I could not expose my hands for an instant. We drove this stage most furiously. Our horses were good as they very frequently have been: and much in the style of our hunting race. In some of the villages knots of Boys and Girls were sitting together at a door and singing. In one a procession of this kind was marching along. The men learn the young people to celebrate the Carnival in this manner while they keep it themselves by getting drunk. We experienced however less inconveniences of this kind than we expected. Every part of the road to Moscow is enlivened by long trains of loaded sledges which seem to go in parties like so many Caravans.

We breakfasted [*Friday*] at Klin (which is a considerable village distinguished by a great number of Domes and Turrets which looked very singular rising from the midst of wooden cottages) and met with very comfortable accommodations. There were several booths erected here on occasion of the Carnival . . . the view of Klin from the eminence which we ascended on leaving it presenting a considerable extent of brown wooden Cottages from which a multitude of towers in so heterogeneous a style raised their heads, was curious and interesting. Not far from Klin we saw on the right a large white Mansion to which an Arch, with a large E over it conducted. We afterwards passed by a brick house which with its farm Yard and Church would not have seemed out of its place in an English Landscape. The face of the country in general was gently undulating, not unlike that about Limber and being either by design or accident prettily diversified with clumps, strongly brought to my mind that part of Lincolnshire. We met in all the villages with lively tokens of the Carnival. . . . The Girls then wore on their head a brown golden fillet standing up in the form of a Diadem with a small hat stuck on fantastically behind, and a coloured handkerchief sometimes over the whole head and sometimes only over the above mentioned fillet. We were followed a good way on the road by a couple of sledges filled with girls dressed in this manner and singing in chorus.

Of the country on the way to Tschernoi I could not help remarking that the ground lies just as one could wish for a Park and that the forest might have been dumped by Eames on purpose to form an agreeable intermixture of lawn and wood. . . . In one of the villages I saw three pretty Girls with Pearl and other fine Necklaces. In the same a party of girls were singing round a Man who was playing to them on a fiddle. While we were waiting at Tschernoi a sledge heavily loaded with singing and full dressed Damsels went out of the yard. Their legs I observed were as warmly cloathed as those of the Men.

We did not set off for Moscow till dark and it was therefore impossible to see the country and what would have pleased me much the approach to the Town. Nothing ever equalled the wretchedness of the roads in this and the preceding stage: I might also include that [from] Klin. But in this and the preceding, in consequence of the late thaw, it was become one continual succession of ridges and holes. The motion of a Kibitka is said at all times to resemble that of a Vessel at Sea; but at present on this road it must certainly have resembled it in a storm. The old man who drove me from Parski pushed along nevertheless with a boldness and address which surprised me. Nor did the young man from Tschernoi acquit himself less well, though I excepted to him at first because they told me that he was drunk. After sitting up for some time, I determined to stretch myself at full length in which position I suffered less from the Jolts, and indeed enjoyed a sound sleep during a good part of the way. *In somnis videbar esse in cubiculo matris meae, ubi illa singulari modo occ. p. bitur. Is qui aderat lumina hac illac mirum ad modum jaculabuntur.** We arrived at Moscow at twelve. . . .

5 Moscow

Saturday, 16th March

We ordered a carriage with six horses and have been this morning to call on M. Tamez's alias Dickenson* (a Letter from Bayley and Cayley to Mr. Dickenson), on Count Razomofsky* (a Letter from his daughter Madame Zagraski) who could not see us being not well but invited us to dinner to morrow, on the Vice Governor (a letter from Somoilow). He had several Birds in the room with him which hindered one from hearing what he said. I remarked his long pipe. The war he seemed to think would prove a bloody one. I was exceedingly struck with the splendour of Count Razomofsky's house. The Town presents a strange jumble of splendid palaces in the Grecian style of architecture, old Churches in a very different style intermingled with the most beggarly hovels. A great many fine houses seem to be building and not yet finished. The others appear modern and entirely in the taste of Petersburg. Upon the whole, the place appears forlorn and uncomfortable, being a much stronger example than the new Capital, of the greatest incongruities.

We dined at our lodgings and in the evening went to a part of the Town where all the people of fashion assemble in their carriages to take the air, a sort of 'Corso'. They assemble about six. It was an immense way from us; not less I should think than four Miles. We arrived however just as all the company were gone. Upon which we returned home, drank tea and repaired about nine to the Masquerade, where in general people wore some dress in addition to their ordinary cloathes but where they were under no necessity to do [so]. In this respect it resembled that at Petersburg but it differed from it materially, as being the resort of all the genteel people in Moscow, whereas the other was chiefly composed of blackguards and of common women, in so much that a female of good character was ashamed to shew her face. It was tolerably full to night, but we were assured that the evening before there had been no less than 2,500 fashionable people present. On Tuesday the Club was shut, and on Wednesday these masked Balls commenced. The rooms opened every day at four in the afternoon, but on Sunday they open in the morning also at nine o'clock, continue open till one, open again at four and continue open till one [in the morning], at which time the signal for the company to depart and of the Carnival being concluded is given by sound of trumpet. A circular room has been built on purpose for these occasions; the dome is supported by a colonnade of the Corinthian order, the company walk about and dance in the Area, and the Arcade which is higher than the Area serves for Card tables and those who wish to be a little out of the crowd. In the Arcade there are some agreeable recesses provided with Sofas etc. to which those who wish to sit quietly together and talk anything over at their leisure, can retire with much satisfaction. There are two or three other apartments besides the circular. Country dances, Cossack and Russ succeeded each other. When the company were doing nothing but walking about, I have seen no entertainment that reminded me so much of Ranelagh. This masquerade is particularly curious, as it gives one an opportunity of seeing several of the national Costume. There was the Laplander, the Samoyede, the Kamptschadale* and a great many others. We came away about one o'clock.

The whole town has exhibited a scene of festivity. The people are all in their best dresses, the streets are crowded with sledges conveying them from one part of the Town to another, and our ears are stunned with the din of their national singing, which I suppose may be heard at this moment in every corner of this immense city.

Sunday, 17th March

We called this morning on Prince Gagarin,* M. Tatischeff and M. Pastell, to all of whom we had letters from the Princess Dashkoff, without finding any of them at home. After this we went to the Masquerade, where we found a great many people, and the ball room lighted up at midday in the same manner as it was afterwards in the evening. A number of smaller lustres encompass a large area, which requires no less than ninety candles. . . . Being desirous of going to Count Razomofsky's in good time, we did not stay so long as I could have wished.

We found the Count at chess, which he suspended for a while in order to converse with us. He has the appearance of being an older man than he is. for he is no more than sixty two or three. He is said to be uncommonly infirm for his age. He wore boots of Russia or Morocco leather, an Epaulette of pearls and a star of diamonds encompassed with Pearls. We were there for a wonder a good while before dinner; as was the rest of the company, who amused themselves, some in one way and some in another, in the spacious and magnificent apartments which open into each other. Among the other attendants on this splendid nobleman I could not help remarking a couple of dwarfs, who stood at his elbow during dinner. A Mad^e Apraxin sat by the Count and did the honours with a great deal of civility and good humour. Both she and the Count were continually inviting us to eat and drink this or that because it was peculiar to this or that part of Russia. The Soup was peculiar to Little Russia, Moscow was famous for its Mutton; the Cherry wine and the Ale came also with similar recommendations. Our wines were Claret, red Burgundy, white Burgundy, Tent, Hungary and Champagne. The Platoon, like that at Mad^e Lleiv's, represented a landscape strewn with Cottages. Immediately after dinner the Count sat down again to Chess. We drank a dish of Coffee, talked a while to two or three people and then hastened away to the Corso, where we met with sledges and carriages in abundance. A very long street was filled with three and sometimes with four rows.

Count Razomofsky is said to have four or five dependants about him. He is considered as the second if not the first man of the Empire in point of property. Some people even say that his income exceeds that of Count Sheremetoff. He receives, I think, 160,000 roubles a year in lieu of his rights and claims as Hetman of the Ukraine. We are told that he and his Brother were originally nothing but Tartar shepherds; that his Brother having come to Moscow as a singer attracted the notice of the Empress Elizabeth, who took him into the office of Favourite; and that to this circumstance together with the share which the Count himself had in the revolution, the family owes its present consequence and wealth.

We came home from the Promenade and drank tea: after which we repaired about nine a second time to the Masquerade, where, though not so numerous as on Friday, the company amounted to 1,600. Several Hussars attended to keep order among the carriages, which, as there were two streets that lead to the landing place, were required to advance alternately, first from one and then the other. The soldiers enforced their orders with whips instead of swords. About twelve or half after twelve Maddox waved a handkerchief as the signal, the trumpets struck up, and the ball concluded. We sat down to supper afterwards with Dr. Cayley and Mr. Maddox. Yet though it must have been three before we rose from table, the Carriages were not all driven off and we were even obliged to wait for a considerable time. A quadrille danced a cotillon to night as well as the night before with this difference that the night before they were all dressed in a sort of uniform. The concluding manœuvre before the trumpets sounded our retreat was a Polonaise which commenced with a very large circle hands round in order to get room. When the trumpets ceased a loud burst of clapping succeeded in compliment to the departing carnival. When we came out from supper we found a poor man in woman's cloaths persecuted by the few people remaining and in a fair way to be insulted, if Mr. Maddox had not called in the assistance of the Major of the Police.

The Princess Viazemsky was in my opinion the prettiest woman there. I think Mr. Maddox said that the saloon is 17 fathoms or 118 feet in Diameter. . . . One of his Prompters is a Prince. . . . Sir Watkin's speech: To see it in perfection you ought to see it danced sans culotte—I only dance to make myself sweat. He turned his back on Mad^e Potemkin; and afterwards fell asleep between her and the Governor.

The Empress has a great dislike to Moscow. When anybody begs leave to retire, she says immediately with an air of chagrin: 'You are going to Moscow I suppose: With Your Majesty's permission: Well go to Moscow then.' Four or five of the Favourites are living here: Mamonoff, —— [?], Yermonhoff, Corsakof and Zoritch, all amply provided for.

Zoritch recommended himself to the Empress's favour by his resolute behaviour when a prisoner in Turky. She still retains a particular regard for him; she bought him the estate on which he lives of 25,000 Peasants for 160,000 ducats when he was dismissed, greatly to the surprise and mortification of Potemkin whom he had highly offended by drawing his sword upon him.

Monday, 18th March

I was much amused with the market where they sell Mushrooms, sour Krout, salted cucumbers, Radishes, Parsnips etc. etc. There were several sledges full of Mushrooms which were sold in strings. The Cucumbers and sour Krout were in large tubs which the dealer stood ready with a wooden ladle in his hand to serve out to the purchaser. The radishes, if that is the proper name for them, were three or four inches at the thickest end in diameter. The people who brought these articles to market seemed more uncouth and savage in their figures than any other Russians I had yet seen.

We dined with Mr. Dickenson, whom I discovered to be a Lincolnshire man. He was born at Glentworth . . . and left Lincolnshire when only thirteen in the year 1755. Dickenson was brought by Thamez from Riga to Moscow . . . he is now become head of the house. Peter the Great had a great regard for Thamez and used to visit him continually. On his death bed I think he expressed a desire to see him. . . . Mr. Dickenson's house, belonging I imagine to the Company which he represents, is situated on an eminence out of the Town, of which it commands a charming view. In the valley between flows the river Mosqua, being of course when it can be distinguished, a great ornament to the Scene.

The expence of carriage from Moscow to Kiakta five roubles a pound. So that the expence of sending American Furs round the Cape is less (Dickenson). The Chinese trade in favour of Russia, which receives from them a lance of silver. Twenty loads of silver had lately arrived. Russia is the only country that can boast of such a balance in her favour with China.

When a man is fixed upon to go as a soldier, he takes leave of his friends as if he was condemned to death, and they accompany him out of the village as if it was his funeral, with tears, lamentations and songs, the purport of which is that they shall never see him more. The Empress can demand as many Men as she pleases. In that respect her power is more unlimited than that of the Sultan. The Master is obliged to cloath them and furnish them at their departure with six months' provisions. A soldier, or a Man sent for a soldier, must be of a certain height. He is stripped stark and examined from head to foot; a decayed tooth or the loss of a tooth is a sufficient reason for refusing him.

If by chance at any time afterwards this man so lamented at his departure happens to pass through the village from which he had been taken, he is the first to plunder the place, out of revenge for having been sent as a soldier: for it often and generally happens that the Starost is governed by pique in his choice of the Men.

Two thirds of the Nobility visit their estates in the summer, even to the distance of 1,000 Versts, and pass three months there. The women amuse themselves with working and teaching their Children to work. The men with hunting. . . . The daughters have but a fourteenth part of their Father's fortune, a widow has a seventh and the Sons divide the rest equally.

Tuesday, 19th March

Our interview with Prince Gagarin was very agreeable. He loaded us with civilities and made us promise when we came back to visit him at his country house. Gagarin travelled in England along with Count Sheremetoff and another Person whose name I forget in the year 1773.

Razomofsky's observation upon the King of France's passing by him without speaking to him, looking at him only, as he was accustomed to do, very attentively, 'what does he take me for, a bear?' The speech had particular force because the King was a great sportsman. He overheard it and made a point of speaking to him ever after. M. Gagarin speaks of him as a man by no means deficient in talents or information. Though of late owing to bad health he had ceased to be what he had formerly been. He receives 200,000 roubles a year in lieu of his rights as Hetman of the Cossacks.

We went in the evening to a German Ball, in favour of which I cannot say very much. The women were not pretty and the Men even over their cards were most of them smoking.

The principal object of Dr. Pallas's tour is to discover whether it is not possible in the desert near the Achtuba to manufacture saltpeter without wood. If he succeeds in that he will remain in that country for some time. Otherwise his plan is to go along the line of Caucase and if he can, but that remains to be known, along the Cuban into the Crimea: from thence to visit the countries lately ceded between the Bug and the Niester; and to return by way of Kiew to Moscow. He has no intention to penetrate into Mount Caucasus, that country having been examined already by Guldenstaed.* A German Merchant to night told me a story of his brother having been taken prisoner thirty miles beyond Kislov by the Tartars twenty years ago, since which time he has never been heard of more.

During the fast they eat nothing that can come under the description of animal food; for which reason they eat their fish with oil instead of butter. Yet I am told that they begin to relax and the Nobility particularly, on these articles. One person considered [that] the Schools which have been established all over the Empire are specially calculated to cure these superstitious practices.

Sheremetof has two country houses* near Moscow where in summer he sees a great deal of company, and where he has a theatre capable of holding two thousand people. . . . Razomofsky, Sheremetof, Golitzine and the Governor [Lopoukin] live in the most handsome style. At the house of the latter as well as at Razomofsky's there is generally a ball once a week.

Wednesday, 20th March

About seven o'clock we called on Count Razomofsky, where we found two parties at cards, one at each end of the drawing room. The Count was playing at one table and Madame Apraxin at the other. We stood for some time by the side of each and then took our departure. After this we drove to Mr. Dickenson's, who invited us to supper; but Bootle not being well we came home.

Dr. Holiday advises us if we perceive the symptoms of a bilious disorder viz. a parched tongue, great lassitude, and Head ach, to take first an emetic, and then every three hours a dose of Bark infused in red wine. Half a dram of Ipececuana is sufficient for an Emetic. He also very strongly recommended Jame's powders, two scruples, mixed up with a dose of glauber salts. The effect of Jame's powders depends on the degree of acid in the Stomach. Where there is no acid they produce no effect whatever.

Notes of a conversation with Dr. Holiday

The Circassians are small and particularly have thin legs. If they perceive a traveller to be armed, being very timid they take to flight. Their legs are generally crooked and they guide their horses with their knees. They speak a variety of languages. They are rather pilferers than highwaymen. They will snatch up a single man in a party and carry him off with surprising address.

A great many Russian Gentlemen live entirely in the country on their estates. Their hospitality to strangers is unbounded. The longer they stay the more welcome they are. They look upon them and treat them as a superior kind of Beings and anxiously listen to their communications. A great many are to be met with particularly in the Governments of Orel, Kursk and Voronetz. Which governments are in a high state of cultivation.

The Governor of Tcherkask a good kind of man but very fond of drinking: in which he expects his guests to join with him; and when he is drunk, he introduces them then to his wives. The Circassian Women are pretty but not visible and very timid.

Dickenson: The Plague in 1770 carried off 100,000 People at Moscow. Thamez's house lost 500 men belonging to their Manufactory. The People stoned the Archbishop to death, because a figure of the Virgin Mary over a gate of the Kremlin, before which the infected, intermixed with those who were not, were continually offering their devotions, [was removed] with great Ceremony to the Cathedral. This was done to remove one cause of the propagation of the evil. Those who were first seized with it died immediately. It became afterwards less malignant. In some the constitution relieved itself by throwing out Bubos, and in that case the patient generally recovered. This terrible disorder shews itself in a great variety of forms. It abated on the approach of winter. Fire was set to the Hospital where it broke out.

Saturday, 23rd March

In my walk this morning I observed the beat Hemp seed which they put into their Soup and which gives it a white colour. I tasted the Sbeten made of honey and warm water which they make in large brass kettles and hawk about in the streets for a Copec a glass. I remarked also the Pancake which they sell upon a stall and eat with oil; also the Cakes made with cabbage etc. and also the cakes soaked with oil. . . . After breakfast we went to see the Nobles' club along with Dr. Cayley and Mr. Anthing. The ball room at the club is 45 of my paces long, 30 broad and as we calculated 60 feet high. A Colonnade encompasses the room and the floor at the back of the pillars is raised above that of the room itself. Behind before and on one side, this large room opens into several others for the accommodation of those who play at cards. The members of this Club are about 2,500, a thousand men and 1,500 ladies. The Subscription for the men is 20 roubles, for the ladies 10. But the supper and other refreshments are not included. The company go to supper at different times in parties; and the charge is a shilling a head. The Club opens, I think, in the month of September and shuts in the month of May. They meet once a week. The Company assembles at seven and sometimes don't break up till four in the morning. We afterwards saw M. Puskof's house which is said to have cost him 250,000 roubles. The only thing that makes it worth seeing is the view; it commands the town and a prodigious extent of country besides. As there are few or no fires in this country, a town is not hid in a Volume of smoke as London is liable to be.

We dined at the great Club as it is called. There [the number of] Members of this, consisting partly of Merchants and partly of Noblesse, is four hundred. They have dinner twice a week; all sorts of Newspapers and not less than three or four Billiard Tables. The rooms are or ought to be open every day.

6 Moscow to Kazan

Sunday, 24th March–Friday, 29th March

It was our intention to have set off early but we were delayed by our Empress's postillion till two o'clock.

The Empress's postillion sat with the peasant on the front of my Kibitka, the soldier on Bootle's and our two servants were in the other. It snowed all the first stage, the badness of the roads was not to be exceeded, and I own that I felt myself very uncomfortable. The face of the country, as far as I could judge, appeared to be gently waving and interspersed with large tracts of woodland. The roads were crowded with Peasants' sledges, to whom neither our peasant nor our driver behaved with much civility. When we arrived at Norwaja there were no horses to be had, Count Worontzoff having engaged fifty at every stage all the way to Wolodimir.

We arrived at Petoska a little after sunrise, but not finding any tolerable accommodations, we were obliged to defer breakfasting till we got to Andola. We never got out of our Kibitkas or went into a house in all this journey to Casan except to breakfast: and though we were obliged to put up with the room where the family slept as well as lived, where the cows were milked and the hens lay their eggs, yet we reckoned of this meal and enjoyed it all the more (at least I can say so for myself) than ever I did the most luxurious dinner. We took this opportunity of washing ourselves and having our hair dressed. I should add that the room in general was so hot that it was impossible to bear it when we stood up. At Andola where we breakfasted this morning two young girls retired to above the stove and employed themselves as long as we staid in spinning. . . . It was eleven o'clock when we arrived at Sugdogda: here we ate our frozen dinner; at this time there were between eight or nine degrees of frost. We changed horses at Moszok at sunrise.

Though it was ten when we stopped for breakfast at Draczimo several of the people were still in bed, if I may call it by that name, over the stove and on the broad shelf within two feet of the top of the room. Some of them having come down and dressed themselves while we were present, we perceived that they sleep in their shirt and a kind of trousers. We observed one person wash himself in the jar which hangs over a large tub for that purpose and pay his devotions to the tutelary figure of the Virgin Mary. The village belongs to Mamonoff who receives ten roubles a head from his people.

Our road lay for twenty-six Versts out of thirty to Monakovo along the bed of the river Vela over the ice, and we went at a prodigious rate. . . . The night was still and beautiful and I left my curtains open a long time.

We passed in the night between St. Pogost and Bogorodskoe by Pavlovna, the celebrated village belonging to Count Shere-metof. Bogorodskoe the village where we breakfasted belongs also to him. The houses appeared neater than usual. The Peasants had also built themselves three years ago a very handsome church. I should like to know whether all the handsome churches which we have seen in different villages have been at the expence of the Peasants. . . . When I first entered the room in which we break-fasted they were milking the cow in it. Sheremetoff's peasants, i.e. those who are poor, pay him five roubles a head; and the rich according to their property. I asked particularly whether they paid in Paper and was told that they did.

We stopped and walked about Nijni Novgorod* for more than two hours, amusing ourselves partly with the Market and partly with the fortress, the bold commanding situation of which we exceedingly admired. From the River this Town has a very shabby and a very singular appearance, seeming to consist of a few scattered huts, which hardly appear sufficient in appurtenances to the splendid churches which tower up amongst them.

As there was more reason to apprehend an attack from robbers between this place and Casan* than in any other part of Russia, I thought it desirable to charge our pistols etc. here and put ourselves in a state of defence.

The view of the Town, innumerable sledges some coming and some going, a long line of cottages at the foot of the steep banks which bound the Wolga on the right; all these circumstances, heightened by the calmness and splendour of the evening, rendered the scene when we set off from Nijni Novgorod one of the most lively imaginable and induced me to stand for a long time out of my Kibitki.

Our Peasants having undertaken to carry us another stage were better than their word and carried us to Yourkina 75 Versts from Novgorod where we arrived at eleven o'clock, very impatient for our frozen dinner. Our road lay all the way on the Wolga as it did afterwards quite to Casan, in all 404 Versts.

During the stage in the night to Fokina the centre horse of the servants' Kibitka plunged into a hole in the ice; and though he recovered himself immediately, the Kibitka followed him into the same and gave such a sudden check to all the horses, that afterwards when it was raised their panic disabled them from proceeding. This village belongs to young Demidoff our acquaintance, who I was told by our driver, in consequence of having lost money at cards, had raised the tax on his Peasants from three roubles to five. They gave him credit however for being a good sort of man but complained of the People whom he set over them. We breakfasted at this place in a room full of Hens. Though the People are very barbarous in their appearance, they do not pay much attention to us, by no means resembling the Norwegians in curiosity.

In this way from Fokino to Kosmodamiansk at Wasil we saw the mouth of the Sura, entered the government of Casan and according to Coxe's Map passed the limits of Europe and Asia. At Wasil the hilly banks of the Wolga began to be covered with wood, and continued so with a few interruptions all the way to Casan. We passed by two or three other large villages at the foot of these lofty banks with several vessels lying near them icebound before we reached Kosmodamiansk, which has the name of a city.

On the way to Czbokzar, after the banks had subsided for a while, they rose again more varied in their form and more beautifully cloathed with wood than they had been before. I could not help comparing my sensation in the Kibitka to that of being at Sea or on a Dutch Canal. The roads in different directions across the river, the little caravans of sledges which we were continually meeting, the semi-circular form of the banks on the right, the contrast of their darkness with the white level plain of snow . . . were circumstances which strongly interested my attention in this stage.

At Czboksar we heard of a cruel murder committed by some people nearby of the same name with this Town. One of the same clan drove us from thence and upon finding that we were English travelling at the Empress's expence as he imagined, he changed the demand from forty Versts [sic] to eighty-five.

We arrived at Kasan just as the sun rose. When we begged the people to say what they expected for breakfasting in their house, with much difficulty the poor woman mentioned thirty Copecs and was ready to bow to the earth when she received it. I admired their stillness and simplicity. The village belongs to the Governor of Viatka and they pay men and women five roubles a head. The Males begin to do this at the age of seventeen and at the same age the females are required to give ten Arcines of cloth which

I

they continue to do until they marry. All persons turned fifty-five are excepted.

We came in view of the Town of Casan at the distance of fifteen Versts and on approaching it it made a handsome appearance: especially the fortress and the churches in it, which are situated on a bold eminence. A soldier stopped us at the entrance of the Town to enquire who we were. We drove to a Russ Tractier's where we met with very good apartments, though without beds, and where we got an excellent dinner. Having dressed ourselves immediately on our arrival, we went and paid our respects as soon as we had dined to the Vice-Governor, whom we had met with both at Petersburg and Moscow. We found a German with him who put our proficiency in his language to the trial. After sitting a little while with him, he conducted us and our German Acquaintance in his Coach and six to the Governor's, Prince Baratiew,* for whom we had a letter from M. Somoilow. He received us very obligingly and as he spoke nothing but Russ the German acted as our interpreter. When we entered there were several·Children and three or four ladies in the room. The Vice-Governor of Perm was also there and having passed us on the road had given notice of our arrival. Prince Baratiew was excessively civil and when we rose to come away invited us first to a meagre Supper and afterwards on our declining that to dinner the next day. He promised to accommodate us with everything in his power for our expedition to Bolghari,* desired a person who speaks French to accompany us the next morning about the Town and made us an offer of his own carriage for that purpose.

Casan, what we have seen of it yet, appears handsomely and regularly built of brick stuccoed white. This was owing to the destruction of it by Pugatcheff.* I enquired the number of inhabitants and was told that they amounted to twenty-two thousand, of whom the Tartars composed between three or four.

Saturday, 30th March

The Governor, as he had promised to do the evening before, sent us his carriage to carry us about the Town for the purpose of seeing its curiosities. An officer, whom we had met at his house the preceding evening accompanied us. We went first to the General Governor's house in the castle. . . . Being in the Governor's carriage we were taken for him, the guard turned out everywhere and we were received with the greatest possible distinction. We were taken afterwards to see a hospital for old people, which certainly was not worth seeing: and then the suburb inhabited by the Tartars.

Several of the Tartars are in affluent circumstances and live in handsome houses. One of these wealthy Tartars shewed us the Mosque, though it happened unluckily not to be at the time of divine service; and afterwards conducted us to his house where he treated us with Eau de vie, with sweetmeats, with Hydromel, with Tea. He also offered [us] coffee, and even carried his complaisance so far as to show us his house, his wife and his daughter-in-law. The ladies before they made their appearance had tricked themselves out in all their finery; and the wife in particular had laid on a whole coating of white and red paint on her face.

We dined at the Governor's, Prince Baratiew's; and in the afternoon about five o'clock set off for Bolghari, an old Tartar Town, in the way to Simbirsk about 114 Versts distant from Casan. As the Governor had furnished us with an Ensign and a soldier who went before to order horses, we got on very fast and arrived at the end of our journey at seven in the morning. The soldier paid nothing for his horses; and the Commission of the Ensign empowered him to take as many as he pleased for the other two Kibitkis, paying only for three. The ruins of Bolghari consist of two towers and seven or eight other ruins scattered over a tract of ground about six Versts in circumference which is surrounded by a ditch. We visited every one of these ruins with all possible attention and ascended both the towers, one of which could not be less than 100 feet high; as the other perhaps might be seventy or seventy-five. Near the latter are thrown about a great number of sepulchral stones with Arabic and Armenian Inscriptions, which we could not see at this time owing to their being covered with snow. The Tartars, we were told, still come every year in the summer on a sort of Pilgrimage in parties of ten or fifteen or fifty to pay their devotions on the spot where the tower stands. They come in Kibitkis and remain there encamped for two or three days. We made our progress through these ruins attended by a crowd of peasants, I counted at one time twenty. When we came back to the cottage where we took up our abode the greatest part of the village were ready to receive us; and what seemed curious, the Men and the women apart. They bowed most respectfully as we passed by. The crowd also that attended to see us set off did the same, standing all of them with their hats off.

We set off about five o'clock and either because the roads were worse or because our military did not exert themselves so much, did not arrive at Casan till between one or two the next day. Our Kibitkis when we set out had each of them six horses, three behind, two in the middle and one before. A peasant sat as usual on the Kibitki and two others rode. Upon our arrival at a little town about

fifteen Versts from Bolghari [? Spassk], the seigneur of the village
as they called him entreated us while our horses were putting to,
to do him the favour of drinking a dish of coffee with him. We
suffered ourselves to be prevailed on and remained for half an
hour in his house, an object of great curiosity to the greatest part
of his acquaintance in the place, who seemed to be assembled for
the purpose of seeing an Englishman for once in their lives. While
we were here the Commandant sent to make his excuses for not
calling upon us owing to illness, but begging that we would do
him the honour of calling upon him. We found him so excessively
ill that it was, I am sure, a very improper thing for us to disturb
him. Here we drank a third strong dish of coffee; to my excess in
which respect I attribute the indisposition which I experienced
afterwards.

7 Kazan to Perm

Tuesday, 2nd April–Sunday, 7th April

The road to Bourouly and afterwards to Arsky was so excessively bad and heavy in consequence of the thaw that I despaired of being able to proceed on sledges. In the second stage the servants' Kibitki repeatedly was at a stand and the peasants were out of Patience with us for having come without wheels. In Bourouly the staple that holds up the apron of my Kibitki came out and occasioned me to pass a very disagreeable night; especially as I was exceedingly indisposed.

Arbasch where we breakfasted is a Tartar village, where at first sight I was struck with the fine countenances of the people, as I was afterwards with the neatness of the houses. The next two I also understood to be Tartar Villages, of which my driver told me that there were upwards of forty in this part of the country, which where they are settled is hilly and Romantic, the steep side of the hills being generally covered with trees. In the way to Melet we walked over the Viatka, and afterwards going a Verst or two farther, descended for a short time into the Bed of that or another river and rattled away upon it at a prodigious rate. At Melet (which I understood at Perm is a Tcheremiss Village as well as the two next), (though John was informed that Wogoukdev Kaksi belongs to the Voltiaki), at Melet we eat some of our patent Soup enriched with a little of the good Princess's Grain, out of the same black pot. A Man was asleep over the stove; and the room so hot and so full of smoke, that it was hardly to be born without sitting down. The Tartars and Tcheremisses are free and only pay a certain capitation Tax to the Crown. The former are Mahometans; the latter are now most of them converted to Xtianity; though some of them still remain totally destitute of all religions, as I was informed by the Governor General.

In our way to Casan I observed that we seemed to excite no curiosity: on the contrary on this road, a crowd of people flocked into the room and stood with their hats quietly looking on all the time we staid. We had here an opportunity of seeing two of their women in their national dress with a high and fantastic coiffure and the outer garment like that of the men reaching down only to the knee. Being asked what we had to pay, they said it would be a shame to take anything. I understand from the Governor that they look on such a visit as an honour and would be offended, many of them, to have anything offered them.

Ever since we left Melet the road had now lain through a continued forest of Firs, Birch and some fine oaks intermixed: often however, and especially about the villages the ground was cleared to a considerable extent on each side and several handsome trees having been left standing had a very parkish appearance. . . . This indeed was the general style of the country ever after to Perm. The Beauty of the forest and the undulations of the ground alternately arrested my attention; and especially in the former the tall white stems of the Birch trees sometimes standing along, and sometimes towering above their associates the firs. The road often gave me the idea of being cut through a newly discovered country as the first step towards improvement and civilization. Whenever we arrived at an eminence we looked always over an immense extent of dark forest. We travelled all this day at a great rate, for instance to Kilmeiserte twenty-nine Versts in two hours, and twenty-five minutes to Zaitzi, which is thirty-eight in under three hours.

At Zaitzi we took our frozen repast and the people, especially I think after they understood us to be English Colonels, flocked in crowds into the room and stood quietly and respectfully looking on. The houses of the Voltiaki do not form a street, have not the Gable end fronting towards the road, and have not the farm yard close by the side of the house as those of the Russians uniformly have. But they are scattered about, the cattle stood in what we should call a sort of Crutch Yard. . . .

From the brow of the hill which we descended to Sesnove the view was prodigiously fine and the contrast between the dark forest and white . . . which lay embosomed in them wonderfully striking. In descending this hill Bootle's Kibitki first and the servants' afterwards were completely overset, and I myself, so very slippery was it, in walking down tumbled flat on my back. . . . Dubofsky belongs to Count Stroganoff, a very comfortable village. We took it into our heads to broil our frozen beef here, which we did each for himself with the help of long fir slips in the presence of near fifty people who flocked into the room to see the odd scene. Curiosity brought hither the Count's Steward amongst the rest. . . . We changed horses at Scholkianiche and Annikowa in the night. Though I had crowded [on] all my cloaths, I found it difficult to keep [warm], which I did not wonder at, when I understood on our arrival at Perm between four and five that there were no less than fifteen degrees of cold.

On our arrival here we found to our astonishment that orders had been given at the Posthouses if two English Gentlemen arrived that they should drive immediately into the Commandant's court, where apartments had been kept aired and in readiness for us for the last three days, in consequence of tidings from the Governor, whom we had seen at Casan, of our coming. He had given us apartments in his own house on account of the unwillingness which the people have to receive strangers into their houses. At first we could hardly believe that we were to take up our abode here and imagined that there must be some mistake. We were soon set right by the Master of the house who sent to enquire what we chose to breakfast and excuse himself for not waiting on us immediately. We got an excellent dish of tea and presently after had a visit from our hospitable commandant, an old German officer disfigured by a goitre, which Bootle taking for an occasional swelling, when we came to sup with him in the evening, tapped with his finger and expressed a hope that it would soon subside.

About two o'clock M. Sokolof* a lieutenant in the Guards who has been settled here a twelvemonth to study Mineralogy waited upon us to offer his services and especially his carriage. He also, though we [were] partly engaged to the commandant, insisted upon our dining with the Governor General. The Commandant excused us on condition of our supping with him. We took a little stroll after this and a quarter before twelve, after having paid our respects to the Governor M. Koltofskoi, we repaired to the house of the Governor General who received us with great politeness. A good deal of time intervened before dinner; and part of the company sat down to Cards; Madame Volkof to Whist and the Governor General himself to trois et trois. They call their hour of dining one but they did not sit down before two. We were about twenty persons. We were not long at table for the Desert, consisting of Postilla of various kinds of several national fruits in the form according to the Russian fashion, was set out in the drawing room. The Governor and Madame Volkof sat down to Cards and in about three quarters of an hour the company dispersed. I ought to mention that there was music in an adjoining room.

We adjourned to M. Sokolof's lodgings to drink and were afterwards accompanied by him to a Copper Forge three Versts off where, as he had taken care to apprise the inspector of our coming, we saw the first and third operations of the Process to great advantage. For the first step of the Process the ore is burnt twenty-four hours mixed with sand and charcoal and at the end of that time run off, an operation to which we were witness. This forge belongs to the Crown and manufactures the produce of all the Imperial mines, which are about ten, in this neighbourhood. The whole quantity made here is 5,000 Poods. The Ore not being rich gives eight pounds of copper in two hundred.

M. Sokolof gave me a more distinct idea of the condition of the Peasants in Russia than I had before, illustrating the two different footings on which they are by the case of two estates belonging to himself. On one of these, where he resides, he has a hundred Peasants from whom he receives nothing but their labour to cultivate the grounds, which he keeps in his own hands, three days in the week. On the other he has seven hundred, who pay him a Capitation Tax and have each of them a portion of land, as large a portion as they are able to manage. If they have not enough they may have more. And when a young man chuses to marry and settle, his Lord is always ready, having land enough, to allot him a piece of ground. He likewise has always a certain number in his service whom he feeds and cloaths but to whom he pays no wages. They are not fond of this situation but like better to live as Peasants.

On our return we supped with our hospitable host, with whom as he spoke nothing but German we had much difficulty to keep up a conversation. A young woman whom he had lately seduced away from her husband was of our party.

They give in Constantinople five thousand roubles for a Georgian Girl. In Persia the Georgian Girls are also in great request but not nearly so dear.

8   Perm to Tobolsk

Monday, 8th April to Wednesday, 10th April. Perm to Ekaterinburg

Finding here the manners, the language, and the luxuries of every other place, I forget that I am at such a distance from England, and I am ready to fancy myself in some great capital rather than in a village on the borders of Siberia.

In Summer the situation of Perm on the banks of the Kama about a Verst broad with an endless extent [of] dark forest at the back of it, must be very agreeable. The Heat in Summer is greater than that in many places much farther to the South, which indeed, as their corn has but two months to ripen in, is very necessary.

The houses at Perm are all of wood, stand apart, have a great and little door into a court after the manner of the villages and on the whole are so much on the model of a peasant's cottage, as to furnish a confirmation of my idea, that the style of building in towns has been always borrowed from the country and that the origin of its peculiarities may always be discovered there.

The good Commandant was angry to find that we were engaged to dine with Sokolof and kindly supplied us with some roast veal, a tart and other things for our journey. He visited us repeatedly before we set off and took a most affectionate leave of us when we came away. Our entertainment at Sokolof's was only to have been a breakfast or a little soup, but it turned out to be a compleat dinner, with which, having twice breakfasted before, partly out of respect to him and partly to the goodness of the things, we made ourselves quite uncomfortable. But really it was a cheerful meal.

The first two villages where we changed horses [Kojanowa Direvne, Innitchage Direvne] are inhabited by the Bachkirs,* a people in religion, customs and dress resembling the Tartars, but not to be compared with them in agreeableness of physiognomy. From Perm to Archonst we only pay a kopek per verst for a horse, and from Archonst where Siberia commences no more than a denier or half a Copec. We sat for some time in the Posthouse at Krulessowa by the light of a fir deal slip of which Bootle took the management. This was a Russian village as all the other stations are I understand from thence to Catharinenbourg, if not to Tobolsk.

117

I was alarmed for some time by the mildness of the evening and therefore very glad to see it begin to snow. We passed through Kunguri, which struck John as being larger than Perm, in the night. We also changed horses in the night at Stritinski. As far as I could observe it, the country was either flat or gently undulating, in a great measure cleared, and often divided by slender wooden fences.

In descending the Hill to Kloutchi where we ate our breakfast, my Kibitki for the first time was overturned; and at the same instant upon looking back I saw the servants' in distress. The cottage at Kloutchi was divided into three little apartments. Archonst is the last place in Russia, and at the next station [Bissertki] we were in Siberia. The country so far had been much the same as yesterday, but I descried hills in this stage at a distance which I took for the outskirts of the Oural Mountains. According to the old and common way of reckoning it appears, therefore, that Siberia is considered as beginning on the west side of that extensive frontier. Krepost, the title given to that and the three following stations, signifies 'fortress', from whence I conclude that on the first conquest of the country these places were fortified in order to overawe the neighbouring people. In the beginning of the stage to Bissertki our road lay over a plain skirted at a distance with dark forests; we afterwards entered a hilly country which presented the most beautiful variety of Ground and was richly wooded in the valleys as well as the declivities with a mixture of birch trees and firs. In this style it continued to Krenoutka. . . . We ate our cold dinner, consisting of the veal and tart which the good Commandant had given us, in a peasant's cottage in company with a Cow, a brewing of quass and several children who in return for a little money that we distributed among [them] were ordered by their mother to kneel down in the Russian fashion and kiss our feet.

It was only a little before sunrise [*Wednesday, 10th*] when we changed horses. About three versts from Witendorski Savode, the Kibitkis going foot pace on account of the horses being knocked up, I lighted and determined to walk the rest of the stage. The morning was bright, calm and pleasant, the road perfectly hard and clean lay over level ground covered with woods and terminated before and on the left hand by dark rising grounds. Having suffered the Kibitkis, however, to go on before me and having taken a wrong division of the road into the village, I was bewildered there for a long time and very near going on and leaving my fellow travellers behind. At the Posthouse where we ate our breakfast, the women were exceedingly amused to see us dress, particularly to see us powder. The Savode [*factory or mill*] is large and belongs to Count Stroganoff. In the next stage our road passed by a gentle ascent and descent over some eminences which commanded a very agreeable view of a diversified and romantic country; in which the hills however had not the smallest pretensions to the title of mountains. We came afterwards to more level ground which being covered with trees, though there were not firs, reminded me continually, especially as one caught now and then the glance of hills at the back of them, of our beloved Norway.

We approached Catherinenbourgh,* distinguishable by its white spires, over flat and extensive tracts of open ground, at the extremity of which the town is situated. The Air about it was darkened by the smoke that issued from the forges. Having sent the Postillion with our letters to the Governor before, he appointed us lodgings and our Messenger met us as we entered with the intelligence. We made up a dinner out of our travelling provisions, and having dispersed our Callers, received a visit in the evening from the governor, with whom we held a broken conversation in German.

Thursday, 11th April

In consequence of the letter to him from M. Volkoff, the inspector of the mint* [*M. Savkoff*] called on us early this morning and was so obliging [as] to go over it with us and shew it himself. We called on the Governor whom we did not find, on M. Van Oyen a Dutch Gentleman who had been making the tour of Siberia. . . . With M. Van Oyen we sat for some time and appointed to go with him in the afternoon to M. Logonoff's, the person who though he understands nothing but Russ had acted as interpreter to Col. Bentham, out of Russ as he humorously said once into Russ. Here we saw a great number of the Stones and other Articles which in a great measure constitute the traffick of this place; and we bought some few. We afterwards went to see the *Pierrerie* or *Fabrique* where the precious stones found in the neighbourhood are manufactured for the use of the Crown. The number of workmen employed is fifty and they work day and night either because by doing so they require fewer instruments or a less consumption of water. We saw a temple valued at 3,000 roubles, the columns etc. of which were composed of various stones, and the rocky foundation was of all the Minerals found at Catherinenbourgh. This was intended as a present to her Majesty. M. Van Oyen invited us to pass the evening and sup with him in company with M. Logonoff who spoke nothing, the Governor, and another who spoke nothing but German. And though we had agreed to set off for M. Touchaninoff's Forge at four o'clock, our supper was not on the table till eleven.

Notes of a conversation with M. Van Oyen.

The two fairs at Macariew and Irbit where Siberian and Chinese Merchandise is exchanged for Russian and European; at the former *de main en main* to the amount of ten millions of roubles; only 400,000 at the last fair of Irbit. During the first week they sell for money but afterwards barter.

The Governors in Siberia, all except Alabica [?] and the one at Irkutsk, Germans and Germans of the Protestant religion. The reason he gave is that the Russians do not like to go into Siberia. But he seemed to admit that the Empress might have more confidence in them than in the Russians.

Siberia far from being without People though thinly inhabited. The Majority are Russians, but the Poles and Exiles form a very numerous body. The Poles were sent thither after the first partition. He spoke highly of their honesty in that country. The Poles the most industrious and best farmers. The Russians as in their country very indolent. Besides these are the wandering tribes of Tongoori, Mongols etc.

Except in Tobolsk none of the Russian Nobility are suffered to have estates or Peasants. They are all subjects to the crown and pay a certain capitation tax as elsewhere.

He was suffered to pass the frontier and visit the Chinese town at Kiachta only once. And then he was desired to pass for a Russian Officer and not to say that he was [a] Dutchman. He imagined this was done for fear the Chinese should ask him some questions with regard to trade. He was positively refused the second time; but he was not permitted to do it without an order, and he conceived it to be attended with some risk.

Friday, 12th April

Though we had agreed to get off at four, a number of obstacles and misunderstandings prevented us from doing it till six. We got a dish of tea at Van Oyen's and likewise stopped at the first stage to take a glass of liqueur and to eat some broiled fish and some bread and cheese which our fellow travellers had brought along with them. We were set down at the house of one of M. Touchaninoff's sons there on a visit at present, who after a while conducted us to his mother's house, introduced us and sat down with us to a very good dinner. The ladies keep the fast and had therefore dined by themselves. I must not forget the dish called Pelmin [*meat dumplings*], which it seems is peculiar to the Government of Perm. Dinner over, we went to see the Forges.* On our return we found the younger brother come home from hunting. And a more compleat character in his way I never saw. He, Bootle and his Brother amused themselves with shooting little birds with Pistols while Van Oyen and I were talking to his pretty wife. This was at the younger Brother's house from which we adjourned again to the mother's where Madams[lle] T. and Mad[e] T. junior entertained us with singing and playing on the Harpsichord . . . . Young Touchaninoff's partiality for the English seemed to have no bounds and when we came away not content with kissing us repeatedly himself, he invited [us] to kiss his pretty wife, once and a second time, which we very readily did. There was no such thing without [delay], in consequence of which we set off so late that it was six in the morning when we got back to Catherinenbourgh. Van Oyen as a Dutchman was not treated with half so much distinction as we were.

Notes

A school at Irkutsk for teaching Japanese; at Tobolsk for teaching Chinese and some other Eastern languages. The Chinese trade was opened last February. It had been interrupted for seven years before.

The Brother told me that he had still 30,000 roubles a year, though he had spent 200,000.

In little Russia he understood, that if a stranger intimate a desire to have a woman, a gentleman would accommodate him. At Moscow the ladies ask the men to dance and even do more than that. Luff a tittle tattle to the Empress. One of the Touchaninoffs gave 100,000 roubles to avoid serving against the Swedes.

Saturday, 13th April

We dined with the Commandant, and afterwards drank Tea and sat for some time with Van Oyen. One thing or another as usual detained us till between five and six.

During the first stage our road [to Tobolsk] lay over a flat uninteresting country cloathed with meagre forests. I felt myself exceedingly out of spirits, partly from observing the badness of the Roads on which in many places there was no snow left and which were become exceedingly heavy owing to the warmth of the day, but chiefly from indisposition, for I had perceived some shudderings before we set out, and I now found myself exceedingly inclined to be feverish. This feverish Habit caused me to pass the whole night uncomfortably. It was just the peep of dawn (I descried through a rent of my curtain) when we changed horses at Pelleskie

Stantie. The Country was still as it had been and as it continued to be all the way to Tobolsk, level and uninteresting. In general it is sufficiently cleared; but I suspect that a great part of this cleared ground is not improved; the brushwood peeping from above the snow continually betrays its forlorn and waste state. In many places also the quality of the trees announced a swampy soil. As to the woods where we passed through them we found them thin and the trees slender.

Sunday, 14th April

Bootle and I walked the last verst stage and a half to Parischena where we breakfasted. I in hopes that it would be of service to me, but I did not find any benefit from it, being attacked by a very extraordinary pain at the pit of my Stomach. The latter part of the next stage was on the River Pyszma by the side of which the road goes I understand for two hundred Versts. In winter we should probably have travelled on the ice but that was objected to. The Drivers in setting out for Tcheremisse being ill advised to a shorter cut across the snow in order to regain the [road], we were very near sticking fast. In the way to Bellajalanskaya I stood up a good deal in my Kibitka which I thought did me a great deal of good. On leaving that place we went a Verst on the river. A party of young girls in their Sunday cloaths were assembled on the elevated bank to see us depart. I made my dinner at the place above mentioned on a glass of milk and water into which I poured a little brandy and a crust of bread. I slept pretty well in the night but I found myself still very feverish in the morning.

During this day's journey we generally passed through one or more villages between the several stations; which gave no bad idea of the population of this part of Siberia; and during the rest of this journey to Tobolsk the case continued everywhere nearly the same. The Farm houses were larger than we had been accustomed to see; and though built on the usual model, do not stand as in Russia in a regular line but dispersed. Their cattle also instead of being under cover are in open Crutch Yards; and each farm Yard is surrounded by a high Palisade. The People themselves have much finer countenances than the Russians have on the other side of the Oural Mountains.

Monday, 15th April

The cottage where we breakfasted this morning in point of neatness would have been no disgrace to Norway; but my indisposition rendered the heat of it insupportable. Several pretty girls who belonged to it could not lessen my impatience to leave it as soon as possible. The windows were made of Mica as they very commonly are in Siberia. Fish bladder is also a material in pretty general use. The sun's power having made the road heavy we proceeded very slowly to Tiumen which seems to [be] a large place with a great number of Churches. Here I made my miserable dinner on a little wretched milk and water. It is but twenty-two Versts to Viliganske yet we were three hours in going them. When we changed horses at the next stage, which was at a very early hour in the morning, to my utter astonishment I observed that it rained. This was the first night it had not froze since we set out.

Several of the women had laid aside the winter cloathing of their legs and were without shoes and stockings; some without the latter only.

Tuesday, 16th April

Where we breakfasted this morning several little children with earrings on of Catherinenbourgh were surveying us from their bed of boards. On the way to Jewlenske we crossed the Tobol whose banks are very steep but whose breadth disappointed, being not more I should think than half a verst. In this day's journey we saw great quantities of hay but piled together in the most slovenly manner. I say nothing of the night which was wretched to me.

Wednesday, 17th April

We travelled four Versts on the Tobol at the latter end of the last stage without perceiving it. Tobolsk, situated partly on a high sand hill and partly on the plain below, makes a singular appearance.

9 Tobolsk

We had sent before to the Commandant to beg quarters, but as those appointed us were not in a condition to receive us on our arrival, we were quartered on a merchant.

Thursday, 18th April

We called on the Commandant, M. Balikoff and Mr. Baktyr,* which last invited us to dinner. We dined at his house with two exiles, one M. Tchoglikoff* a State Prisoner, the other M. Samorokoff who had been banished to this place with his two associates for forgery. He is a grandson of the Poet. In the evening I was seized with a shivering which was followed by heat and perspiration, which was increased to a violent degree by a dose of Dr. James's powders.

Tchoglikoff was only eighteen years old when he returned to Russia and offended Prince Orloff by taking a chair and sitting down at his *levée*. His mother being *Gouvernante* to the Empress, then Grand Dutchess, he was constantly in the house with her till he was five years old. He was then sent away for peeping at the Empress as she was dressing. The Empress at that time was about twenty, pale, for she used no paint, and with what he called an English Physiognomy. It was in the year '70 that he was put under arrest. His young brother had been banished to Turachansk at the age of fourteen two years before. There he continued till his death, which happened last year. Another Brother was put into confinement three or four years after him at Schlussenburgh, where he still continues rather a close prisoner on account of its Vicinity to Petersburgh. He writes to him through the medium of Count Osterman, who is the trustee of his affairs. A daughter of this brother's died in [the] Count's house.

While Lieutenant Colonel of the 13 regiment of Cossacs he ingratiated himself with them in a manner which furnished matter of accusation against him by dividing amongst them the booty which they took. He has two cousins who are one of them in the Ukraine and the other obliged to live on his estates, both of them in a sort of exile of imprisonment. He is related to Count Stro-

JOHN PARKINSON
REPRODUCED FROM A MINIATURE IN SCUNTHORPE
MUSEUM AND ART GALLERY

JACOB JOHAN ANKARSTRÖM

Afſkedad Capitain 30 år gammal. Giorde Miſsgärningen d. 16. mart. Häcktad d. 11 Dº Fick ſin dom d. 16 apr. Stod i halsjern på 3 Torg 3ꝛe dagar å rad näml. d. 19, 20, 21. apr. och hvarje gång af Bödelsknecten hudſtruken med 5 par ſpö, ſamt vid galgen miſtade högra handen blef halshuggen och ſteglad d. 27 apr. 1792.

A CONTEMPORARY SWEDISH PRINT OF THE EXECUTION OF JACOB
JOHAN ANKARSTROM, ASSASSIN OF GUSTAVUS III

MORT DU PRINCE POTEMKIN.T.
Le 5. Octobre 1791.

Inventé, dessiné et gravé par I.C.Nabbok. 1793.

THE DEATH OF PRINCE POTEMKIN, FROM AN ENGRAVING
BY I. C. NABBOV

A VIEW OF THE GARDEN OF THE SUMMER PALACE AT ST. PETERSBURG

An artificial ruin in the park of the Imperial Palace at Tsarskoye Selo

The Red Gate in Moscow in the late Eighteenth Century

A RUSSIAN ORTHODOX PRIEST IN HIS ORDINARY COSTUME AND
CEREMONIAL ROBES

The Cathedral of St. Basil in Moscow as it appeared before the restoration of 1839–45

ganoff by his wife who was a Trubetskoi; and he is of the same family as the Saltikoffs.

Tchoglikoff while at Berosow wrote several things which were taken away from him. The summer lasts, he says, at that place only three weeks; in which time they are obliged to cut, rake and get in their Corn and Hay. While it lasts the summer is insufferably sultry. The Samoyedes of that country, when they kill a Rein deer put the blood into their broth, and eat the heart and liver reeking hot, which T. remarked was very good.

He remembers the Empress Elizabeth when 35 years old; she was then a very handsome woman and was remarkable for the fineness of her bosom, which she always wore bare. The present Empress used to employ a watch for measuring her steps; and to make a point of walking fifteen Versts a day. He seems to hold the Grand Duke in great contempt, having a strong idea of his Tyrannical disposition, which will never be borne he says in Russia and on which account he does not believe that his reign will be of four months' duration. A firm and mild Government is the only one which the Russians are capable of submitting to.

Andrew Razomofsky* gave the first Grand Dutchess the venereal disease, and she communicated it to the Grand Duke. This disease was even the cause of her death in childbed, for she would not reveal it to anybody. Andrew Razomofsky has been in a kind of exile for this offence ever since.

M. Derzhavin* the only man at present in her Majesty's Cabinet who had the courage to speak his mind. He is a poet and was brought first into notice by his poetical talents. He wrote particularly an ode addressed to Felista,* meaning the Empress, the glories of whose reign he celebrates in this ode.

Baktyr told Bootle that two Persons last year had been carried away no body knew whither for carrying on a treasonable correspondence with the National Convention.

His father in law Glaboff* was Procureur General before Viazemsky. The Empress dismissed him because she did not chuse, she said, to have a procureur general wiser than herself. As to Viazemsky, he turned the Government upside down and destroyed all order, which had [not] yet and could not soon be reestablished.

Count Skavronski* the present Russian Minister at Naples, having quarrelled with a Frenchman in the good graces of his mother, was provoked by her to give her a blow. By the laws of Russia a blow given to a Parent is punished by the loss of a hand. The enraged mother being determined to prosecute her son according to the rigours of the law, he laid his case before Prince Potemkin, who promised him his protection on condition that he would marry

K

one of his nieces whom the Prince was known to have debauched. This alternative almost drove him to commit violence on himself; but at length he determined to accept it and the Prince, as good as his word, gave orders that the countess should not be admitted to the Empress's presence, which enraged her to such a degree that she left Russia and at present resides at Naples. The Count's private fortune is calculated at 120,000 roubles a year.

Tchoglikoff told me that the people of this country being in good plight are exceedingly independent and refractory. They are ready, they say, to comply with the law and the Ukases of the Empress but not with the arbitrary pleasure and capricious commands of those who are set over them. He spoke of the Peasants between Tobolsk and Orenburgh as in particularly good circumstances.

At Berosow they give three Reindeer for a good leading dog. A Reindeer is worth fifty squirrels; and a squirrel ten copecs. Their dogs are a kind of wolf dog. The Samoyedes of Berosow smoke the skins they wear to a reddish yellow. Over that they wear a cloathing of Rein deer skin with the hair on the outside.

Saturday, 20th April

Bootle dined with M. Baktyr: and before he came back I was seized with another shivering fit.

Monday, 22nd April

Though I had rose surprisingly well, I was again attacked by a shivering fit about two o'clock. It was followed as before with heat perspiration and clearly determined my complaint to be a second day's ague.*

Tuesday, 23rd April

Bootle is gone to day to dine at Mr. Baktyr. Though almost perfectly well, I am not in a state of health to accompany him.

Wednesday, 24th April

I had a slight return of my fever to day but it did not assume an aguish form. It only took away my appetite and rendered me exceedingly lethargic.

Thursday, 25th April

I sent this morning, being at a loss how to treat myself, for Mr. Peterson, who encouraged me to go and dine at Mr. Baktyr's, and said that my complaint was what the people of this country were very subject to in Spring. Mr. Peterson lived thirteen years at Astracan and has been twenty here. He spoke of the waters at Zarepta as excellent for the bowels.

We met him, Mr. Balikoff and another gentleman at Mr. Baktyr's. Baktyr observed that in this country everything led to everything. That is, that in appointing persons to particular situations they little considered how far his former way of life qualified him for it. Yet if a Man was raised from the military line to a department in the law, they would not [on that] account make any allowance for his ignorance of the laws, or be less severe on the errors which he might commit.

Agreeably to the advice of Van Oyen we make a point now of kissing the ladies' hands; which, when they happen to be as pretty as Mrs. Baktyr, is a very agreeable ceremony.

Friday, 26th April

In this country one scarcely meets with anybody who has not served [in the army]. Peterson served as a surgeon in the war of 1756 from '60 to '63, and Baktyr served in the first Russian war that happened in this reign. Baktyr and Balikoff yesterday spoke in a very different strain of Viazemsky from Tchoglikoff.

Note: Mr. Tchoglikoff . . . gave the following account of himself.—

His father was Governor of Peter the 3^d, his Mother *Gouvernante* of the present Empress while Grand Dutchess—at thirteen he was sent (unwisely enough, he observes, considering that he was a Russian) to Geneva, where he studied five years and where he knew Lord Abingdon, his Brother Captain Bertie, Lord Macartney, Lords William and George Gordon, a Mr. Dundas, a Mr. Crawford, Mr. Stephen Fox, the Duke of Richmond, Lord George Lennox and Lord Gainsborough, who was his particular friend.— He came to Russia for a short time after the death of Peter but having quarrelled with Prince Orloff (who, as well as his brothers, when he was a boy at the Cadet Corps used to go about begging and borrowing money to subsist on and had often been at that time supplied by him), he went abroad again and spent several years in travelling.—Having a great desire to go to India in the English service, his friends the Princes of Meckleburgh promised to get him an appointment by means of their sister the Queen—in full reliance on these assurances at the end of ten years from the time of his first departure from Russia he returned to take leave of his friends.—But there being a war, he was required either to serve or to quit the country in twenty-four hours—being offered his rank he took that of Major, went into Poland, was ordered to apply a petard to the gate of Cracow (a service usually imposed on those who have committed some crime), did it and was wounded— being sent either from Poland or from the campaign against the Turks with some advices to Petersburgh he was remarkably well received by the Empress, and I think on his return to the Army made lieutenant Colonel of the 13th Regiment of Cossacs, a very hazardous and fatiguing situation. He was with the Russian Army at Choizim and Jassy, and offered Marshal Romanzoff [*Rumyantsev*] to sell his estate and with the money make a diversion by raising a revolt in Monte Negri near Scutari, with which proposition he was sent to her Majesty. The proposition was not listened [to] but he was dispatched to the Army in Georgia with a private commission to arrest the Commander there if he found him guilty of the Misdemeanours which were laid to his charge. The Orloffs apprized the Commander of this and directed him to arrest Mr. Tchoglikoff, which was done. This happened in the year '70. While under arrest he made his escape and paid a visit to Prince Heraclius,* but returned in a few weeks. When first taken he might have escaped into [Persia] where a friend of his was Grand Master of the Artillery of Kerim Khan; and could he have foreseen the length of his punishment, he would certainly have done so. He was conveyed first after being made a prisoner to a place where the plague raged; and half or more of his guard officers and men died but he and his suite escaped, either from accident or from having had it before with the army in Walachia. From Georgia he was sent to Casan and there confined for about four months, but upon Pugatcheff's rebellion breaking out, by an order from Petersburg [he] was hurried away to Tobolsk where the Governor told him he was to remain ten years, which news he heard with much *sang froid*. After two years' residence at Tobolsk a courier came from Petersburg to order his removal to Berosof on the Oby where people are sent who are to be forgotten, where Prince Dolgorucki* had been sent before and where Prince Menchikof* and Count Osterman,* the father of the present Vice Chancellor, died. The place is 1,000 Versts north of Tobolsk. Here he lived for eight years amusing himself by hunting, fishing and shooting squirrels with the Samoyedes, its wild inhabitants. Except his guards (for till the last eight years he had always a guard about him) nobody was with him there. In this cold spot he never wore a pelisse though he has witnessed cold of 36 degrees which broke his Thermometer. When brought back to Tobolsk his guard was soon discontinued and for the last eight years he has been left at liberty to live as he pleases. He is even permitted to write to his friends. However notwithstanding repeated applications of his friends, for he is too proud to solicit it in any other way, though the time of his exile has been long expired, he could never get the sentence of his banishment recalled. His youngest brother being lately dead at Turachansk, a town on the Yenissey three or four thousand Versts to the East of Tobolsk, his large property devolves to him and his brother confined in Schlussenburgh, and he is going to ask permission to come to Petersburgh in order to settle his affairs, the Procurer General having offered to present the Petition to the Empress and his brother in law, M. Zagraski, having advised him to take this measure. Provided he is permitted to settle and take possession of this property, it will be afterwards a matter of indifference to him whether he resides at Tobolsk or elsewhere. He is now become a Philosopher and not [at] all anxious what becomes of him. He reads and writes a good deal but goes little into company. What hurts him most is the being on the footing with those people who are banished for Crimes.

M. Zagraski married one of his sisters for his first wife and the Countess Munich was another. He was very intimate with Potemkin and he wrote to him in his exile to use his good offices, but the Prince could do nothing against the Orloffs whom he feared. The Prince during their intimacy placed so much confidence [in him], that being sent on some occasion by the Empress as a spy on the conduct of the General, he communicated to T. the errand on which he was come. He had the indiscretion at Paris to take the device of 'Chacun à son tour' which was converted into an article of accusation against him. He drew his sword upon Prince Orloff on some occasion and the Prince he says ran away. He was requested to preside in the Novogorod deputation (when the convention was assembled to deliberate upon a new code of laws), which honour he declined, but being desired to name a person, he named an old General. He was requested at least to assist them with his counsels and one day, the General being ill, he supplied his place and got into a warm altercation with Prince Orloff with regard to the degree of liberty which it might be proper to bestow on the Peasants. He contrived in the warmth of the altercation to advance till he neared a window where he knew that the Empress was attending to hear what passed. His confutation of Orloff was so compleat, and Orloff was reduced to so entire a nonplus that her Majesty sent to him and desired him to say no more. When sent to the Empress to read his father-in-law's plan for dividing the Senate he disputed with the Empress, who asked him how he dared to do [so], to which he replied that her Majesty had only to recollect the character of his mother, who never was known to give a point up.

That part of his property which he had in Russia was embezzled when he fell into disgrace; he has the property at Geneva and at Amsterdam, but all communication having been prohibited him with his agents at those places, he derives no benefit from that property and subsists on money supplied to him by his relations. When he was first arrested the Russian Court applied through their Minister Count Panin to have the money belonging to him in the bank of Amsterdam delivered up, which the bank refused to do without a certificate from their Minister at Petersburgh to say that Mr. Tchoglikoff was dead. He married in a singular manner the first woman whom he met with one day in the street, the daughter of an officer: he took her immediately to a convent some versts off where the ceremony was performed without her relatives knowing it. He had been neglected in an illness by his servants and wanted a person to take care of him. He was a pupil of Rousseau and passed four months in the same house with him at Iverdan.*

This was the account which Mr. Tchoglikoff gave of himself, but we understood from the Procurer General that his commission to arrest the Procurer General was a pretended [one], that under the sanction of it he had succeeded in debauching a great number of the soldiery, and that he had formed connections with the Princes of that country [Georgia]: and that this conduct was the cause of his being seized. That when brought to Tobolsk he lived on bad terms with the Governor and allowed his tongue liberties against the Empress, which being repeated, occasioned him to be sent to Berosow. That the same indiscretion in speaking too freely has been the means of prolonging his exile.

There are exiles of different sorts. Some have lands allotted to them which they cultivate but they can never rise above the rank of Peasant. Others are kept in confinement and are allowed something to subsist on: those however are great prisoners. The gentlemen banished are for the most part sent to live in Siberia and are not allowed anything. From Bootle.

N. Somorokoff whom we dined with the first day at Mr. Baktyr's was five years ago a lieutenant in the guards. He has a talent for drawing and having one day copied a bank note for amusement, a friend of his came in and begged the copy in order to pass it as money. He gave it and afterwards passed one himself. His two accomplices are here with him. He is a great nephew of the Poet* He amuses himself with writing books and receives 1,000 roubles a year for composing what they call the rural and Oeconomical repository, which is printed at the Tobolsk press.

Saturday, 27th April

We took a good long walk in the morning about the town and dined afterwards with Mr. Peterson, at whose house in the afternoon there was the rehearsal of a play, viz. Beverley,* which they are employed in getting up. Mr. Tchoglikoff there conducted and presented us at Madam Poushkin's, who is preparing since the death of her husband to leave this place to which she accompanied him at the age of twenty, though the Empress would have suffered her to marry again. Her Son was entirely brought up at Moscow and when he paid his parents a visit here last year, he did not know his father. M. Poushkin was sent hither for a forgery of two millions, and he remained here twenty years. His library before the fire consisted of 2,000 volumes. She speaks with detestation of Moscow [? Tobolsk] where there are no amusements, and nine months of winter. We returned from Madame Poushkin's to Mr. Peterson's and had a long conversation with Baktyr and Balikoff, whose surprise to hear that the integrity of an English judge was not so much as suspected, I could not help remarking. Baktyr told Bootle that the present Empress had done one thing which Peter the Great could not effect; i.e. a regard for a man's word which till of late a Russian thought himself under no obligation to keep. Peterson in speaking of Astracan advised us to avoid Melons, to drink a spoonful of Vinegar in our water. . . . He added that in the month of June the innundations would be over.

A M. Radiskef* has been sent two years ago to Ilinsk for writing a book called 'A Journey from Moscow to Petersbourgh'. He writes a letter from several different stations, where he remarks a great number of abuses and traces them all up to a despotic government. Has his Bust been put up by the National Assembly? He is banished for ten years. He is about forty.

Baktyr's office as Procurer General is independent of every other power in the Government. He is in this capacity inspector of all the tribunals and is assisted by several subassessors fixed in different districts, who when anything contrary to law, according to their judgment, is done within their department, make their report to him. Though he cannot arrest judgment, he warns the Tribunals; if they do not give him satisfaction, he has recourse to [the] Governor General; and lastly if the Governor General sides with the Tribunals, he appeals to the Procurer General and the Senate; a step which he had occasion to take last year.

The Fire happened here April the 23ᵈ, 1788. It broke out in a shopkeeper's house where they were making Quass, and being increased by a high wind not only baffled every attempt to stop [it], but spread by a hollow way, across which a wall is built with doors, to the higher Town. In the higher town it consumed the Archbishop's and Governor General's houses. The boarded streets contributed to extend its ravages. There were 3,000 houses in Tobolsk before the calamity, but it reduced them to 1,500; and the best were destroyed. They have begun to rebuild but they go on slowly, especially as on account of the war the Crown was obliged to withhold its allowance of 20,000 roubles a year. The Archbishop resides in a part of the Palace which he has caused to be fitted up.

In speaking of the Empress it is very much the fashion to say *c'est un grand homme*. Tchoglikoff in speaking of the Princess Dashkoff said likewise *'c'est un grand homme'*.

In the Government of Tobolsk, Tchoglikoff told me that there are 300,000 Russians, 50,000 Tartars and 20,000 of other nations, Tongousi, Ostiacks, Samoyedes etc.

The ladies having carried the height of their headdresses to an enormous degree, an Ukase was published reducing [them] to the moderate height of three Verschocks, which are equal to about two of our inches.

The Governor gives us leave to order his carriage with six horses whenever we please, furnished us with a Dragoon on horseback to execute our Messages, and has sent us several bottles of Ale and Wine.

Sunday, 28th April

At the Governor's we were obliged to talk with him, his lady and his sister by an interpreter. Baktyr, Peterson, Balikoff and several persons in the uniform of the Government composed the company. Here as at almost every other dinner we had rein deer Venison.

A Frenchman who lives with the Governor as Tutor to his Children told me that he had been in the employ of the Farmers General of France, who to his certain knowledge though they squeezed 1,500 millions out of the people paid no more than 600 into the public Treasury. So that there remained a surplus of 900 millions to be divided between the Farmers General who consisted of 100 Persons, viz. 49 Farmers General, 40 Intendants etc.*

My French friend represented their treatment of the peasants in this country as little better than that of the Negroes. Though under the crown they suffer as much vexation or more from the crown agents as if they were under Lords. They are attached to the soil and most severely punished if they attempt at any time to make their escape, i.e. with a bastinado and three or four years' confinement. They only seek to have just corn enough for their own service; if they have more, there are no means of disposing it. A Canal, however, from the Kama to the Dwina is in agitation. The people knowing no better are not unhappy under their oppression. The French Peasantry live on fruit or fruit and vegetables in summer and on flesh meat in winter. A Russian consumes as much bread in a month as a Frenchman in a year.

They are subject to fevers here, particularly in the spring. But the complaint which they suffer from most is the Rheumatism and the *lues Venerea*, which last is exceedingly difficult to cure, Mercury from the coldness of the climate not producing the desired effect. In order to assist it, the Patient is obliged to be put into a warm bath. Peterson represented the *lues venerea* as not only very fatal but also an increasing evil in these northern regions. Peterson advised us to bath at Astracan.

They are exceedingly subject in Russia to haemorroides owing to the frequent use of the bath. The Governor's children today had been in the bath and Peterson told me that they went in about once a week.

Monday, 29th April

We dined at M. Baktyr's where we met Balikoff and the Frenchman. In the afternoon we called at Madame Poushkin's. . . .

Before the fire the number of inhabitants here was about 15,000, at present about 10,000. Writers in mentioning the population often speak only of the Men paying the Capitation tax.

Tuesday, 30th April

We dined at the Governor's . . . and staid till near six o'clock unable to speak with our good hosts but by an interpreter.

The Archbishop speaks no language but Latin besides Russ; and of Latin he understands only a few words. The Archimandrite understands both French and Latin perfectly well. They make very little account of their Clergy. The Archbishop has not more than 2,000 roubles a year and the Archimandrite not more than 400 (Frenchman).

To say Mr. Baktyr instead of Ivan Ivanovitch is uncivil from an equal; it implies a superior; and even from a superior it is not taken well (Baktyr).

Wednesday, 1st May

... Supped with Madame Poushkin who treated us among other good things with Jelly of a fruit, called by some such name as Kniaz, i.e. Prince, a fruit very plentiful in Siberia and peculiar, smaller than but resembling a strawberry, with one side red and the other green, and with the most delightful fragrance in the world. I admired the coolness with which Madame Poushkin spoke of Bentham's Mistress, a woman who was cook in his house. She fancied that I had left some attachment behind me in England.

Baktyr set off from here the 12th of April with Bentham for Petro Pawlowsk and had a terrible journey. He returned on the 23rd and found no difficulties. One river had to be passed three or four times.

M. Somorokoff made his confession in an adjoining room within our hearing. They confess once a year. They are bound most solemnly to reveal the whole. If the sins are of a very heinous nature the Priest refuses the communion. It is generally made in the Church.

M. Somorokoff and his wife who had resided two years at St. Pierre gave me some curious details concerning the Kirghese. They approach the frontiers in winter to purchase corn and are on a friendly footing with the Russians; in summer they retire to a distance. Their food a kind of gruel made of meal on which they pour hot water; Kummis or sour mare's milk, and horseflesh; but they eat only the flesh of horses that die; they have also cheese, but that they melt on their gruel. In summer they appear in companies of two or three hundred: they have a Sultan who has but the shadow of any authority in each company; and they have a Khan who is considered to preside over the whole Horde. He has however little or no power and their Government, such as it is, ought to be called Patriarchal. They often have wars among themselves; and every family lives in a kind of warfare, regarding it as meritorious to steal and pillage when they can. They buy a great deal of corn of the Russians and pay with their cattle.

The Garrison of the fortress of St. Pierre is encamped during the Summer months in divisions of two or three hundred men.

Thursday, 2nd May

... dined at the Governor's. ... Balikoff followed to our lodgings from the Governor's and talked me asleep.

The Governor accompanied only by two Persons made a visit once to a Khan of the Kirghese. The Khan desired his excellence to be asked how many cattle he wished to be killed. The Governor having declined that compliment, a number of women was produced and he was desired to make a Choice. The Governor declining also this compliment, was told that he must at least accept of a pair of Kirghese horses.

There are three Khans and the subjects of each may amount to 40,000 souls. They all, i.e. all the three hordes, hold themselves under the protection of Russia.

They had a pure race of horses, a race peculiar to themselves till Pugatcheff's rebellion, at which time having seized all the stallions that came in their way, English, Russian, Polish etc., the breed is now mixed and corrupted.

The Governor gives a horse-race every year to the Tartars who come to it from the distance of 600 Versts. A great many start, they run twice round the ground, in all about six versts and there are prizes I think for the first thirteen or fourteen. When the Tartars run races among themselves, it is from one village to another.

The Governor mentioned a town in the Government of Tobolsk (I think Turakinsk), to and from which eight months are necessary to receive advices and send an answer.

The Governor has a great deal of power over the exiles; he can dispose of them as he thinks fit; and can give them permission to settle in any part of his government. Several thousands are sent as exiles into Siberia every year. Those who are fixed as Peasants pay no tribute during the first three years, in consideration of their having a house to build etc. They can never rise beyond the rank of peasants and are regarded with contempt. Some are sent to the mines but these are great offenders. Those who have their noses split have been guilty of murder. An exile is considered as dead in law, and his heirs take possession of his fortune. He loses his rank, and if an officer, he is reduced to the level of a common soldier. A Person has been lately condemned to exile for having sold eighteen deserted Guards at the rate of seven or eight hundred roubles apiece for recruits. Others are sent into exile for selling estates which do not belong to them.

The pay of a Russian soldier is six roubles a year; but he is provided with bread, meal . . . two pairs of boots, three shirts, an uniform once in two years etc. With the six roubles he has to buy chalk to clean his girdle, hair powder, and soap: so that he has not much left to purchase flesh meat. His chief expense is in camp in summer. In winter he has a right to eat with the people of the house where he is quartered, on condition that he contributes his allowance of meal.

Tchoglikoff offended the first governor by seducing his mistresses, which caused him to send word that he could [not] answer for the tranquillity unless the Tchoglikoffs (for the younger brother was here also at that time) were removed to a greater distance. One of his brother's many offences was the beating of a Priest for refusing to baptize a cat. The other brother was imprisoned for drawing his sword on somebody. Tchoglikoff has been married twice and both times to common women which together with his taking to drinking has occasioned his conduct to be represented in unfavourable colours. The Empress allows him through the medium of the Governor a pension of 100 roubles a year.

The appointment of the Governor General is 9,000 roubles, that of the Governor 3,000, that of the Procureur General 600, that of the three other Procureurs 300. There is still corruption in the administration of justice on account of the smallness of the salaries, but formerly in the time of the Voyvodes it was carried to a much greater length.

Friday, 3rd May

Yesterday, that is holy Thursday, as our Saviour washed the feet of his disciples on that day, is a day on which it is thought either pious or fortunate to cut the hair. Both the Mad[selles] Poushkin where we called for a short time after leaving Mr. Baktyr, had undergone that ceremony.

Somoilow* wrote to Baktyr some time ago to know the number of prisoners; and on observing it to be very great, he reprimanded Baktyr for not seeing that they were brought to Justice. Baktyr stated in his justification that he made sixty-five representations on that head, and that the great number of delinquents arose from the great number of exiles sent hither, which did not amount in a year to less than a thousand.

Baktyr and Balikoff represented the Peasants in Siberia as on a better footing than those in Russia. They intimated also that we must not imagine those out of the great road to be so well off as those on it. The Peasants in Siberia were on a better footing because after paying a certain sum to the crown they had no Lord at whose mercy the rest of their property lay. They did not know what the effects of the late regulations might have been, but before then, none of the Russian Peasants were so well off as those in little Russia. In white Russia and in Livonia the Peasants furnish no recruits. A Lord can sell any number of his peasants and often does for recruits. The only restriction he lies under in regard to the sale of his Peasants is that he must [not] separate a husband and his wife. A Lord is suffered to beat his own Peasants, but the Law punishes those who take that liberty with Peasants that do not belong to him.

If the Empress wishes to ameliorate the condition of the Peasants and give them liberty by degrees, why reduce the Peasants of little Russia to the same footing as the other Russian Peasants, why attach them to the soil which was not the case till lately? I was answered from a desire to establish throughout the whole Empire an uniformity of constitution: which is so much the object of Government, that although the subdivisions of a district in this Government are so remote from the residence of the Capitaine Isprovnic that it is extremely difficult for a plaintiff to carry his grievances to such a distance, to a distance for instance of 500 or 1,000 Versts, yet it was not till after representations from a Governor General, that permission could be obtained to establish an inferior kind of legislator [*or magistrate*] in each subdivision for the purpose of hearing the evidence and stating the case to the Capitaine above-mentioned.

Saturday, 4th May

At twelve o'clock midnight the bells of all the churches began to jingle, signifying that the fast was over, and at the same time summoning every body to church; a summons very generally attended to. The Governor and his family continued there from one o'clock to four. Bootle sat up after me and was pestered the whole time with an incessant jingling. The day has been close and warm.

Sunday, 5th May

The Governor called upon us this morning before we were up; it being a custom on this occasion to pay the compliment of a visit to all their acquaintance. We had a visit also from the Post Master, M. Baktyr and M. Balikoff. The Governor's carriage came for us to dinner very early, and the servants begged us to make haste, because they had been up all night, and should sleep after dinner. We found the ladies at the Governor's sitting round a table, with an immense lump of butter and a large loaf upon it. With this collation they had I believe concluded the fast and commenced the festival. This festival continues eight days. The additional ladies were the Vice Governor's wife and his three daughters. When we came away, having professed an intention to take a walk, the Frenchman begged leave to accompany us.

In this walk we were overtaken by a shower of rain which obliged us to take refuge in a house where the master of it, his wife and two other men saluted us on occasion of the day. After which we were treated with Eau de vie, Quass and Cider. . . . Honey and water was mixed with the Eau de vie. We were also invited on coming away to drink a glass of wine. The hospitality and civility of our hosts was very dramatic and oriental. Our French compagnon was the only one who spoke a little Russ: they asked him to what country we belonged, and when he told them that he was French and we English, they observed that we were at a great distance from our homes. They recommended the short way to Orenburgh which is no more than 1,200 miles.

N.B. Every person in France who wore a *culotte* was an Abbé. A person took the Tonsure frequently at the age of eleven, after which he was able to hold a benefice of any value. The only form consisted in the Bishop's saying when he was presented to him and knelt down before him 'His dabitur una pars [?] et calicis meae, tu Deus es; etc.' If he married he forfeited his benefice. There were several thousands of these Abbés: he said either five or eight.

This fast lasts seven weeks. They have three others. . . . During these fasts on Thursdays, Wednesdays and Fridays they abstain even from fish. The People were many of them dressed in a glazed dark blue gown of the usual form tied round with a sash. . . . We saw salutations happen repeatedly in the street. They say to one another on this occasion 'Christ is risen from the dead', to which the other replies 'he is indeed'. They then salute each other, and exchange in many cases a red egg. The red Egg is symbolical of the resurrection. This custom explains the custom of the present which the soldier and the Postillion made us. Even at the Governor's the salutation and this form of words was observed. And I believe we ought when we entered to have saluted all the company both Gentlemen and ladies.

Monday, 6th May

As the Empress's birthday had fallen in the fast it was kept today. Seventy or eighty persons, all men, dined at the Governor's; and at about six a ball opened, which was concluded between eleven and twelve with a supper. Polonaises, English country dances and Minuets succeeded each other. The whole was finished with a Siberian dance. Their best Musician and several young ladies were ill so that the ball was not quite so gay as it might have been. Yet there were a hundred persons present of whom forty-five were ladies. There are about ten or twelve balls in the year at the Governor's and these are the only opportunities the ladies have of dancing. . . . Upon expressing to the Governor my surprise to see so gay a ball in so remote a part of the world, he told me that the new regulations which had so much increased the number of Officers in civil departments sent from Russia had given an entirely new face to the capital of every government. For that now instead of the Governor, the Procurer General and two or three others, there were not less than forty or fifty persons who had each his wife and his daughters.

Tuesday, 7th May

When I awoke this morning, I was exceedingly surprised to see it snowing very hard, the ground all white and the wind very high. There were this morning no less than seven degrees of cold, whereas the day before yesterday we had had seventeen degrees of heat. We dined again at the Governor's and again met our friends Messrs. Baktyr, Balikoff and Peterson. In the evening we went to the theatre, where the performance, considering that the actors are chiefly soldiers and girls of no education, was better than I expected. The only female Actress that appeared in the first piece, was the daughter of a soldier, who could neither read nor write and who received fifteen roubles a year for her services. Of three other soldiers, one received twelve, another fifteen and the third thirty. To an exile who was sent hither for assuming the name of Prince Volkonski, they pay 150. The theatre has been built about two years. In general they act once a week, namely on Sundays. Mr. Balikoff gave us places in his box from which however we removed presently to the Governor's, who was so obliging as to desire that we would, under an idea that we should see better there.

Wednesday, 8th May

We dined at the Vice Governor's, M. Selifontoff, who was so obliging as to send his carriage for us and give us the use of it afterwards to the theatre. . . . The name of our play was the Brigadier* which was followed by a ballet, which considering the circumstances of the house, both exceeded my expectations. Before the entertainment began our friend Balikoff conducted us behind the Scenes even into the ladies' dressing room, one of whom was an exile sent hither, he said, for a little *sottise*: which turned out to be *nothing less than* causing a maid servant to be whipped to death.

15 soldiers, 6 actrices, 6 writers, an old man who had acted formerly on the German stage at Petersburgh, 14 dancing Girls and
the man who personated Prince Volkonski compose the greatest
part of the troop. The old German was sent here for poignarding
his wife.

Observing blinds in Balikoff's Box I asked him the reason for
them: he had them put up, he said, on account of the Archimandrite and an Abbé of his acquaintance who liked to come to the
theatre now and then but could not in decency be seen.

Saturday, 11th May

We stepped into a travelling Italian's shop and then accompanied Baktyr in his carriage to the lower Town. . . . The first
class of Merchants must have a Capital of 10,000 roubles. They
are at liberty to trade with foreign Merchants; and their grandsons become nobles. The second class are at liberty to traffic all
over Russia: the third only in his own district. A *Negociant
Renommé* reports his property to be 50,000 roubles: he has a
right to drive four horses in his carriage etc. Baktyr.

The trade of Kiachta is carried on the whole year. But the
month of February which the Chinese call the 'White Month' and
the months of September or August are the principal seasons for
it. The whole trade is carried on by barter. *Pelleterie* and the Horns
of a particular kind of stag are the chief articles exported by
Russia; *Thé*, cottons etc. the chief [ones] given in exchange by the
Chinese. He [Peterson] had no idea of the balance being so much
in favour of Russia. If Potemkin had lived Russia would have had
a war with China.* The number of troops was augmented with
this view in this Government and [that] of Kolyvan [by] 30,000
troops.

Sunday, 12th May

There was an opera in the evening at the theatre which did
not go off ill. Their prettiest and best actress was a common girl
taken from the Streets. An old Abbé accompanied by a younger
religious came and sat with us in Balikoff's box.

Monday, 13th May

A person just arrived from Petersburgh dined at the Governor's
and brought the news of the victory gained over the French and
also of the Partition of Poland.

At Berosow they descend by steps cut in the Ice to get their water: often as many as five. Peterson has known the Ice here two Toises thick, or three of our yards. In winter they go from Tiumen to Tobolsk, 250 Versts, in 16 hours; the Governor had done it in 18.

If a Person has a reprobate son he denounces him to a tribunal; and the son loses after this his claim to his share of his father's Property. It is but the property which a man receives from his father which [he must divide] equally among his sons. That which he acquires he may dispose of as he pleases. He may also if he [wishes] dissipate and sell either one or the other. The Governor.

The Women all ride astride.

Tuesday, 14th May

I went this morning to the market in a Drosky, the first time I had made use of that conveyance. We dine with the Governor who has put off his journey to Tiumen till the day after to-morrow. He and the ladies repaired at an early hour to the house of [a] Gentleman who gave a supper this evening in honour of his wife's nameday. We drank tea with Baktyr and did [not] go till between six and seven. The ladies were playing at Lottery tickets in one room and the men at some game in the other. In the room where the ladies were a table was set out with Sweetmeats. . . . Some of the Sweetmeats above mentioned were from China. Among other good things that were handed about at supper was what we should call Rose brandy. They deal here very much in that sort of liqueurs.

Wednesday, 15th May

It snowed this morning and was so cold that I did not venture out, especially as I felt a return of my fever which made me very uncomfortable all the day. Peterson gave me a call and brought the German papers. We dined as usual at the Governor's and in the afternoon paid farewell visits, as it is determined to set off tomorrow. . . .

L

10 Sarepta

Sunday, 16th June

We stopped at an inn where the accommodations would do credit to a good inn in England. After ordering dinner, we determined to call on Dr. Pallas, having heard with much satisfaction at Zaritzin that he was here. Both he and Mrs. Pallas were exceedingly glad to see us. We drank a dish of Coffee with them and returned to our Inn, where we received a visit from the Master of the Police inviting us to attend a little concert which they have every Sunday between the hours of six and eight. The performers consist of the Brethren* themselves, who amused themselves in this way, and as many as chuse to attend them twice a week, viz. on Sundays and Tuesdays.

I met an old painter here who had passed three or four years in England and spoke English perfectly well. One of these years he resided in Oxford, where he did not learn much; though he preferred it to Cambridge, which appeared he said to be a dirty place.

One of the Anciens was a Swiss and came from the Grisons. With him we conversed in French. They were all very civil and well behaved. At eight the bell rang and they went to Church.

[Dr. Pallas] has been on an excursion of ten days into the Oural Desert (and he was fifteen days in this desert), as far as Lake Kamysch, where contrary to his expectations he met with several hills of gypsum. He and his party consumed here all their bread and were reduced to a short allowance of Grain. They had depended upon wild fowl, of which however they met with hardly any, the Kirghese having destroyed it all. There are a few Calmucs left in this Desert, who however would be glad to depart, but the Russians are unwilling they should because they regard them as disaffected; and they themselves are at a loss which way to [turn]. Their Brethren who made their escape and are settled on the Irtisch are laid under a necessity very disagreeable to them to quit their roving life and live in fixed habitations. The reason of their disaffection to the Russians is the oppressions and pillages they have suffered, particularly from the late Prince Potemkin and from General Paul. For that reason they fly away now (he was speaking I think when he said this of the Calmucks in the Steppes of Kama) at the sight of a stranger: whereas formerly they were rejoiced at the sight and gladly went to meet him.

There is an Ukase for the preservation of Bulgari; otherwise the Russians would have soon destroyed the remains of Antiquity there; as they have done at Zarewo Podi, being the most destructive people in the world: destruction being an enjoyment and pleasure to them.

M. Agappa [*Alexander Agathi*] Master of the Schools at Astracan is the greatest traveller Dr. Pallas ever met with. Besides most of the countries of Europe he has travelled by the way of Agypt and Persia to India and from thence back through Cashmir, Bocharia etc. to Russia. He has made several curious observations in his travels. He visited the mines in the country of the Turkwas. He means to publish. He is a native of Smyrna.

At the Empress's death all may not go well perhaps. A Person so well acquainted with the country as Dr. Pallas will not be suffered to go out of it. After Orloff's [death] Dr. Pallas sat with the Empress several evenings and had many serious conversations with her (Mad[e] Pallas).

Monday, 17th June

I rose early, drank a glass of water at the Well in the Yard of our Inn and took a walk out of the Town into the fields as far as the Calmuc Tents. I met a party of six or seven well mounted and well dressed coming hither. The morning was delightful. The party, which I took for Calmucks, were Astracan Tartars who employ themselves in trading with the Calmucks.

Before our breakfast was over the Master of the Police called upon us to accompany us to the house where the Sisters or unmarried women live altogether. They were at different kinds of work in separate rooms and in small parties: some spinning, others sowing, some embroidering, others weaving. The Children divided into two classes were with their respective School Mistresses. The whole number including the children is about seventy and without them fifty. The children sleep at home.

Besides the rooms where they work [we] went into their chapel, their eating room, their bedroom, the Bakehouse and the kitchen, in every one of which we were struck with their great neatness and comfort. [In the chapel] they have prayers every evening at seven, and at nine the Children go to prayers in the Church. They breakfast at six, dine at eleven, sup at six, go to bed at ten, rise at five.

The garden is managed by two of the Sisters. Here the little society walk, breakfast and drink their coffee. We sat for a considerable time in one of the arbours with our obliging conductors. There were a great many Water Melons coming up; to which, as well as to fruit in general, the gentle rains with which they have been blessed are likely to be very favourable.

We went from the Sisters' house to the Shop, which contains articles of every kind and particularly a great many from England. The profits belong to the Society.

The next thing we saw was the Brothers' house, where we found them divided into a number of little parties according to their respective trades, for instance of Shoemakers, Weavers, Taylors, joiners etc. These little [parties] dine as the whole society does in the Hall or Eating room; but they breakfast and drink their coffee in their own apartment. They received us everywhere with great civility and a sort of unaffected politeness which was very pleasing and which reminded me of the manners of the people at Chaux de fonds and Locle. It was curious to recognize among the Taylors and the Shoemakers, for instance, several of the faces which we had seen at the concert on Sunday evening. The whole Number including the Children may be a hundred and without them eighty.

Mr. Brandt . . . accompanied us home and sat by us while we dined. He told us that when the Colony first settled here it was entirely a step and that they were obliged to send a thousand Versts for wood. Pugatcheff attempted fire to the Colony in three places, in none of which it kindled. The only thing he respected was a picture of our Saviour in the Church. At the first settlement of the Colony none of the trading boats from the Wolga called here but now they find it worth their while.

Several of brethren and particularly Christian Petrovitch, Conrad, the Surgeon etc. have told me that they look on the Tartars, the Calmucs, the Tchovashes and the Mordvans to be better people than the Russians. Our Landlord told me that more mischief was done to this place in the time of Pugatcheff's rebellion by them than by him; in short that in their passage through Sarrepta they carried away more property.

Tuesday, 18th June

I think Dr. Pallas told us this evening that [the] original design of establishing the Society was the Conversion of the Calmucs. The May[or] was employed as a Missionary and lived with them two years, at the end of which time it was found that the Scheme was not practicable.

He told us that there are about six principal hordes in this Desert between the Wolga and the Don; that the one encamped at present fifty Versts from Sarrepta is the largest consisting of 5,000 Kibitkas and perhaps 20,000 souls; that there are besides the great hordes some straggling ones of less consideration, a hundred or two hundred in number.

In the evening we walked with the Mayor of the place, our good friend who had accompanied us everywhere, to the Calmuc Tents. We entered one of them, in the midst of which a fire was burning with a pan of milk over it, and we tasted their sour Milk or Koumiss. But this was from the cow; the Mare Koumiss, he told us, was thinner, more wholesome and more agreeable to the palate. [The pan] as soon as it was boiled was to be poured into the leather bag where by mixing with the sour milk already there it soon became the same. Before the Dish was handed to us, the Calmuc woman stirred it well about with a kind of Mill. This [Koumiss] and meal mixed up with the same constitutes the whole luxury of their Table. Yet our friend assured us that a rich Calmuc imagines no people in the world live so well, and are in general so well off, as themselves.

Two Priests, visitors from the great Horde who had come upon business to Sarrepta, were sitting at the foot of one of the Tents in which they proposed they [should] pass the night. There were four tents on this spot in all; and the People by whom they were inhabited were employed to look after the Cattle. There are several [Calmucs] who when they have no property quit their horde for a time and even let themselves to do menial services or to work as labourers. They are the best people to entrust with the Care of Cattle.

When a stranger is known and recommended to them they treat him with great attention and take pains to satisfy his curiosity; but otherwise they take but little notice of him. The women do all the labourers' work. Except the woodwork they have all the trouble of fitting up the Tent. When they are under no apprehension of rain they frequently sleep in the open Air.

In our way to these Tents we stopped several times and listened to the Concert in the Brothers' house, which sounded charmingly at a distance.

On our return it being nine o'clock, their hour of Prayers, we stepped into the Church. The Service consisted of a hymn accompanied by an Organ, in which the whole congregation joined and which lasted about quarter of an hour.

Made Pallas observed to-day that the People of Sarrepta when treated civilly will do anything to serve you; but when treated otherwise will do nothing in the world.

Wednesday, 19th June

Their water at Sarrepta comes from the hills two miles off and is conveyed to no less than twenty Wells; the most delicious water imaginable. The Square in the middle of Sarrepta is composed on the North side of the Brothers' house, the Church and the Sisters' house, on the South by the Inn and the shop; on the East by the Widows' house and the Candle Manufactory, and on the West by the Comptoir and the ——. A single row of Poplar trees and Aspern are planted near the buildings all round; and there is an enclosure planted with trees of the same kind, but not kept in very nice order.

Dr. Pallas called upon us in his Droosky and conducted [us] to the top of the hills at the back of this plain where he shewed [us] a quantity of concretions on the edge of these heights which had evidently been cast up by the waves of the sea, when the desert made a part of the Caspian. He had dug here himself for the purpose of making the experiment and somebody had followed his example with the same success. We coasted the brow of the hills a considerable way enjoying a fine view of the serpentine Wolga, of the wooded plain on the other side of it, and of the desert beyond, not to mention the plain below us, the Town of Sarrepta, the Calmuc Tents, Zarizin, and on the right the Sarpa with the Desert at the back of that river. We returned by what they call the Turm from which the water comes which supplies the Town, and as it was already ten o'clock we deferred our visit to the mineral waters till after dinner.

The Germans came into the country 29,000 men and now the number is increased to 32,000. The Kirghese and Pugatcheff destroyed and carried off about 2,000. A Scotchman concerned in the rebellion has often sung a Rebellious Song to him [Pallas], the tune of which he knew perfectly well; as he was travelling through the country of the Baschkirs, who have rebelled two or three times, he heard a Peasant singing a song to exactly the same tune, but upon desiring his soldier and interpreter to observe the words, he was told that this also was a rebellious song. 'Over the hills and far away etc.'

The Turks attempted twice to cut a way from Zarizin across to the Don. But if, as Lowitz told Dr. Pallas, the level of the Don is forty feet higher than that of the Wolga, the Don might have flowed into the Wolga and left its own channel empty.

The Kirghese, whom he calls Tartars in contradistinction to the Calmucs, enjoy much greater freedom than the latter, who are under abject submission to their Princes. In order to know whether any Kirghese have passed the frontier they place twigs with both ends stuck in the ground, and if they see them removed in a certain way they know immediately that it is the Kirghese and go in pursuit of them.

The Calmucs hang up in the wind a piece of cloth with a prayer written upon it and when the wind shakes it about they think the efficacy as great as if they had uttered it themselves. We saw a piece of cloth of this kind to-day at one of the Calmuc Tents. They even [have] Mills which answer the same purpose. Their religion prohibits them from washing any of their utensils, perhaps on a principle of saving their water. On his late excursion his party consisted of no more than twenty Persons, yet they were often too many to be supplied from the scanty Provisions of the Country. The Calmuc Priests [are] rich and oppress the People.

He shewed us a Moss which in an emergency the People eat. There is also another of a dark colour. The taste like that of Morelles. Liquorice grows wild and might be a profitable article of exportation to England. Dr. Pallas collected several of the flies which were used as Spanish flies by the Ancients. When Potemkin at one time was out of favour, his amusement consisted in shooting knats and flies in his apartment with a Pistol (Dr. Pallas).

Old Brandt gave us his company while we were at dinner and Dr. Sedler* called upon us before the cloth was removed. He told us several curious things of the Calmucs and their language. . . . By way of paying him a great compliment a Calmuc chief told him that his (the Doctor's) wife was his (the chief's) sister. If you ask whether a child is a boy and it is a girl, they reply that it is a 'blunt boy'.

We . . . walked in the afternoon to Dr. Sedler's Garden. As well as several others it is situated on the Sarpa. He has planted a good many trees and Vines enough to furnish last year two hundred Eimer* of wine; each of which contains sixteen bottles.

We were told by the good people at the Inn that thirty thousand Calmucks left the steppes between the Don and the Ural at the time of their Migration. That they were driven to this Measure by the oppressions of the Russians. That they traversed both the Steps without distinction. That the remainder at present does not consist of more than 1,500 families: exclusive, I understood, of those settled on the Cama, whom they endeavour to withdraw from their roving mode of life. . . . When the Colony first came here the country was crowded with Calmucs.

Thursday, 20th June

I got up early, the wind was high and the whole morning cool and pleasant. We passed the greatest part in doubt whether we should go with Dr. Pallas or not to the Mineral Wells. About noon we called on our friend the Doctor where we got decided by a brother whom we met with there to abandon our project of visiting the Calmuc camp. For he assured us (and his authority seemed good), that it was but a part of a great horde, the bulk of which was near Tcherkask, whereas there were not more than a hundred families here. He added that the whole number of Calmuc Families who had migrated from the Steppes amounted to 70,000 families. (Pallas told me afterwards the same day that they amounted to 120,000.) That about 15,000 remained. (I understand from Pallas that these had gone over to and put themselves under the protection of the Don Cossacks; because the Russians had endeavoured to subject to the general laws of the kingdom and confine to fixed habitations this particular Horde, the line of its Princes having become extinct. With those who were still governed by their Princes they did not pretend to do the same. He thought that this mode of proceeding towards them would drive them all away. He was sorry for it because they are of great benefit to the Country.) That a very few, and those such only who had belonged [in] it always, were remaining in the Steppe of Irik. That the Calmucs of the Steppe on this side of the Wolga were no longer permitted to pass the river. That the horde to which the Camp on the Sarpa belonged had been very much diminished by desertion to the Don Cossacks. He promised us also a letter to a Calmuc Chief, a Major in the Russian Service who had very much distinguished himself against the Cuban Tartars* or in Caucase. He has a house at Astracan and also on our road; but he is sometimes with his Horde and probably so at this time; and therefore may possibly be at a great distance. The letter is to be open in order that we may avail ourselves of it with any other Calmucs who fall in our way.

I cannot help [remarking] that I never saw countenances in my life which seemed to indicate greater peace of mind, greater Philanthropy, greater contentment than those of the good people here, Men as well as Women. Their behaviour and their conversation accord with their looks. I have not heard a syllable fall from any of them which intimates dissatisfaction with their state or disaffection to one another.

We drank tea at Dr. Pallas's and accompanied him and Madame
in the evening to the Mineral waters, eight versts off on the way to
Zarizin. The building consists of a long covered walk which leads
to the wells of the Baths and [a] few cottages besides. If the Colony
could have obtained a grant of the spot, they would have put
themselves to some expence to prepare it for the reception of
company. But hitherto they have not been able to obtain a grant.
There has however now and then been a considerable concourse
of strangers who are obliged to live in tents. The waters have a
brackish taste, are of an opening quality and when tasted leave
a dryness on the palate. We wandered about near an hour and a
half while the Dr. and Mrs. Pallas were bathing and then came
home in the cool, almost too much in the cool, of the evening.

Friday, 21st June

Having given orders last night to have two baths ready we set
off in a Drooska at six o'clock this morning to go and bathe. We
enjoyed our scouring exceedingly and returned to breakfast about
nine.

. . . Christian Petrovitch and I took a walk with Madame
[Pallas] along the banks of the Sarpi, which are covered with
gardens made at a great expence, because they are obliged to
remove the earth to a considerable depth. We met two Calmuc
Priests with whom Christian conversed a considerable [time]. They
wore caps almost in the form of a dish, the upper part yellow,
Boots of Russian leather etc. and were not ill looking. On our
return we amused ourselves for a while watching the Motions of
a Scorpion Spider, a dangerous Spider found in the houses at
Sarrepta, and then went home, hastened away by the prospect of
an approaching Storm. . . . I sat for a considerable time at the
door of our Inn observing the lightning and conversing in German
with our Landlord, who is a Swiss from the Canton of Zurich.

Saturday, 22nd June

There were twenty-eight degrees of heat in the course of this
day . . . I don't know whether it was because the next day was
Sunday; but the Town today was crowded with Calmucs, who on
account of the heat wore their upper garment turned down and
had nothing over their body but their shirt.

Mr. Brandt came to sit with us as usual after dinner and re-
counted some curious instances of Russian Corruption. A very
respectable man was sent by the Empress to enquire into some

abuses at Casan. The wife of one of the persons concerned in
these abuses was employed to present him with 100 Ducats. He
rejected the offer with disdain; they then made him an offer in
the same way of a thousand and upon his testifying still greater
indignation, they set to work certain persons in Petersburg who
represented the conduct of this upright man to the Empress in
so unfavourable a light that he was soon recalled and not even
admitted to her Majesty's presence.

A Person was appointed to levy the Penalty at Jaroslaff on the
boats which passed there made with hewn planks or carrying such,
and being an honest man he exacted for the Government 50,000
roubles in the course of the year instead of 5,000. But this did
not suit the interests of the Governor and others connected with
him, who therefore persecuted this man in such a manner that he
was obliged to quit his post; and Brandt saw [him] soon after
at Moscow without a penny in his Pocket; whereas if he had
been a dishonest man he might easily have acquired a fortune of
20,000 roubles.

The G[overnor] General of Saratow and Voronetch, who is a
very honest man, declares that it is with the greatest difficulty he
can discharge the duties of his situation consistently with a pure
conscience. He has now left Saratow and resides at Voronetsch.

G[eneral] Nicholson assured them here that he could not prevent the irregularities of his Army, for if he had not permitted
[them] to do almost what they pleased, he was afraid of their going
over to the enemy.

A man's rule in Russia should be to have nothing to do with
Justice. He had better submit to an injury.

When the new regulations were made an old Peasant with tears
in his eyes lamented to him the alteration; we had but one man,
the Voyvode to maintain before, but now we have a legion.

We drank tea at Dr. Pallas's and were witnesses to [a] curious
battle between the Scorpion Spider and a large common spider of
the field. We all of us stood a long time at the door observing the
continual flashes of lightning in the horizon towards the south-west.
The Storm at last appeared to be advancing towards us and
hastened our departure. It took place soon after accompanied with
such a whirlwind that we were glad to shut our windows, and
rejoiced that it had not caught us in the desert.

The Empress proposed to Pallas the Work which has since been
executed by another Person, viz. a Dictionary* with the words
beginning with the same letter in a variety of languages placed in
columns by the side of each other. This work is in four Volumes.
Pallas told the Empress plainly that it would be of no use. But

when she has once taken a thing into her head, she is not easily persuaded to relinquish [it]. Her idea was that this would shew the relation of all the languages in the world to the Schlavonian, which she was fond of considering as the most ancient and the Mother tongue of all the others.

A favourite diversion among the Russians is Goose fighting. They have Geese partly of the Chinese breed to be seen on the Wolga which they make use of for that Purpose. In little [Russian] Provinces where the Gentry are rich they lay great wagers on these battles. The Chinese fight grasshoppers. Grasshoppers of this kind near Kiachta. They are also fond of Crane fighting and lay great sums of money on a battle.

Sunday, 23rd June

As it was a festival, in order to announce it to the Congregation, a hymn was performed from the Tower of the church at six o'clock in the morning by a concert of instrumental Music, chiefly Clarinets. The congregation also was summoned to Church by something of the same kind. We had been invited to go the day before for the sake of seeing the whole congregation. . . . There were about 120 of each sex present all dressed, especially the women, in the neatest manner. It was impossible not to admire the service as extremely decent and truly evangelical.

Carlo —— the Doctor came out of his house as we passed by it to wish us a good journey. . . . We . . . took our departure from Sarrepta to which I never saw a place equal for the goodness of the people and for all the comforts of life.

11 Sarepta to Astrakhan

Sunday, 23rd June, continued

When Pallas took his leave of us he said he should be very happy to meet us anywhere again except in Russia.

We set off between eight and nine and the evening was cool and pleasant. The country as long as [I] continued awake was a dead level . . . and our road lay not far from the Wolga, of which we were frequently in sight. I fell asleep before the end of the first stage and did not awake till we were changing horses at the third, viz. at Kaminskoy, where the posthouse was a temporary building a little beyond the village near the vestiges of a small fortress.

Monday, 24th June

In the first stage, while our Kibitkas were passing a piece of water on a wretched raft, at three different times I observed a troop of three or four hundred horses accompanied by their Calmuc Master swim across the same like the stags at Lime.* We breakfasted at Poddy [Direvna] in a miserable hut surrounded by half a score of wondering and curious spectators and exceedingly teazed with flies. A bad room in a bad inn at a close Manufacturing town in England may be thought a luxury after this.

In the stage to Czernoijar we saw three or four small Calmuc Encampments, as we did afterwards in almost every stage to Astracan, and also a flock of goats and several herds of cattle belonging to that people.

The banks of the Wolga are lofty and steep where Czernoijar is situated, which causes the Town, the buildings whereof, except the Churches, are all of wood, to look handsome as one approaches. It being a holiday the People were all in their best cloaths and I could [not] help comparing the goodness and neatness of their cloaths with the rags and tatters of the populace in Italy. While we were waiting for horses, it seeemed to be the appointed time for all the young Girls in the place to fetch water from the Wolga.

As they were all in their national dress and very neat it was a very agreeable and picturesque sight.

Our road in this stage and in general all the way to Astracan lay near the Wolga of which we frequently got views. The wood[s] and green Meadows and inundations presented a strong and pleasant contrast to dry sandy Desert thinly cloaked with bitter plants which we had through this whole stage. At Gorodschok, Coindet wakened me at between eleven and twelve to dine, i.e. to eat some bread and cheese, which together with the irregular driving of the soldier prevented me from falling asleep again. We were driven to Czernoijar, Gorodschok and Wetlianke by Don Cossacks, fifty of whom are constantly on duty at Czernoijar and the two other places.

I take Wetlianke to be the first Stanitza* colonized by the Dubofka Cossacks. Early as the hour was the people were out of their beds and the houses appeared comfortable, as they did ever after in the Stanitzes belonging to this People.

Tuesday, 25th June

We breakfasted in the lobby of a poor hut with only a single floor at Enotaewsk where we were terribly infested as usual with flies. The Dolmetcher* of the Calmucs, Michael C—— Vesilev lives at E[notaevsk] in a large handsome wooden house having a gallery running round it. . . . We had a letter to him from Christian Petrovitch, and not finding him here determined to call upon him at his Country house a little out of the road seven miles off. He received us in a hayloft which being open on all sides let the air through and being situated close by the side of the river was perfectly delightful to us come from travelling over the sunburnt dusty steppe. We drank a dish and he not only gave us a good deal of information about the Calmucs but furnished us with a letter of recommendation to the Princess in case we should not find Prince Tiumen with his Horde.

One of the Calmuc Encampments between C[ernoijar] and E[notaevsk] consisted of thirty tents but the number in general was from ten to that number. We understood from the Dolmetcher that we see none but the poorer Calmucs on the Wolga, that all the richer are encamped on the rivers that fall into the Don. Soon after we left the Dolmetcher we were witness to the breaking up of a tent and the conveying it away on the back of two Camels together with the family and their cattle. On the way to Sereglatske their horses and cattle being assembled about the Camp served very much to enliven and animate the scene.

At the Stations the Commander of the Cossacks constantly attended and discovered great civility. We arrived at Sereglatske and having determined to visit Prince Tiumen who was with his horde near our route six or seven versts forward, we determined to stop here till break of day (damned bore, what the Devil is there to see).

Wednesday, 26th June

We actually set off at break of day as we had proposed, understanding that the Prince was up always early, and arrived at the Camp, which consisted of about 120 tents, soon after. . . . His tents were three in number in the centre of the Camp and were distinguishable by their whiteness. We halted at some distance from [them] and sent John in quest of him with our letters. He requested us to wait a little while till his tent was ready for our reception; which it was not just then owing to his having had company to pass the night with him. In fact, however, I believe that the Princesses, viz. his wife and daughters, were asleep in it; for we saw two ladies presently after passing from this tent to another in a great hurry and dressing themselves as they went.

He received us with great politeness. The tent . . . being open at the top and a little all round underneath was very cool and pleasant. A Carpet of white clean felt was spread all over the ground except a round space in the middle over which stood a Semi-globular Vessel covered with a Mat whereon lay a ladle. This was for their Koumiss. A Sopha, which I suspect had served for one of the beds (the other was on the floor), three Camp Chairs and two Carpets, on one [of] which his chair was placed and ours were intended to be [on] the other, composed the furniture.

After conversing for some time, we were served out of a wooden vessel, in the form almost of a short boot, with a dish of tea prepared in the Calmuc way, that is with tea, water, butter and salt. Our dishes were also of wood and by way of signifying that they were prohibited from washing their Utensils, a handful of shavings were brought in along with them to rub and clean the inside. This kind of tea, he assured us, was wholesome and I was so far from finding it unpalatable that I begged for a second dish. Before the Tea was brought in, his son had entered very neatly dressed and took his seat on a carpet which was spread for him on one side. He also partook of our fare, smoked his pipe as his father did (it was extraordinary that the Prince never once invited us to smoke) and seemed to be treated with much distinction. We observed that the Servants in handing anything to the Prince were very cautious

not to set their foot on his Carpet. We were afterwards served
with tea in our own way, with lemon juice to supply the place of
Milk.

Upon begging leave, when we had sat for some time, to walk
about the Camp, he conducted us to their places of worship, which
consisted of four tents standing by themselves, where everything
had evidently been prepared for our reception. In every one of
these there was a kind of altar on which, beside some tinsel ornaments, were placed in several small pewter cups offerings of water
barley, barley mixed with beans, cheese made of sour milk and
sugar. At the back of the altar were either their religious books
covered with a carpet (at least this was the case in one) or a
Cabinet, the doors of which being open exhibited a variety of
idols each in his niche sitting squat and often decorated with a
string of Pearls. These Cabinets reminded me of the pictures over
altars in Roman Catholic Churches which are often shut up in
this manner with folding doors. On each side of the altar were
hung the holy pictures containing a great number of extravagant
figures, and dangling like so many colours. The faces in these were
all in the Chinese style, as indeed those of the Calmucs are. It
was remarkable that there was a glory round each of the heads.
Some of these paintings, or rather tapestries, come from Tibet
but in general they are manufactured at home.

The Prince and his son on entering each tent as a mark of
reverence touched some or all of the holy pictures with their
head[s]. We were shewn in one the Drums and trumpets which
they make use of sometimes in their service; and also the Standard
with a figure of the God of Battles and a long inscription upon it
in Tangut,* which they take with them when they go to war. The
Prince took this very standard with him I understand when he
served in the Cuban. Each of these tents is superintended by a certain number of Priests, who I suspect sleep and live in them.

When we had satisfied our curiosity here he invited us to visit
the tent of the Lama. He used to be appointed by the Lama of
Thibet. But of late it has been usual on account of the length and
danger of the journey for the old Lama to fix before his death
without sending to Thibet on some person properly qualified for
his successor. Formerly also Pilgrimages were usual to that country
but of late they have been discontinued, he said, for the same
reason.

We found him sitting in the posture of his God which he did not
alter in the smallest degree by way of return to our bows. Carpets
were laid for us and we sat down crosslegged in the eastern fashion.
What shall I offer you, he said; we seemed inclined to decline

everything but upon the Prince's saying that their religion required us to take something, we accepted of some Koumiss or Mare's milk which was handed to us in a neat bason out of a wooden Vessel in the form of a short Churn that was standing by the Altar. It was thin, acid but by no means disagreeable having as Dr. Pallas observed rather a vinous taste and resembling that, particularly white wine Whey. He enquired about our religion whether it was the same with that of the Germans; and about our language, whether that of our religion and of common life were the same, and about the size of our country. It was news to him that Great Britain was an island. . . . He conversed with great composure and when we were coming away wished us a safe return to our native country and to the presence of our Sovereign. We bowed very respectfully on parting but he did not on this occasion or any other make the smallest movement in return.

The Lama seldom stirs out except to ride about once a week and walk in their processions. The Calmucs in general by being continually on horseback and at other times sitting generally in their manner, become feeble to such a degree that many of them can scarcely bear to be on their feet for an hour together. The Prince I think mentioned this. N.B. Their way is to give Names to their Children according to circumstances. For instance [said the Prince] if my wife had happened to be delivered of a son at this time, perhaps I should have given him the name of one of you in honour of this visit. The Prince told us that their Custom is to reckon the age of a Person from the time of his Mother's being with Child.

I shall now mention the arrangement of the Lama's Apartment and his dress. At his back was placed a thick roll of black leather which we took for his bed, and behind that a kind of sopha : before [this] was a little low form like what the Priests had before them when we saw them at divine service. On his right hand a little advanced stood an altar with the usual offerings upon [it], particularly several small conical lumps of sugar wrapped in paper, and in a cup on a stand by itself a dish of Calmuc tea, which he had probably presented this morning, as the primitie* of his breakfast. Close by the Altar I observed the little Churn already mentioned and two boots like what had contained our Calmuc tea. On his left opposite to the Altar stood a pile of Boxes containing I suppose the holy things. Several Utensils of different kinds were scattered about the room, which however on the whole was very neat.

His dress consisted of a Calmuc Cap, a red outer Garment, an under one of yellow (B[ootle] calls it a Petticoat) and a shirt under that. What he had on his legs we could not see because they were hid.

The Prince before we went to the Lama had invited us to dine; and upon our expressing a wish to dress and wash ourselves first, had ordered a tent to be erected near our Kibitkas for that purpose to which we now retired. I forgot to mention that on rising from my awkward posture on the Carpet in the Lama's tent I had entirely lost the use of my limbs and could hardly scramble out.

The dinner was already serving up when we returned. A table was laid in the Tent on the Spot where the Koumiss had stood, the top of the tent was covered [?] down, the sides were opened all round in order to let thro' a current of air, and a canopy was raised over the Sopha. While we were at dinner, several spiders dropped upon us from the top of the Tent. Our dinner was in the Russian style, being preceded by a savoury collation and followed by Tea instead of Coffee. Caviare, dried fish, cheese made of cows milk, cheese made of sour milk such as we had seen on the altars, twisted white bread, butter, Eau de vie and a Medicine to mix with it composed the collation. Minced meat or rather soup, something between both, the fat of Mutton cut in slices, some slices of fat beef; pigskin filled with rice tasting strong[ly] of Garlic, Curry and Roast Mutton with lemon composed our dinner. The art of making the minced Meat or Soup above mentioned consists in boiling it very gently. The ingredients besides the Mutton are only water and salt. It was richly sprinkled with little pieces of fat. It was curious to meet with Rhine wine, English beer and English knives and forks in a Calmuc tent. Besides the Rhine wine and the English Beer he treated us with some wine that came out of his own Garden.

He did the honours of his table with great politeness and propriety and we were never at a loss for conversation. To account for which I must mention that our interpreter John was present all the while and even sat down with us to dinner. I forgot to mention that an old Musician played during our whole dinner time on an Instrument somewhat resembling a guittar and accompanied his playing with the Voice. One of his tunes was exactly a French one Bootle [knew], which was curious after what Pallas had remarked in general of their Music. Most of the songs were Love Songs, the ditties of despairing lovers. He [the Prince] told us that the Calmucs in their national meals sit on carpets and are helped according to Seniority.

When word was brought us that divine service was ready we rose from table and hastened to the consecrated tents; in one of which we found thirteen Priests forming two rows, six on one

M

side and seven on the other, chanting in a low hoarse voice accompanied with the most ridiculous gruntings. They likewise twirled
their hands round one another and snapped their fingers in a
curious manner. But they presently took into their hands a bell
and a sort of short staple [?], after which a tinkling of their bells
in Chorus supplied the place of the latter of these operations. The
Psalm or hymn or verse seemed continually to come to an end;
there was then a pause, and a new beginning was made always
by one particular Priest. When we had attended about three
quarters of an hour the Prince inquired whether our curiosity was
satisfied; observing at the same time that it would last an hour
longer, and without any variation. We of course found ourselves
disposed not to stay any longer. The Dress of the Priests was a
cap turned up with five wings and having [a] shaft or spire in the
middle of black twisted round with string in several places, an
outer garment like a pair of stays, an under one not coming much
below it, and a third somewhat in the form of a petticoat. There
were little low benches before them and they all preserved the
most unmoveable gravity of countenance and did not once turn
their gaze towards us. . . . I understand that there are four services
in a day, one in the morning, two in the middle of the day and one
in the evening.

We now ordered our Kibitkas and returned with the Prince
to his tent where we again drank tea. In the meantime he entertained us with a sight of two of their sacred Volumes, one in the
Tangut the other in the Mongol language, by an exhibition of four
dromedaries, and lastly of the Calmuc way of wrestling. The two
combatants were perfectly naked except about the loins. Their
contest resembled the old Palaestra: the object being, one to throw
the other down.

Those Volumes I understand from him contain a history of
God Almighty's gracious dispensations to their nation. I understood also that there are a great many of them. The Calmucs all
ran to kiss them as soon as they saw them before they were brought
in to us. They resembled in shape a book of accounts. The Mongol
language was written in the same manner as the Calmuc and is I
imagine the same. The Tangut was written from left to right like
ours. But the letters very much resembled the Hebrew. This I
understand to be the language of their religion and totally different
from that of common life: as different, to use the Prince's expression, as Russian from Greek.

They have in all about a hundred and twenty [camels]. Two
are sufficient to carry away a tent. These Dromedaries have each
two benches. The four which we saw were very tall. Awkward

as is their Motion, they can upon occasion outrun a swift horse. They will subsist fifteen days without eating or drinking.

He [the Prince] had before shewn us his hawks and dogs, one of which though only fifteen months old, a prodigious powerful creature, had killed eighteen Wolves for him last winter; one of the hawks he had made a present of to the Governor General. When we took our leave of him he begged us in the Russian style not to forget him and desired if ever we came into these parts again to give him two or three days Notice in order that he might be able to receive us in a better manner. We agreed in thinking the behaviour of this Calmuc perfectly polite: yet he always went out of his tent before us, a piece of etiquette which I have since imagined he may have learnt from her Majesty's representatives the Governors and Governors general.

The Prince's horde consists he told us of about 3,000 families or Kibitkis. He had about 120 with him at present in this spot which his ancestors had been in the habit of frequenting for a century past. He proposed to remain here a fortnight, then to remove to his island in which he passes another fortnight; and from thence to the other side of the Wolga. For this purpose however, as we were informed by the Brigadier, he is obliged to obtain permission of the Governor, though he dissembled that to us, and insinuated that the Calmucs were all at full liberty to cross the river. Yet I remember that he seemed to be rather chagrined by the Question. The rest of his horde are dispersed all over the Steppe; but they are obliged to procure leave to go from him. Many individuals are possessed of a thousand horses and other cattle in proportion. Not more than four or five of these can be accommodated, he said, in the same place. He asserted also that the number of Calmuc families was 50,000, that there are 22,000 on this side towards the Wolga and 10,000 in the neighbourhood of Tcherkask. Yet the Brigadier, who pretends to be well informed, asserts that the whole number is not more than 15,000 or 20,000. He also maintains in opposition to Pallas and Vesilef that there are no Calmucs in the Steppe of Ural; and that the number of families who made their escape did not amount to more than 40 or 50,000. Yet he calculated that they amounted to 400,000 souls.

He says that the only people there [i.e. in the Ural Steppe] are a few Tartars. His account of the Calmucs who made their escape out of Russia* is that the greatest part of them were destroyed by the Kirghese, owing to the want of fodder for their horses, and that no more than twenty thousand escaped with their lives. The Prince's account was the same except that they had received no intelligence of those who had escaped with their lives and did not know where they were. Now as it seems to be well understood that they are settled in the Irtish in the Chinese Territories, I imagined that this ignorance of his was pretended. He was but eleven at the time of this secession. Some of his horde was in the number, he said, of the seceders. I thought that he spoke of this event with evident marks of concern. This Horde is called the horde of Chachioutoch, and the Prince's name is as he gave it himself after we had written ours by his desire 'Wladell i Knes Premier Major Tiumen'. He seemed to make a great point of his title of Premier Major. I could not help remarking the Piety with which the Prince spoke of every future enterprise and future intention: adding also if it pleased God to prolong his life, by leave of Providence and so on.

12 Astrakhan

Thursday, 27th June

We called in the evening upon the Governor with whom as he speaks no language but Russ we were obliged to converse by means of an interpreter. He was extremely civil, remarking that Astracan was seldom visited by such strangers as ourselves, and offering us all the services in his power. He mentioned as objects for our curiosity, the fishery which was carrying on at this time, the sight of some Kirghese, and a Persian Khan who had taken refuge from the disorders in his country under the protection of Russia. While we were with him the Commander of the Ural Cossacks came in and also the Vice-Governor, which last invited us to dinner with him the next day. The conversation turning on the Salubrity of the Climate, a medical man, Pargold, who was there observed I think that as long as the marshy ground was left in the middle of the Town, it must on that account and on that account only be in some degree unhealthy. Before we went away the Governor shewed us a very beautiful Turcomanian horse three years old which he had bought for three hundred roubles. The Vice-Governor made us an offer of his carriage but we preferred our Drooski and went next to deliver our letters to our friends the Armenian Merchants. They were brothers and as their houses are opposite, he on whom we called sent for the other.

We were treated here in the first place with English Beer, of which all they knew was that it came from Petersburgh. As we had had no dinner I begged a little bread to eat with it, and they brought us what they called Asiatic bread, though the difference from European was so little that if they had not told us I should not have suspected. We were afterwards invited to drink a glass of Ispahan Wine which in its flavour and taste was entirely new to me and perhaps superior to anything I had ever met with of the kind. It had been in Astracan I think between twenty and thirty years. After this the tablecloth was spread and a Dessert brought in consisting of Figs, Pistachio Nuts, Raisins and Bread, all from Persia. We were likewise asked to take another glass of Ispahan,

161

which we could not refuse, although by some means or other, we were understood to have done so and did not get one.

With regard to the trade of Persia they told that there had been five Persian Ships here this year and that the goods which they brought to Astracan from that country were chiefly silks, half silks and Cottons. In answer to Bootle's Question how far it was to India they said that it was a voyage in the first place of two or three days to Resht a port on the Caspian, a thousand Versts from thence to Ispahan, seven hundred from Ispahan to Shiraz and 2,300 from Shiraz to Bassora. Before we came away the Gentleman whom we dined upon invited us to dine with him the day after tomorrow and promised that it should be altogether in the Asiatic style: one circumstance of which is that we dine at eleven o'clock.

The way which they take to have good water here is to let it stand for several days in a cellar and to keep it in Ice. The Sand or whatever it is loaded with settles then and leaves it perfectly good. We begged some water of this kind last night from the Master of the house. N.B. When there is no wind here what renders the heat insupportable are the Saline Particles which rise out of the earth and load the Air. These . . . penetrate into the skin and cause fevers. The heat of day was universally complained of though the Thermometer was supposed to be up only to 30 and it rises sometimes to 36. The People resident here are only here for a time and therefore do not adopt the Methods observed in other countries to guard themselves against the heat. They also come from a part of the world where these precautions are not necessary and not practised and therefore they go on here as they have been used to do in a very different climate. They ought to do as the Italians do at Venice and Naples, i.e. turn night into day; shut their doors and windows in the former and open them in the latter.

Friday, 28th June

Our company [at dinner at the Vice Governor's] was about thirty-six Persons. There was a band of Music in the adjoining room. Our first dish was a thing I had never tasted before, viz. iced Soup, the same nearly I believe as the soup we had been used to meet with at Petersburgh. We had a great variety of the country's Wines, one particularly with a strong taste of Cloves, two or three that resembled Champaign and one exactly like Tent.* Towards the latter end of dinner several toasts were drunk by all the company in the same wine and out of the same glass. First the health of the Governor and Vice Governor, secondly the lady of the Vice

Governor; thirdly all the ladies; fourthly all the Gentlemen and lastly the Vice Governor himself whose name day it was. A servant went round with the bottle and glass to present these toasts which there was no possibility of refusing. The same thing was repeated in the evening at supper, for the company passed the whole day here, as they generally do when a dinner is given. Their number however was much reduced. Not very long after dinner they began to dance and continued to do so with some interruptions till supper and even afterwards till midnight. The day was insupportably hot. I hardly ever suffered more from heat; yet during supper from being placed in a through air I was under apprehension of being chilled.

In the afternoon the refugee Khan from Persia made his appearance accompanied by his Russian interpreter: so that we were obliged to converse with him by means of a third Person. One of his attendants brought him from time to time a pipe in water which after two or three inspirations he returned, or when he meant to pay a compliment, offered to some person near him. We came in each of us for the honour of a whiff. He kept his cap or turban on the whole time; his robe was red cloth tied round with a sash; his slippers were blue, he wore a cloak over his robe when he entered which he afterwards laid aside. His Nose was aquiline, his Eyes full and his Countenance expressive with the most handsome black beard I ever saw. What struck me as much as anything was the inharmonious vulgar tone of his voice. He invited us to go and see him. Several Persian Merchants came and presented him with flowers which he gave to the ladies. One who stuck very close to him was known, the Ober-Commandant said, to carry on a correspondence with his brother.

I understand that he was the Khan of Astrabad* and that his eldest brother being desirous of subjecting the whole kingdom to himself had attacked this his younger brother and obliged him to fly for his life. At this moment he is at war with all the other Khans. Several battles have been fought and he has been often wounded. This eldest brother has no children and indeed as I was told by one person has been rendered incapable of having any. On the contrary the younger brother has several.

The Empress makes him an allowance of 12,000 roubles a year. I think he has about sixty Persons with him. It is in contemplation to remove him to Kislar: to which he is very averse because then he would not meet with the same society, he would not be treated with the same respect and he dreads the Climate. The Russian Government neither wishes to offend the brother by taking him too decidedly under its protection; nor to offend him by a want of attention; for fear that either one or the other should in process of time be in a situation to revenge the affront.

He and his Persians rise at three in the morning, pay their adoration, smoke, drink their sherbet and go to bed again. They rise again either at six or nine and the rest of the day is divided between smoking and sleeping. To see Women come into society as they do here is a new sight to him and they say that he is much amused with it.

There was also an Armenian Merchant and his wife present in the afternoon, both in their national dress. In general the Armenian Women do not come into company; but the husband of this lady is a fine Gentleman or rather is a lively young man who chuses to break through the customs of his countrymen in this respect. N.B. Upon asking the Vice-Governor what the population of Astracan was he told me that there were 4,000 houses and that the number of Armenians was 10,000.

In the afternoon we took a little walk out with the Ober Commandant to the Persian Shops and the quarter of the Indians. . . . The Persian habitations are very uncomfortable. We went into one consisting of a single Apartment, dark and stinking, two thirds of which was taken up with the Divan on which they sleep. The richest Merchants when unmarried live in this way. When married they have a house and quit their shops.

The Indians* carry on no commerce but live on the interest of their money being literally like the Jews Usurers by profession. The Vice-Governor told me that their number was about a hundred: that they burn their dead and regard an interment as a subject of rejoicing. The Ober Commandant had written to the G[overnor] General that they were an useless sort of people and ought to be driven out of the country. They seem to live within the precincts of one great inclosure, as far as I could observe in the most uncomfortable way imaginable. We entered and walked a good way in a long alley where we understood that they lived and where we were almost suffocated with Smoke. We saw several perched on the walls of their inclosure where they often appear, I understand, perfectly naked.

They eat no meat but subsist chiefly on vegetables and have a great respect for dogs, believing that the souls of those who die migrate into the bodies of those animals. We met a party who were well dressed: and when after what I had seen and heard I expressed my surprise at seeing them so, I was told that several of them are very rich. I understand that they have no women of their own and their principal expence is in that Article.

Astracan not being paved* the streets are deep in dust which

the wind blows about and renders very unpleasant. Yet they are
still worse, the Ober Commandant says, after rain, for then it is
not possible to conceive how dirty and nasty they are. The houses
in general are of wood and make a very shabby appearance. The
Churches, however, as well as a good many houses, are of brick
stuccoed white and in the style of Petersbourgh embellished with
architectural ornament. A good part of a street is now and then
built in this way and looks rather handsome; though as the stucco
is become dirty and begun to peel off everywhere more or less,
those buildings have at the same time a ruinous, neglected, slovenly
Appearance.

Saturday, 29th June

We staid at home this morning and ordered ourselves to be
denied, by which we avoided a visit from the Governor and two
officers of the Guards, M. De Ligne* and M. Sovolofski, who came
to call upon us. Our morning indeed was not very long for we
were invited to dine with our Armenian Friend at eleven o'clock.

We did not sit down, however, till near one. Our party consisted of the Ober Commandant, three other Russian officers
including our crazy countryman* Mr. ——, a Russian Merchant,
and four Armenian Merchants viz. our host, his brother, his son
in law and an old man who had been in England and Holland.
It was remarkable that in this little party there were no less than
five languages spoken alternately, viz. Russ, Armenian, French,
German and English. A table was set out before dinner according
to the Russian fashion: two sorts of dried Caviar, Eau de vie, and
a Persian wine. It is the custom of the Armenians to begin their
dinner with Eggs. We had a great variety of dishes, some Russian
and some Armenian, a great variety of Wines, some Persian
(particularly Wine of Shiraz and Ispahan) and some Russian, and
a great variety of fruits in the dessert which were chiefly Persian:
Apples, Citron of a great size, Dates, Acid preserved plums etc.
etc. I counted twenty-four Articles. The same custom of drinking
healths which I had remarked at the Vice-Governor's was observed
also here. As strangers our health was drunk first and afterwards
those of the other company, three at a time. Coffee was followed by
the introduction of a water Pipe of which we most of us took a
few whiffs. The String or whatever it ought to be called, was near
three yards long. It was pliant and ornamented with rings of silver.
The fireplace also was of silver. I do not understand the Mechanism
but the smoke by some means passes I believe through the water.
The form was the same as that of the Khan's.

Our Armenian friend having lent us his carriage we made another attempt to find M. Agathi and at last succeeded. He is a native of Smyrna, was educated at Padua, and being employed by a society (whose object was to make enquiries into the interior state of Africa) to travel in that country. Under this idea he disembarked at Algiers and went by land to Grand Cairo, where he met with Bruce,* who gave him a very exaggerated account of what he had seen and done in Abyssinia. From Grand Cairo he went to Gedda, from thence to Surat, from Surat to Madrass, from Madrass through the Kingdoms of Cashmire and Persia to Russia. He receives five hundred roubles a year here as Director of the Schools; but besides that he is a considerable Merchant. We sat with him a good while and were much amused by his conversation.

He met at Gedda with an Armenian who having gone into Abyssinia with his son for the purpose of trading, had been sent by the Queen* on some commission but was obliged to leave his son in pawn behind as a security for his return. He asked this man whether he had heard of Bruce. The Armenian replied that he had not, though he embarked from the port where Bruce pretends to have landed. This Armenian gave Agathi such an account of the diffiiculties of getting out of Abyssinia that he deterred him from undertaking the journey. None of Bruce's Companions returned with Bruce to bear true witness to the truth of his relations.

Agathi met Worthley Montague* at Rosetta and [was] induced by a false representation of his to visit Mount Sinai. For he assured him, what he also published to the world, that the Pentateuch was to be seen written there in the rocks. He asked him in what language but that he could not tell. Agathi in fact found the rocks covered with Inscriptions in different Eastern characters as Montague had mentioned; but these inscriptions were only the names of the persons who had been here, written by way of recording that they had.

Montague under an idea that he was a son of the Grand Signior having during his residence at Rosetta observed several of the Mahometan Ceremonies, was waited upon by four Doctors to inquire whether he was a believer in Mahomet or no. He durst not deny it, for after what he had done he would certainly have lost his life. On the other hand he did not chuse to declare himself a Musselman on account of his relations. He contrived to get himself out of this scrape by putting the Doctors into good humour with Sherbet, Pipes and Chocolate; and then raising a dispute among them on this question whether a person with so short a —— as his, which he produced, was under any obligation to be circumcised. While they were disputing with great warmth, he begged them to retire for the present and to consider the question coolly and at their leisure. In the mean time he took care to take himself off.

The Country of Cashmire, he says, is a mountainous country which never was subject to any despots; where the people enjoy a sort of liberty, though he did not explain what. But he mentioned a remarkable Republic in that country of some such name as Set-leek,* composed of people from all countries; the only condition required of those who wish to incorporate themselves being the taking of an Oath of aversion and hostility to all Kings.

He travelled through Persia in the habit of a Dervise in perfect security understanding as he did the Turkish, Arabic and Persian languages. . . . He says that there is great simplicity in several parts of the Mahometan Religion . . . the inequalities in the style of the Alcorn [i.e. the Koran], some part being so very low and others so very sublime, convincing him that it was not all written by the same person. He spoke of it, I think, as being in some respects exceedingly majestic and grand. He mentioned two places, Yeist or something like it [? Yazd], where there are still —— or worshippers of the sun in Persia.

From him we went to the O[ver] Commandant who would gladly give us apartments in his house. While he, Bootle and M. De Ligne took a walk, I employed myself in bathing. He has a band of Music which was playing the greatest part of the afternoon. After bathing I was served with an excellent dish of Chocolate. When we were coming away, he insisted upon our stepping into the adjoining room, where the supper being on the table; it was impossible to refrain from taking something, especially as English Beer, English Porter and some excellent Butter made a part of the entertainment.

The Over-Commandant told me that the number of Armenian houses here was 1,600 and the number of people he imagined not less than 10,000. The Persians are about 100: three or four of them are married and live in convenient houses; but the rest, being here a certain time only for the purpose of trading, content themselves with Cabines such as we saw last night.

The great number of Mills which one sees about this Town are for the Purpose of watering their Gardens. I have just counted near thirty which I can see from the window of our Apartments. All their wood for building and burning comes from Casan and Viatka, which causes it to [be] very dear. It costs, I think he said, six roubles a month to heat a single stove. And yet I think he said at another time that though he dines at home every day and has generally ten Persons to dine with him, his table costs him no

168   A TOUR OF RUSSIA, SIBERIA AND THE CRIMEA

more than twelve roubles a month. All the necessaries of life are
so cheap that his income of 3,000 roubles will go farther, he says,
than 20,000 at Petersburgh.

Sunday, 30th June

I waked uneasy having dreamt that the Vestal was going to be
married.

I had a visit early this morning from Mr. Kelly, an American
Englishman in this service, who though a wild impetuous man,
threw a good deal of light on the corruption of those who are
entrusted with power, on the rascality of the Navy officers in
Russia, and in some respects on the nature of military rank.

Nothing can be sold without the Governor's permission. He
permits them to sell their commodities for more or less according
as they are paid. Hence the high price of many of the common
Articles of life at Astracan. Meat which ought to be no more here
than one Copeck a pound is three or four, and so on. The Boats
that come from Moscow are drawn up close to his own house in
order that they lie the more at his Mercy.

At the first foreign Port they [*the naval officers*] come to they
sell the Cables, Sailcloth and Anchors, which they bring out with
them to serve in case of emergencies and account for them as they
think proper in their log book. A Russian Vessel upon arriving
at Copenhagen, was actually obliged to purchase an Anchor in
consequence of having really lost one after having sold all the rest.
Mr. Kelly had often received innuendos from the Russians on
board that he ought to do as other people in this respect.

Till a person arrives to the rank of Premier Major, which is the
first commission signed by the Empress he is regarded as nothing.
A Captain even is regarded as nothing. But having once obtained
the rank of Premier Major, he is considered on the road to preferment: he is looked upon as a Gentleman.

As an instance of Oppression he mentioned that if a Peasant
has the misfortune to lose half a dozen Brothers, and as many
children, he must pay himself the Capitation Tax for them all, till
I suppose a given time. Or was it the tax to the Lord? Another
instance was that if a Peasant has a handsome daughter, it is in the
power of the Lord to take her and treat her as he thinks proper.
The Question always is, [Agathi] says, what rank has a Man; the
character of a Sçavant or anything of that sort is not in the least
regarded.

While he was still with us we were called upon by Mr. Agathi.
He told me I think the Indians [? Persians] are about 70, the

Indians about 100 and the Chvintzi about 250. These last come from Chiva and Usbeck, two places between the Caspian Sea and Bocharia, the trade of which country they carry on. They come and go as the Persians do without establishing themselves. The Indians, he assured me, are Sodomites and have their boys from Casan. The Governor's lady told me that there are fresh Indians constantly and that they lend their money at the enormous interest of five Copecks a rouble per month. At the same time they live at no expense.

Before dinner we called on Sovolofski and De Ligne, two officers of the Guards, at the house of the former who is married to a daughter of General Beketof and receives an income of 50 or 60,000 roubles from his Fishery. He told me that he possessed 200 Versts of coast on the Caspian Sea near Kislar to which he had transported about 200 Peasants who however did not enjoy their health, being very subject to the Scurvy and to inflammatory as well as intermittent fevers. He shewed [us] a Cave where their fish is kept. A Cave of this kind is surrounded with Ice in order to preserve it cool. The Fish is laid in piles and a Canal in the middle receives the water which flows from the place. This stank most insufferably. But he had several in the Country, he told me, which were kept in the nicest possible order. The whole number of fishing and transport Vessels belonging to this place were he said 200. He had five of his own. Kelly told me that the Russians had three frigates and four other small armed Vessels in the Caspian.

We dined at the O[ver] Commandant's very uncomfortably, devoured almost with flies, stupified with the Noise and fooleries of a Russian Soldier who had lost his understanding, and in the midst of spectators who having already dined themselves, came in and sat by while we were at dinner. I could not help observing that the Russians and others submitted to pull off their hats at the requisition of this fool and especially so while he was preaching.

The Over Commandant accompanied us after dinner on a visit to the Khan, who not being come out of the bath or not having an interpreter at hand, could not immediately receive us. We were treated in the first place with tea; a cloth was then spread on a table and half a score dishes of fruit were put upon it. These were handed to us one after another. Besides which we had sherbet and a whiff of his Pipe. The Over Commandant says that he has been an exile at the courts of different Khans for the last nine years. The young man who handed the Pipe to him is supposed to supply the place of a mistress.

He sat in the eastern manner all this time on his Divan which has some resemblance to a taylor's Bench. Several of his Ministers were in the room, particularly his Mufti and his Visier. The Mufti had superintended both his and his brother's education. A Curtain covered a window which looked into a chamber adjoining where he kept an Uncle and another Person in Chains. As we went out all his attendants were in waiting and formed a lane. Their dress in general was a long outward garment of red Cloth, a close garment of Stuff for the most part of some other colour tied with a sash under that, a Turban, Trowsers and slippers. His whole Suite is about seventy. Every man has a Divan to himself. He recollected the Persian who came to England with Mr. Elliott and said that he was an Ecrivain. The Visier also recollected Mr. Elliott who, he said, had travelled over the greatest part of Persia. They saluted us when we came away by putting their hand to their forehead.

We met him [*the Vizier*] again in the evening at the Governor's, where a splendid supper and ball was given and where we were treated with not less distinction at least than the exiled sovereign. Besides him and his Suite, there was an Indian present at this assembly, as likewise the gay Armenian and his wife in their national dresses.

This Indian for four years having been in love with a lady, has every day during all that time placed himself opposite to her windows for four hours. Why don't you declare your love, Agathi said to him? Like the moth, said he, I chuse rather to flutter about the flame till I am consumed and say nothing. His complexion was very tawny, his black hair cut very close on all the fore part of his head, and tied behind in a little tail curling up, his outer garment was red, he wore Pantaloons and slippers. Under his outer Garment, he wore a loose flowery dress of Indian stuff and under that a shirt. This is the style nearly of all their dresses.

Two young ladies just arrived from Petersburgh amused the Company by dancing the Russian, the Bohemian and the Cossack dances: and after supper a band of Armenian Music was provided and two Armenians who danced to it the Armenian dances. The horrid custom of drinking toasts was introduced likewise here and the poor Khan as well as ourselves were [*sic*] obliged to submit to it.

I came away in a drooski with Agathi though the Governor's carriage it seems was ready for us; but I was glad not to depend upon B's coming away. Agathi says that the Russian Character is not naturally gay. That their attendance on Balls like that at the Governor's to night is by way of paying their court; or balls would be more common in other houses. That in fact the Russians have no Character at all, or if any that the strongest trait of it is a blind servility to the good pleasure of the Court and their superiors. Play and ——, Agathi says, are the two things in which the Russians make the chief enjoyment to consist.

Upon my observing that we had too many things at the Russian Entertainments, he said that the Profusion in the house of [a] Russian Merchant was three times as great, and their importunities for you to eat and drink the same also. They fall upon their knees and entreat you, thinking that they cannot entertain you kindly without behaving in this manner. M. Agathi told me that no dancing was equal to that of the Egyptian ——: the Women there made a profession of it; that they were cloathed in a thin dress of gauze; that they move any part of the body in such a manner as notwithstanding this veil to make it appear almost naked; and that they did so particularly with the *partes Genitales*.

Agathi told me that by bribing two sets of People in the way to Tiflis with ten Copecks each we might be conducted with the greatest security. The number of inhabitants is not more than 10,000 at Tiflis. The distance from Mosdok 270 Wersts.

The O[ver] Commandant assured us that grants of Fisheries had been made to several Russian Nobles on condition that they peopled the Country adjoining. He mentioned particularly the Names of Saltikoff and Besborodko. Saltikoff's estate lies in an Island in the Caspian Sea which belongs properly to Persia. He derives a revenue of 1,500 roubles a year from it. Others enjoy a much greater revenue. Yet not one single Peasant have they planted in these lands agreeably to the conditions of the Grant. The O[ver] Commandant has sent an account of all this. The Fisheries are carried on by People sent from Astracan who are able if industrious to earn a great deal of money. I imagine that it does not answer to plant Colonies in these parts. Sovolofski had settled two hundred Peasants on his estate; but they had been a great many of them carried off. The 20,000 colonists settled on the line, the Vice-Governor told me, had been reduced to 10 [? 10,000].

Monday, 1st July

Our whole morning was lost in receiving visitants. The first was Agathi with the Gorodishni to beg pardon for having put us into such bad lodgings. Then came the crazy Irish American Captain Kelly: and lastly the Governor with his interpreter. The latter called upon us again on his return and took us with him to dinner.

We dined about four and twenty. He does not speak any language but Russ. But his wife speaks French and is a well bred, agreeable woman. She told me that there arrive Indians here from time to time, very poor at first and obliged to act in the capacity of servants: that they get rich however by degrees, and then follow the trade of the rest, namely that of Usury. That some of them are married to Tartar women but that the issue of such marriages are brought up in the Mahometan Religion. That they give two great entertainments, the married people one and the unmarried People another, to all the Town in their respective abodes. On which occasion they treat with a great variety of fruits, vegetables and such other things as their religion permits them to eat. That in their funeral piles they make use of a great quantity of incense: that the ashes of the dead are collected, put into an urn and sent to their relations in India; which practice, Agathi observed, prevails all along the Coast of Malabar.

Tuesday, 2nd July

I walked out early this morning to the Cathedral* (where I loitered for some time on the terrace), through the Persian Shops and into the Indian Caravansera. This is a long square of one floor, covered after the manner of the East with Soil. Several windows open to the roof, flowers or plants in pots stand there, and the Indians themselves are frequently to be seen on the roof. There was a schism among them some time ago, they separated, and a part of them removed to another habitation. They live in a very dirty way and are almost devoured by Vermin (which their religion forbids them to kill), especially the Dervises. The wives of those who are married to Tartar women continue to reside in the Tartar abode and their husbands visit them there but never pass the night with them for fear of being murdered.

Though I returned from my walk at seven o'clock the heat had begun to be insupportable. It begins, I understand, at six. They reckon the heat not less here than at Naples. In winter the cold is sometimes twenty-six Degrees; and the Ice of the Wolga two feet thick. Last Winter the greatest was twenty-three. In summer the heat rises as high as thirty-six. Pallas called it a pays de diable.

We dined at Mr. Agathi's who was so obliging as to send his carriage for us. The company was genteel and the dinner excellent. I had some conversation . . . with a Person now resident here but a native of Achaia. He told me that the whole trade of Astracan is in the hands of the Armenians and the Persians. That the

Armenians called themselves subjects of Russia at Astracan and subjects of Persia when they are in that country. That the trade is spoilt by being carried on by People who are not resident in the country but who come only to sell their goods. That the Government does not bestow a thought or stir a finger for the benefit of the Commerce here. That the Russians are wholly occupied by the Fishery.

The Meynots who inhabit the mountainous country along the sea in the Morea have never been conquered by the Turks. The Plain lying between these and the opposite mountains is therefore a Wilderness and full of wild Cattle.

We remained here till between six and seven o'clock, when our obliging Landlord furnished us with his Drooski to call on our Armenian friends and Captain Kelly. The latter we found at home. His wife is an American as well as himself and speaks English with a very foreign pronunciation. They took us into the opposite house which is inhabited by Tartars, as a Curiosity. More than two-thirds of the room was occupied by a Stage or Divan covered with a Carpet. Here they sit in the day and sleep at night. Upon our entering the Women all retired. Every thing was very neat; the bedding was put aside in the day time, two shelves above were filled with a variety of Pottery and China ware; and a row of Cushions were laid along the back of the Divan. The whole Tartar abode appeared neat and particularly the People. We saw several Armenian Women in this excursion walking about cloathed in a long white veil.

Upon traversing the Town one finds a great many stone houses interspersed among the houses of wood. . . . The evening was fine and the shipping looked beautiful with a rosy western sky behind it. It had been settled that we should go along with M. Agathi to see the Indian form of worship. But when we came back from paying these visits it was too late. Their service commences always at Sunset.

Wednesday, 3rd July

We drank tea in the Balcony at the Governor's and called afterwards on the O. Commandant where I begged leave to bath. The Governor makes 100,000 roubles of his place; the Vice G[overnor] 40,000. Though two millions of roubles worth of Salt is made here in the year, the revenue receives no more than 400,000 roubles. The Over Commandant told this [to] Bootle, adding: I have written an account of all this to Petersburgh. The Governor desired 150 soldiers for some public building and sent them into his Garden.

N

Thursday, 4th July

. . . It was then time to fulfil our appointment with Mr. Agathi, who had promised to accompany us to see the Indian Service. We found a learned Persian of Sallian* with him who passes the summer at Astracan in selling the Merchandise which he brings from Persia and returns for the winter to his own country. The Khan had wished to engage him as his Secretary which he had refused. I admired the softness of the Persian language as he spoke it and the gentleness of his manners. While we were sitting before the Persian Shops and waiting till the service began we were surrounded with Indians, Persians, Chivoutz etc. with all of whom M. Agathi was able to converse. He speaks Turkish, Arabic, Persian, which are all entirely distinct languages, Armenian, Modern Greek, Russ, French, Italian, Spanish, and a little Portughese and he understands Latin, Greek and English. The distinction between the dress of the Persians and Chivoutz is that the latter have the breasts of their shirts open and the former have them closed in the way of the Russians. The Indians wear most of them the Persian Dress. A dirty young fellow who walked with us from the service was worth, Agathi said, 20,000 Guineas and several of them were worth from ten to that sum.

When we entered the Indian place of worship we found a Bramin on his hams before the altar preparing himself. One of his Assistants soon after handed a small pot of incense to him, which he continued afterwards to fan. Before he rose to present it I observed him twirling round his hands in the same manner exactly as the Calmuc Priests did. A few drops of water were thrown on the incense in order to produce a vapour which is considered as a representation of the air, one of the four elements and that which on this occasion is intended to be offered. The presentation of this element as well as those which came after, was accompanied by the whole congregation chaunting together with the tinkling of Bells and Cymbals. The Dervise next as a symbol of fire lighted a row of six wicks and presented them in the same manner as the incense (he raised and lowered it alternately) chaunting and tinkling the bell which he held in his left hand as before. To represent water he poured a little on the ground at several different times and to represent earth he held up a small square piece of doubled linen. When the offering[s] were finished the bells and the Cymbals ceased.

The second part of the Ceremony was to taste all the Elements. For this purpose the consecrated water in the first place was sprinkled on each of the Congregation: then the lighted wicks were

handed round and each person put his hand into the flame. Afterwards a small spoonful of water was poured into the hand of every
one which he immediately sucked up: and lastly by way of tasting
Earth a plate of cut cucumbers went round and every one took a
little. The Service then ended and we were immediately presented
with a plate of Sugar Candy.

Sometime during the latter part of the service (this was after
the tasting of the Fire) they all fell on their faces and remained
in that position for some time. After which, rising on their hams,
a prayer was said by the Dervise for their country. The rest of
the service being chaunted, it was only on this occasion that we
had an opportunity of remarking the tones of their pronunciation,
which struck me as not unlike those of the French.

The Congregation consisted of about sixteen Persons who
dropped in one after another, and as they entered squatted down
first on their hams and then touched the ground with their fore-
heads.

The greatest part of the temple was occupied by a matted Divan
upon which they all stood. Upon an inclined plane rising from
what I call the altar were placed their Idols in two rows, ornamented
several of them like the Calmuc with Chains of Pearls. On the
upper row were I think five of these. The largest in the middle.
Their size that of a Doll. Below there was a short one with a
Baskir cap which has the preeminence. Another was in the form
of a dog etc. etc. Another with several arms. Two with goats heads
etc. etc. The Idols are in a frame suspended from the ceiling. Their
faces are of metal and their garments flowered. On the left hand
upon the Altar, as well as by two black stones lying also upon it
the genetal parts of the two Sexes were represented. [On the left]
an upright Penis was in the middle and two representations of the
female Parts were placed one on each side of it. On [the stones]
the female parts were represented by white streaks which were
[meant] to be natural but probably were artificial. Several of the
Utensils employed in the service were on the ground below. We
were warned not to touch anything.

They had the complaisance to offer us a dish of tea and behaved
to us with great civility.

Friday, 5th July

The Governor's carriage was ready for us this morning at half
past three in order to go in a party down the river to an Utschug
thirty versts off and see the Astracan Fishery. This Utschug belongs
to a company consisting of all the Merchants in Astracan, i.e. of

all those who register themselves as such to the amount of 2,000. Their right of fishing extended formerly over all the several [branches] of the river between the capital Town and the Sea; but the town has curtailed them from time to time by grants to private Persons. . . . Yet notwithstanding these retrenchments, the fishery in question is capable (as Nikita K. told me) of producing a profit of 100,000 roubles.

Our party was the Dr., M. Agathi, an Italian Architect . . . the Governor, ourselves, two or three Russian Officers and two or three Persons belonging to the Governor. The flotilla consisted of three boats, all rowed by Tartars, some converted and others not. Our navigation was for some time down the Wolga in all breadth and Majesty, but afterwards, for the greatest part of the way, down one of the numerous Arms into which it divides itself. . . . Our Tartars amused us from time to time with their singing. The encampments also of their countrymen close on the edge of the river had a very agreeable effect. The flatness of the country and the border of reeds which we had on each hand after we quitted the Wolga reminded me exceedingly of Holland. As the wind was favourable we were generally able to use sails and arrived in Utschug in good time.

Having regaled ourselves with a glass of brandy and some excellent fresh Caviare, we walked out to see the houses in which they deposit their barrels of Caviare, and the Cave in which they lay up their fish. The cold was so great and the Stink so horrible that I could not bear to stay long. It is encompassed as the Cave we saw before with Ice, and filled with Piles of salted fish.

On our return dinner was ready and having all of us taken a nap after it, which our jollity rendered very necessary, we reimbarked in order to go back; hoping to see some of the fish taken in the way, in which owing to the stormy weather we were disappointed. . . . At setting out the wind was against us, presently after which there fell a dead calm; a little before we reached however the end of our voyage a favourable breeze struck up and we were able to use sails, but with so light a Vessel, such unskilful sailors and so much canvas, not I believe without danger.

We landed at one spot and walked a considerable way till we came to a Tartar encampment where the Governor married a couple, where I ate some excellent Macaroni Soup and where they invited us to have some Koumis. The evening was uncommonly fine, the setting sun and the objects on the bank of the river were charmingly reflected by the water and our Tartars, especially as we passed by the Encampments in sight of the young Girls, sang merrily. We landed in the Tartar Suburb and were conveyed home from thence six in a carriage. I was glad to get home in any way, being excessively sleepy and tired.

Saturday, 6th July

We dined today with Maker K. where our company except little Agathi consisted entirely of Armenians, though of Armenians born in very different parts of the world; for instance one at Ispahan, another at Schamachie and so on. His way of talking about our Armenian friends before their face was curious. Nikita, said he, loves Boys and therefore has taken care to place himself by you viz. Bootle. It's the same with every body in the East—Non eadem atetas non eadem mens.*

The dinner began as usual with eggs and concluded with a dessert of twenty-four Articles. We were invited at eleven and I think dinner was over and we came away between one and two.

About five o'clock we sallied out to call on the Vice-Governor. . . . On our way we stept into a Tartar Mosque and saw the form of their worship which consists chiefly in repeated solemn prostrations. On our return . . . we repaired to the Indian Caravansera in hopes of seeing their service again but they had none tonight.

Sunday, 7th July

We were present this morning at the public examination of the young persons who are educated in the schools of Astracan. I was surprised to see four girls in the first class. The Governor and a great crowd of people attended. The Examination was held in the refectory of an old dissolved convent near the Cathedral. They are about two hundred in number and divided into four classes, of which the first said their catechism, the second was examined in Arithmetic and Grammar, the third in Geography and ancient history and the fourth in Geometry, Fractions, Algebra and Fortification. To those who were raised to a higher class the Governor distributed the proper books. A number of drawings as specimens of their improvement were laid on the table. The young Persons were examined by their respective Masters. To three or four who had completed their education a sort of testimonium was given. This examination takes place twice a year and not only in the Capital but wherever Schools are established. The Masters dined afterwards at the Governor's. The examination lasted from nine to near twelve and concluded with a little cold collation given by M. Agathi the director of the Schools.

The Tartar Shops are built at their own expense. It is in contemplation to erect a new Caravansera for the Indians with the public Money. What they call the Russian Shops, those I mean opposite to the Shops of Moscow and decorated in front with arcades, are handsome and have a good effect. The Walls of the Kremlin and the Bielogorod* are of brick and in many places fallen to decay.

Monday, 8th July

Kelly introduced his friend this morning and bored us as usual. We dined a small party at the Governor's of which [one] was Prince Tiumen, who did not seem to be treated with much distinction but considered as a premier Major and nothing more. He played at Chess and his gentlemanlike manners discovered themselves no less here than in his tent. I came home after dinner and remained at home all the evening. Bootle suffered me to return in the Governor's Phaeton by myself and accompanied the Doctor: with whom he also supped. Prince Tiumen's outward dress is a short robe of cloth edged with broad gold lace and tied round with a sash. His cap was also finely gilt. There is a reserve and gravity in his deportment which I could fancy denotes dissatisfaction.

Tuesday, 9th July

It being the Anniversary of the Empress's accession to the throne every body made a point of being at [the] Cathedral, whither we also went in a carriage sent us by the Governor. The Archbishop was ill and therefore his place was supplied by the Protopope, who stood on the raised stage where the Archbishop dresses himself, at the end of [a] lane formed by two rows of priests. . . . The Archbishop's disorder was indolence and Drunkenness. When in the country he devotes himself to those vices. He [is] obliged in the Town to be more on the reserve and therefore prefers the country.

We were too late for the beginning of the Service. When we entered they were chaunting and continued to do for some time. A sumptuous Volume accompanied by two tapers was then carried to [the] Protopope, who read something out of it. The prayer for the Royal family followed, on which occasion the whole congregation knelt down and we after some little hesitation did the same, by which we got no small credit. The Monks at last separated into two parties, and a rich cross being brought to the Protopope, who now took his stand at the foot of the [stage], every body approached to kiss [it] in two places. The priests were dressed in very rich Garments; with something like a Dr.'s Hood, except that it was parti-coloured hanging down before. It was immediately after the prayer I think that the Guns were fired.

A Person whom I sat by at dinner today told [me] that the Sermons which the Clergy preach contained rather Panegyrics on the virtues of the royal family than religious instruction. He mentioned some Churchman who had in disgust with this practice laid aside his profession. This is only the case however in Towns. In the villages, far from being able to preach, [they] are often not able to read. They are instructed, instead of attempting oratory, to read printed sermons.

Wednesday, 10th July

This being St. Peter and Paul['s day], it was kept, as the day before had been, in honour of the Grand Duke. The service in the Cathedral was performed by the Archbishop. . . . The Gorodichni came and invited us to attend it but we were obliged to call on the Coloustoffs. . . . Between forty and fifty Persons dined, in which number were three Calmuc Princes, of whom Prince Tiumen was one, a young Prince was another, and the third was chief of a larger horde than P. Tiumen's. We were detained a long time for our Podorosne and the Governor begged us at last to wait till eleven o'clock for two letters which he had to send.

The Governor told me that the number of the Calmucs at one time was 300,000; that they are [now] 30 or 40: that Tiumen may have 3,000 Kibitkis but it must be including those belonging to the crown who are put under his protection as a person whom they can depend on. I understood at the same time that there come back every year some of the Seceders owing to the unkind treatment they meet with from the Chinese; and that their reports have checked every wish in those who remained to follow them. Tiumen has the manners and sentiments of a Gentleman but the rest are 'cochons'.

13 Georgievsk

We arrived at Georgiew early in the morning and found a lodging prepared for us, which, though only consisting of a single room, was the best the place afforded and the same as was given to people of the first consequence. We had scarcely entered before a Messenger arrived to inquire of our Servants who we were, but Coindet only being in the way, he was unable to satisfy his curiosity. Not long after we were waited on by a Lieutenant Col. on the part of the Governor General to find out who [we] were and to invite us to dinner, which as usual was early, and as he called it in the military style. The first apartment which we passed through was filled with officers but we found him in the second or third encompassed by a small party of persons of the first consequence such as the Mufti, the General of the Cossacks Ivan Dimitrevitch, and one or two other Generals with stars. He treated us with great politeness and affability and our conference was held in the midst of a large circle, very few of whom however understood our conversation, which was in French.

G[eneral] Goudovitch* appears to be about fifty and in his manners has more the air of a man of fashion than any one we have seen since we left Petersburgh, as much perhaps as any one we have seen in Russia. The Mufti sat on his right hand at dinner and Bootle on his left. He talked incessantly himself and very little was said by any one else. We retired after dinner to our apartments and remained there till between five and six, at which time he had invited us to accompany him on an airing, which when he has not business he takes every afternoon.

We sallied forth with all the parade of an Eastern Prince in view of his enemy, with an escort of between twenty and thirty Cossacks, with two carriages and half a score horses for those who chose to ride when we arrived on open ground. As I had silk stockings and silk Breeches on I chose to continue in the carriage and was attended by our acquaintance Boranow. We paraded up and down the Steppe in hopes of seeing the Mountains of Snow and particularly Elburus, which at last we had the pleasure of doing, though rather indistinctly, but by accident pointed out [to] us in a most singular manner, by having [a] diadem of white cloud. This extraordinary Mountain rises like an immense pyramidical Mass and towers above all the rest. Its distance from G[eorgiew] is calculated to be a hundred and eighty Versts. A notion prevails that Noah's Ark rested upon it and as it is forked, caused the gap between the forks, which is twelve Versts in width. As the Elburus was not generally visible, the Baschtagh [peak] was the most striking and conspicuous object in the gay and delightful landscape, which was also enlivened by a little encampment at the back of the Kuma, whose course like that of all the other rivers in this country is marked by a tract of woodland abounding with all sorts of game. The rest of the country is Stepp, here and there dotted with haystacks, sprinkled as usual with barrows, and in a few places cultivated a little; the produce Oats, *Grütze* [*i.e. crushed oat grain*], Barley, Melons and Cucumbers.

On our return we drank tea, went out to hear the military Music of the Grand Guard, again returned with the General into the house, where he shewed us some stag and buck horns, as also some furniture made of the red wood of the country. We took our leave after and sauntered for some time about the town. We committed to paper when we came back the substance of what we had heard in conversation with the Governor. There is a great deal of parade in the Governor's whole style of living and particularly of military parade. He evidently affects the Character and reputation of a soldier, besides which the idea of being constantly on these frontiers in a state of war, gives a colour and apology for all this. Affable as he is, his behaviour to those about him is distant; and we have seen no Person hitherto treated with an equal degree of deference and respect.

The Music introduced by the Grand Veneur Narischin made a part of the band. This Music consists of as many instruments as there are Notes. The instruments are of brass, nearly in the form of Bugle horns and produce an effect similar to that of an Organ. They differ in size according to the notes from six inches long to as many feet. They played several Russian Airs and concluded with two hymns, both inchantingly fine. Bootle compared the latter to some of Handel's Choruses. The last part of the Ceremony was to shoulder their Musquets and raise their caps for a few instants a little above their head, by way of offering up prayer. The Balls at the Club* always concluded with these horns: we had it also one night at Golofkin's. Bootle had an opportunity of examining it on one of his visits at Mad^e Watkofsky's.

Notes of the Governor's conversation

When any Person who has pretensions to a private Audience of the Empress wishes to avail himself of that priviledge, he repairs to a particular apartment, where a valet de chambre having asked him whether he comes on business and announced him to her Majesty, he is admitted to her presence as soon as she is at leisure. At the private Hermitages a great number of those who are admissible to them rendezvous in a certain Apartment and the Empress causes as many as she thinks proper to be invited. If there are any who do not play at Cards, the goodness and condescension of her Majesty is shewn by her endeavours to amuse them.

At her private dinners none of the Royal family ever appear. There are about twenty who compose these parties and they arrange matters in such a manner that twelve sit down at the Majesty's table. They all rendezvous and those who mean to dine deliver their names to Baratinski, who if by mistake more than twelve announce themselves, informs the youngest that the table is full. Zeuboff is always of the Party. His Brother Valerian also is one of the twenty. They take their places according to their rank. The Empress helps the Soup and each person on receiving it rises from his Seat. In all the other respects Ceremony is banished. Strangers, such as Goudovitch when he comes from his Government is expected to attend all the private Hermitages. Zeuboff reads a great deal, says little and is very dry in his manner.

Sunday, 21st July

The G[overnor] G[eneral] as he had provided us with wax candles, with Wine and Mead yesterday evening, very unexpectedly sent us tea and Coffee for breakfast this morning. About ten we received a message inviting us after divine service was over to the Parade, where we saw the troops and his Arabian horses in their fine Trappings.

A very numerous company dined at the General's because it was Sunday, and the dinner was accompanied by the Music of the Horns, which obstructed very much my conversation in German with my neighbours the Colonel and the Lieutenant Colonel. In the afternoon the General paid us a visit. . . . He then invited us to take an airing with him; on which as yesterday we sat in a Droosky attended by a large suite of Gentlemen, servants and Cossacks, and then got on horseback. My horse was a Georgian and one of the General's hunters, a very nice creature. He conducted us through a low woody tract by the side of the Kuma, where I could have fancied myself in an English forest and where we forgot that we were in a country of Stepp.

On our return we drank tea at the General's and came home, where my repose was disturbed by a visit from the Surgeon [?] Major who was unfortunately very drunk. I never saw military subserviency carried to such a length as in the presence of the Governor General. A General does not speak without pulling off his hat; in the field whenever we stopped all the officers pulled off their hats; in his house Col. and Lieut. Col.ˢ seem to consider it as unlawful to open their mouths before him, and if they were speaking, if he came towards them, were immediately silent. His house, the Parade and the fields had all the appearance of a great School in this respect.

Two thirds of the Garrison at Anapa* consisting of 25,000 men were killed. Goudovitch coolly observed that there were literally ruisseaux de sang. The 14,000 Prisoners, Bootle says, comprised the Women etc.

Monday, 22nd July

We set out today on an expedition to see the Mountains of Bestovie or the five Mountains.* It was our plan over night to get off by six or seven, but owing partly to a General of Artillery who accompanied us, it was between ten and eleven. We changed horses at a redoubt eighteen Versts from Georgiew and at the distance of a few Versts from Constantinogrost, a fortress near the above mentioned mountains, we were met by two young Chasseur officers with saddle horses for the purpose of visiting the hot wells. We ascended first the reservoir lately made to serve as a bath and supplied by several little rivulets which flow down the rock incrusting their little channels with sulphur. I put my hand into the reservoir but it seemed as if I could not have borne to keep it there for many seconds.

We proceeded from hence on horseback by one of the most perilous roads I ever passed to several natural reservoirs of the same water where we found bathing Circassians of both sexes. [The ride had been] over smooth uneven rocks by the side of Precipices where a slip must have been fatal. Bootle who was before me repeatedly stopped and thereby increased my danger who was mounted on a very sure but a very impatient horse belonging to the premier Major, who had given 180 roubles for it.

Had the Atmosphere been clear we should have commanded a fine view of the mountains. Our next and last object in this eminence, was a circular aperture in the rock twenty fathoms deep and four or five yards in diameter filled at the bottom with some kind of mineral water. At the foot of the mountains we saw and afterwards [went] through a couple of Circassian Villages. . . . The Materials of their houses were the same as those of the Russian Villages, Mud for the walls and reeds or straw for the roof. Another thing which struck me in this ride were the Tartar burial places, which are for the most part on an eminence, often on one of those which in ancient times had been raised as a funereal Monument, and which being of a square form and composed of white stones contrasts very agreeably often with the verdant lawn on which they stand. The heat of the day was excessive and we rode very fast.

N.B. The Circassians are so exceedingly addicted to robbery that I heard a story of them stealing in the night a present of horses, or some such present, which they had made to a friend on the preceding day.

We [were] received at the fortress with all the honours of war. Several officers were of our party for dinner which was agreeable enough. Amongst other attendants when we arrived were four or five Circassian Princes. In the afternoon we took an airing and paid a visit to their Village. It was our intention also to have visited a Prince of the Nogai Tartars; but as his brother had died on this day a twelvemonth before, it was kept as a day of mourning and he could not receive us. These Nogai Tartars fled from the Crimea to M. Caucasus, from whence they have ventured back into these plains and fixed their habitations.

On our way to the Tartar Village through the Circassian, I exchanged hands with the Circassian Prince, was shewn the stump or naked tree, at which his guests bring their horses, and went into his house. A Carpet being spread on the Ground near this tree, three Persons in which number the General was one, sat down and had water poured in their hands with which they dipped their face and stroked their whiskers to shew us the way of receiving their guests. In the house, which consisted of a single room and was open to the top, there was a wooden Divan about a foot high at one end and this constituted all the furniture. There was also, as in the Princess's house which was also open to the top, a Chimney Piece.

When we returned to this village we stopped there again, and though we were invited to sup, for which purpose to oblige us a brother Prince offered to roast his very soul, we contented ourselves with begging leave to be introduced to the Princess, who lives apart in a house by herself. The husband did not accompany us, it being contrary to their ideas of Propriety for the husband to visit his wife in the day. When he steals to her even in the night it is with the utmost privacy. She received us standing on her divan without moving in the least in answer to the bows which we made on entering. Carpets were spread [for] us and we sat down crosslegged as she also did; and in a short time we were served out of a sort of kettle with a little bason full of Maxomi, a very strong fermented liquor obtained from meal, said to be very wholesome and which I did not find disagreeable. The Princess had with her, standing by her, a little child belonging to some other Prince whom she had taken to bring up. It is a singular Custom of these People not to educate their own children; but to do it one for the other. Two or three dirty women attended as Domestics and one sat down I think on the same Divan. About the tent and peeping in at the door we observed several young Girls, whose faces were very beautiful and confirmed the notions commonly entertained of Circassian Beauty.

I was told that when the old women of the Village dine with the Princess, which I believe they do every day, they must all be satisfied before she is permitted to eat a Morsel: for the purpose of shewing that they are all equal. The Dress of the Circassians is a cap in the form of a Melon cut in two, a loose Asiatic robe fastened round with a girdle to which hang their knives, trowsers down to the Ankles; and red slippers nicely fitted to their little feet. The Princes and the Usdens* wear Sabres, Pistols and coats of Mail. The Princes have no property of their own but can demand whatever they please.* The Usdens live wholly a life of pleasure and idleness and are many of them in their way very rich.

When we came away the Circassian Princes made an offer if we wished to travel about the country to be our conductors and were ready to answer for our security. Our journey to these villages passed through a charming scene, sometimes Woodland in which I was shewn several [kinds of trees] and especially [groves?] of wild Olive, but generally over plains enamelled and cloathed with the greatest luxuriance of Vegetation. These plains wind round several isolated Mountains, of which the Beschtagh is one, the Montagne chaude where we had seen the hot bath a second, and the Montagne des chamois de serpents and la Montagne chauve others. The sides of the Mountains were in some places naked rock, in others rock sparingly wooded and in others again, Wood or lawn or Wood and lawn intermingled.

We supped with the Commandant of the Fortress M. Vrerofkin, as we had dined with him.

Tuesday, 23rd July

The General, M. Vrerofkin, the two Georgian Princes, ourselves and one of the young officers who had conducted us to the hot baths, set off this morning on an excursion thirty two Versts farther towards the Mountains, in order to visit the Eaus aigres,* where we found L^t. Col^1. Manseroff and his lady, L. Col^1. Liwoff and his lady with her mother residing on account of their health. We were accompanied by a guard of a hundred Dragoons partly for security and partly out of respect for us and the General. The Circassians are so apt to revolt and can be relied on so little that the company had a guard of thirty men. In this expedition we presently quitted the plains and entered a hilly country which though more destitute of wood, indeed altogether so, reminded me, particularly as we [were] now coming nearer to M. Caucasus, of the face of the country between Besancon and Pontarlier which may be considered as the approach to M. Jura or the Alps. The face of the whole country is broken into hills, which though destitute of trees owing perhaps to the practice of burning the grass yet are pleasing by their verdure and the variety of their contour. We stopped in the way to visit a subterranean passage or Cavern such as one meets with in all calcareous Mountains as these are; which they pretended had formerly served as the resort or asylum of Banditti, and which the Circassians assert is fifty Versts in length. The Patent lantern which was to have lighted us was fortunately broken as we were entering; I said fortunately for there was I could find little or nothing to see, the cavern was very cold and we were very hot. Several of those Tartar burial places which I have mentioned presented themselves as we went along. . . .

The company received us in the most obliging manner; we dined with the Lieutenant Colonel Manserof, a small party in a tent built like a house which he transported hither in two Kibitkis; and in the evening we took an airing to a Bassar Village at the distance of a few Versts. . . . During dinner as well as after our tent was surrounded by Circassians, Bassars and Abbaizas* of all descriptions, Princes, Usdens and Peasants leaning on their staffs and observing with great attention every thing that passed. They danced at the request of the company several Circassian dances, the greatest excellence whereof consists in poising themselves on the toes. A little semicircle of half a score sing and clap their hands, the dancer performs immediately before them, chimes in towards the end with the singers in [a] menacing kind of tone and concludes with challenging one of them to follow him by clapping him on the back.

The arrangement of our encampment was thus. At a small distance from the Wells were the Tents of the two Colonels and four or five Tents opposite to them for their Guard; on an eminence about one hundred yards off was a large Tent for us and another for the two Armenian [?Georgian] Princes. Beyond and farther slept our hundred Dragoons on the ground. In our airing this evening I was struck with the appearance of Elburus, with the population of the village, and particularly with the figures of several Circassians who stood on the hills and looked at us leaning on their staffs.

I observed a great deal of Indian Wheat in the neighbourhood of this village. The Waters of this Spring raised a sort of sand or gravel in such a manner that one takes up a good deal of it with every glass. It sinks however immediately to the bottom; the water sparkles and has a brisk champagne taste which it loses in some degree if not immediately drunk. They prescribe it for all kinds of obstructions. The two Colonels had both come hither for disorders of that kind and received great benefit. It generally goes off in urine and after clearing the body afterwards fortifies it. The People of the country have long had a confidence in its medicinal virtues, but they are capable of spoiling it for fear the Russians should be induced to create a fortress there, because this would retrench their liberty by taking from them the power of stealing and pilfering, their most favourite occupation.

Considering the remoteness of the Spot, I never was in a place where I enjoyed less privacy. One seemed to live altogether in public. Soldiers and Sentinels met one at every turn and distressed me by their attitudes of respect. Being in a low situation, i.e. being encompassed on all sides by hills, the heat was greater notwithstanding our vicinity to M. Caucasus than either at Constantinogrosk or Georgiew; and we were entirely out of sight of the Snow Mountains, which except the top of Elburus in our excursion this evening, were perfectly invisible to us during the whole of our stay.

Wednesday, 24th July

I found my bed in the Tent comfortable enough except that in the morning I experienced a disagreeable chillness. The Alertness of our Cham the General and the beating of the Drum at four o'clock likewise disturbed us. After Tea and Coffee as usual in [our] tent we walked down to the Wells and very foolishly undertook an expedition of two Versts on foot to visit a Cascade which it was not worth while to go two Yards to see. This expedition threw me into such a violent perspiration that I found myself under the necessity of changing my Under Waistcoat. We stayed here today on purpose to go and see the ruins of an ancient fortress supposed to have belonged to the Huns when they were in possession of the Country: yet though [there was] so much anxiety to see it over night, it was never once thought of or mentioned till it was too late.

We dined again surrounded by Circassians who remained here all the day and amused us with a great variety of their national dances, which they accompanied besides the voice with a shabby kind of Fife. A Pole, a lieutenant in the Army, who has the arrangement of the band and particularly that of the Horns at Georgiew, played several tunes in the evening on the Violin, one of which I may call an historical tune, for he told a story at the same time, the events and circumstances of which the tune with great humour illustrated. Some of the company also employed themselves in firing at an egg. Yet notwithstanding all these efforts, the ladies had the Headach and the day went off heavily, perhaps owing in a great measure to the heat. After dinner I retired to my tent as I had done the day before and took a nap. The Conversation between two Persons in the evening had strongly the appearance of a Courtship.

Thursday, 25th July

We were greatly solicited to stay and visit Bourgsang the fortress alluded to above, but we resisted the importunities. . . . A fine view this morning of Erdburus, but we were too low for seeing any others. Our dinner at Constantinogrosk was agreeable as it had been before. Indeed everything was done that could be in order to amuse us. A servant who was with the Georgian Princes, as also an Armenian gentleman who played on the Balilaka, entertained [us] with several Georgian dances; as did afterwards up stairs a little Turkish Girl taken at Anapa and kept by the Prince Arbilianoff. Another young Girl, who had been taken at the same place and was kept by Vrerofkin, made also a part of the company. Being desperately wounded himself with a sabre in the right hand, the young girl was brought to him by his officers. She was then fourteen or fifteen. He has a child by her and she is become a Christian.

The Armenian had been one of Potemkin's buffoons. He played extremely well on the 'Balilaka' if that is the name of it. This instrument has only two strings and is played upon like the Harp with the finger. There is another [type] with three [strings]. The back Steps of the Georgian Dances, and the Management of the hands are graceful. In one part of the Dance, the performer squats down on his hams and dances in that posture. They bear some small resemblance to the Circassian in the manœuvres with the toes.

[The Prince G. Arbilianoff] gave Bootle a very curious Circassian Staff and also a rich Turkish dagger taken at Anapa. He gave me one also taken at the same place and called a Kingall, from Korasan, calculated for quick defence. [He] presented Bootle also with a dagger of the Mountains made at Tiflis: as he did each of us afterwards with a pair of Georgian Slippers which he [?Bootle] got on with much ado and wore for the rest of the day.

N.B. The Prince G. Arbilianoff's dress was as follows. First a Cap turned up with black lamb skin. Secondly a white Shirt next the skin; above that a blue silk robe which reached down like a petticoat below the knee; over that another white shirt which came down below the outward robe a little way; over all when full dressed a coat of Mail and over that the outward robe. . . . A robber lately attempted when he was travelling to lift up his Coat of Mail and wound him under it but he seized him by the throat and throttled him.

We did not get away until between six and seven . . . our host honoured us with a strong convoy headed by an Officer. . . . The Moon shone bright but did not keep us awake. Our strong escort accompanied [us] no farther than the first stage.

Friday, 26th July

After breakfast [at Georgiew] we waited on the General to thank [him] for the excellent arrangements he had made for us in our late expedition. Though busily occupied himself, we found his apartments crowded with Officers come either to lounge or to pay their court. After being admitted to the honour of a short audience, we went as he advised us to take a view of the Mountains; which were visible as the white ridge both to the left and the right of Erdburus, though rather indistinctly seen on account of the haze which entirely hid the black Mountains from our view and rendered the Chain at a distance to the left almost imperceptible. I should like to know whether Erdburus is nearer than the rest* or whether its apparent proximity arises from the clearness of the Air into which it soars. . . . The Point opposite Mosdok appears very lofty. Erdburus itself stands like a Governor General in the midst of this range of Mountains, divided into forks rounded at the top (if one of these is not flat). . . . These two forks unite below the interstice and spread themselves out on all sides to a great distance like the

o

cloth of a Tent, leaving the spectator at a loss to ascertain whether he sees the extremity of the Snowy-region or not. The ridges on each side appear like lofty piles or walls of Snow with rugged side and an irregular outline towering above the dark border at their feet (which the haziness of the Air prevents one from seeing distinctly) and worthy to serve as a boundary between two different quarters of the World.

When we went to dinner we found the General giving Audience to a Circassian Princess. A man came in afterwards who was going to touch the ground with his head before him. The same good order prevails at the little table in the Drawing room as at dinner and elsewhere. Every one approaches in due order: a Colonel does not dare to approach till the Generals have served, nor the inferior Officers before the Col[1]. General Ferroy beseeched us not to mention to the General the visit which we had had from the drunken Surgeon: and the Georgian Prince today entreated us not to mention Verofkin's visit to Stavropol. In the evening when we returned to the General in order to take the usual airing with him, he was giving audience to some Turkoman Tartars* whom he complained of for their excessive talkativeness.

Saturday, 27th July

Both yesterday and today I observed that we had a soup and a wine which the rest of the Company did not partake of. General Ferroy and the two Georgian Princes were of our party today. These Georgian Princes are of a great family and related by their Mother's side to Prince Heracles.

When an Ambassador goes to Constantinople he is received and treated as a Petitioner. The Etiquette is for the Visir to send word by letter to the Sultan that a stranger is arrived from a foreign country in want of cloathes and provisions and desired to be admitted to his presence. An appointment of cloathes and provisions is made in consequence of this representation; and when he has his audience, the interpreter gives to his letter (for instance to the Empress's letter) the form of a supplication. The Ambassador is introduced between two persons who take care, when he retires, to prevent him from turning his back on his serene highness.

Goudovitch has very much the air of a man of fashion and he has behaved to us, collectively considered, with great kindness and hospitality. At the same time no person in Russia or during our voyage has made such a pointed distinction between my companion and me. His whole conversation is addressed to him: when I speak he seldom hears me and when he does, often with so little attention as to misapprehend what I say. On this account I own that my abode here has not been pleasant but very mortifying; and if these are the manners of what are called People of the first fashion, the Lord protect me from such People. I do not believe however that a man of very good sense and very nice feeling would act in this way. I strongly suspect that the General's excellence consists principally in stringing pedigrees and ascertaining the etiquette, when he ventures out of that tract and attempts to converse like a man of knowledge, reflection and profound good sense, he appears to get out of his Element.

We have our breakfast from him every morning and he generally sends a bottle or two of Hydromel after us when we leave him in the evening.

It turned out at last that the General intended to send his sons to England where he recommended them to my fellow traveller's friendship. Hence the source of all those extraordinary attentions to him. It is not the first time that when the interest of a child has been in question I have witnessed similar civilities and endearments on the part of the Parent. I myself have been repeatedly the object of them, when no sooner had the views of the Parent been changed, than they have given place to coldness and indifference.

We took our airing again today the same way as we had done the first day in the Drooski and took our stand on a barrow in view of the Mountains on one side and the Stepp on the other, in which there was a fire. . . . Erdburus raised his two heads above the clouds, which however rose like a wall at their back to a vast height above them. . . . The other mountains were seen intermingled with the white clouds which concealed the greatest part of them from our sight. The jagged outline however was discernible.

Before we set out the General had treated us with some Hydromel mixed with Gluckwa syrup and on our return we had Tea as usual qualified with Lemonjuice and Khinine. After half or three quarter of an hour's very pleasant conversation we took our leave of him, with an assurance that he had made a provision; which we found indeed he had in a very handsome manner—two Bottles of French Wine, two of Rhine Wine, Bottles of English Beer, a Cruse of Eau de Vie, some Cheese and plenty of bread.

We could see from [the hill] some large villages which gave the General occasion to say that in the hands of Individuals the Colonies did not prosper. If a grant of land was made to an Individual he was apt to take the fish and cut down the wood without making any establishment. That they had a class of People in Russia, a sort of Yeomanry, between the Peasant and the Gentleman, who succeeded much better because they settled on the spot and addicted themselves to husbandry. There were some Colonies I think of this kind which were very prosperous. He had villages where there was not land enough for his Peasants. Yet it was not worth his while to transport them hither. There would be the expense of the transport, the building of houses, the loss of what they pay annually etc. etc. Besides which the Village from which they came would continue under the necessity of paying the Capitation Tax of the emigrés to Government. In one of his villages his Peasants in the last war had bought several recruits at the rate of 650 roubles a piece rather [than] part with their sons and relations.

From M. Goudovitch we went to take our leave of General Ferroy and the two Georgian Princes who seemed to have conceived a great affection for us. . . . We sat after this a short time and then betook ourselves to our beds in the Kibitkis, where I slept very soundly. The Court as usual and the Tops of the houses were crowded with people sleeping in the open Air. There were thirty one degrees of heat today in the shade.

14 Bakchiserai

Friday, 23rd August

We came suddenly in sight of Bakchiserai* and were therefore exceedingly struck with its situation in a bottom between two mountains. Having stopped at a Caravansera not yet entirely finished, we sent a note with the news of our arrival to Major Cobley, Mad⁵ Mordvinoff's brother, who obligingly invited us to dinner and sent us word that being in expectation of us he had already prepared apartments for us in the palace.*

As soon as we had dressed therefore, we repaired thither and were very obligingly received by Mad⁵ Mordvinoff and the rest of the company, which consisted of the Admiral's brother, General Spied, two widow ladies, the Admiral's sister, two other young ladies and Major Cobley. Mr. Willis of the Alma and Dr. McDougal were also of the party to dinner. Unfortunately on going down stairs from Mad⁵ Mordvinoff's Apartments to the dining [room] Bootle missed a step and fell by which he strained his Ankle and hurt both his knees in such a manner that he was obliged to retire to his chamber. We dined in a large lofty room on the ground floor which had served in the Khan's time for the State audience chamber. Our own quarters are his other state rooms, and that part of the Palace which the Admiral and Mad⁵ Mordvinoff inhabit were his private apartments. When the Empress was here she put them all to their proper use. After dinner M. Mordvinoff* carried me through several parts of the palace, particularly that which was allotted to the ladies, of whom the favourites lived in a separate building from the rest. In order to come to this part of the palace it was necessary to pass through the apartment of the chief Eunuch, who corresponded with the Kislar Aga of [the] Grand Signior's Seraglio; and he took care that no improper persons should go that way.

Towards the evening Cobley took me up to the top of the Mountain on the south side of the Town to see the view, which is indeed enchanting and pleased the Empress so much that she remained here three hours. The Town lay at our feet interspersed with Minarets, Domes and Gardens in which the Poplars have a very agreeable effect. Though exceedingly reduced in its dimensions it still fills up the whole hollow between the two mountains; of which the opposite one puts out on its side or terminates in some very picturesque as well as very tremendous rocks, for they overhang the town and seem likely one day to break from their hold and overwhelm the houses underneath. A Jew Village on an eminence* on the right at the distance and a narrow woody romantic Valley in which the Khan had a country seat not far from it add interesting features to the Prospect.

We returned by a different way and through more of the Town which is traversed by a small clear stream and abounds in fountains of delicious water. The service at the great Mosque belonging to the palace was just over when we entered. There is a charming fountain near the entrance rushing out in twenty different places where the Tartars wash themselves before they go in. The rest of the evening was passed in Made Mordvinoff's apartments where we drank tea and supped. She is very affable and unaffected and withal a pretty woman, with manners perfectly English.

Bakchiserai pleased the Empress so much that she staid here three days. The Mountain during her stay was illuminated.

Saturday, 24th August

The General, M. Mordvinoff, Made, her two sisters in law and her brother set off this morning on an excursion to Sevastopol, in [which] Bootle's accident prevented us from joining them. . . . In the afternoon I was at the Mosque, paid a visit to the ladies residing in another part of the palace, and took a long walk in the Town. There only seems to be one street, that which passes through the centre and the whole length of the Town, in which a carriage can go; the rest being all too narrow and uneven: they have many of them however a kind of raised trottoir on the sides for the convenience of foot passengers. As they keep their women so close, the back of their houses is generally turned to the street. Indeed the houses and gardens are interspersed in such a manner that in walking along one almost forgets it is a town and is ready to fancy oneself in a straggling irregular Village. The clear babbling rivulet that steals through the heart of the City, the murmurs of the fountains which [one] comes to at every step, and the great number of trees interspersed up and down, have a very refreshing sound and appearance. The Tartars seem to be fond of Balconies and many of the houses are provided with them. They have the Character of being lazy and fond of indulgence; and so one might imagine from seeing them sitting on their hams everywhere and smoking their long Pipes. In general however they are very neatly dressed. Several of the old men look exceedingly venerable with their long beards.

The Turkish women are all concealed but I met some Armenian and Greek Women in the streets, the latter of whom were pretty. The Market was crowded with Cucumbers, water Melons and Melons, all which they sell very cheap by the weight. The Summons from the minarets to divine service did not suffer me to forget that I was in a Tartar or Mahometan Town. . . . When I returned from my walk we had Tea, which served us for supper, and I employed the evening in describing our apartments.

Here follows a plan of the palace.

A. The Chamber in which the Khan gave audience to his subjects: and in which we lived. The two 'o' are two slender painted gilded wooden columns which mark the limits of the Divan, which is raised two thirds of a foot above the space between them and the wall, which space is about six feet broad. The large O is the Chimney, which has so much the appearance of a seat or throne that Bootle actually asked whether the Khan did not sit there. The upper part or Canopy is made of stone painted and is decorated at top with artificial flowers seen through a glass. All the other chimneys are constructed in the same manner. The floor of the Divan as well as the lower space is covered with matting. A sopha about five feet wide and two thirds of a foot high runs along three sides of the Divan. Mattrasses being laid on a raised platform . . . are covered with green cloth reaching down to the floor and edged with a broad border of gold lace. The Cushions against which they lean with the back are large and covered with crimson sattin embroidered with silk and silver. Three sides of the room have each a double row of four windows; in the upper of which the glass is stained. There are windows even in the upper part of the partition wall behind which are seen artificial flowers and which I am inclined to think can be opened in order to make a free circulation of air. That part of the sides of the room which is not occupied by windows is embellished with gildings and paintings. The Ceiling over the Divan is distinct from the other and is decorated in a simple manner with red lozenges, has a handsome chandelier hanging down from the middle, and its corniche on all the four sides adorned with striking views of Constantinople. In the partition wall under the artificial flowers and on each side of the Chimney are Cupboards.

N.B. In these apartments one hears the fountain in the Hall

below and they have at least at this time of the year a most charming effect. It would have been thought a great rudeness for any one to come upon [the Divan] with his slippers on. They were left in the lower space; and a person would leave them as a mark of great humility without the door. We found in our apartment the table which the Khan made use [of] to dine: it was about a foot and a half high and the same in width; the materials wood painted. They have only one dish set on at a time and use neither Knives nor Forks. . . .

Monday, 26th August

Having early in the morning stumbled accidently on the Officer of the house, a captain who submits to fill the department of maitre d'Hotel to the Admiral, he made an offer to accompany me to a Greek Church cut out of a rock* at a distance of two Versts, observing that it would be particularly an object of curiosity this morning, because as it was the Assumption of the Virgin Mary, to whom the Church was dedicated, all the Greeks of the Crimea made a point of resorting thither on a sort of Pilgrimage to pay their devotions. As the service was over before we arrived we met accordingly with a long train of these Men, women and Children, some on horseback but the greatest part not, returning from the Church.

The way lay through a continuation of the valley at the end of the Town till where, after going about a verst and a half, it divides into two branches, in one of which (that on the right) we ascended first by a narrow path and afterwards by a long flight of steps cut out of the rock to the Church. It was formerly, I understand, the Church of a Monastery but at present is served by two priests who live in cells cut also out of the rock not far from it. There are several others of the same kind which were I imagine the habitations of the Monks. Adjoining to it is a building of wood supported by posts, in case of which giving way it would fall headlong into the valley. A service of some kind was still going on; and the person officiating seemed to be exhausted with heat and fatigue.

In the bottom of the Valley a view was commanded here of the ruins of a town which belonged to the Greeks before they were transported out of the Crimea agreeably to an Article in the peace of 1774. Both this valley and the other was bounded on each side by naked and perpendicular rocks in a style more romantic and bold than anything I have seen in the Crimea. I passed by a great number of Fountains now dry on the side of the mountain and

saw others among the ruins. The two branches above mentioned
of the valley inclose the imperial Park and the road to the Jewish
Town lies through that in which I visited the Church. In coming
back [we saw] the Mausoleum of a Mullah and the walls of a palace
which formerly belonged to a Tartar Nobleman, both going to
decay.

I ate my breakfast with great pleasure after the morning's exercise. . . . In the afternoon we were visited repeatedly by parties of
Greek Strangers come to Bakchiserai on occasion of the Assumption, and who were taking a survey of the palace. Men, women
and Children were of these parties, who all bowed very respectfully
on coming in and going out. Several of the women were pretty. I
recollected that these were all emigrant from ancient Greece. The
Men wear a Jacket, Trowsers and slippers. The women a ribband
round their head, a long loose robe reaching to the ground and
garnished with gold lace, a gown under that fastened round with
a sash, and sometimes a kind of belt buckled with two large round
clasps before.

The Khan, Mr. Willis said, never lived more than a fortnight
at Bakchiserai. Caffa and General Schatz's house near the old Crim
were the usual places of his residence. He was a Captain in the
Russian Guards and had passed some time at Petersburg. His
dissatisfaction with the court of Russia arose from his Pension
being ill paid. The dissatisfaction of his subjects with him [arose]
from a suspicion that it was his intention to sell them and put
himself under the protection of Russia. I did not know before Mr.
Willis mentioned it that he was beheaded by order of the Porte
in the island of Rhodes soon after his arrival.

Six divisions of Tartars consisting of a hundred Men each, as
they could not be employed against the Turks, were sent to serve
in Sweden. Two of these mutinied against their Officers and two
hundred and fifty of them took refuge in Poland, from whence
the remains of these fugitives to the number of sixty have been sent
back lately hither. In what manner they are to be disposed of is
not yet known; as no answer from her Majesty has yet been
received to the report of their return.

The apartments which the Admiral makes use of consisted of
several small ones and were thrown into their present form against
the Empress's coming. In those which we occupy, and which were
the Audience Chambers of the Khan, the Empress also gave
Audience. Mamonoff the favourite lived in Mrs. Hawk's apartments
and the Empress gave him the meeting in a room with latticed
windows, communicating with hers as well as his. Potemkin did
not like Mordvinoff because he was above flattering him and

because he would not give up his opinions: because he had too clear a head and too good a heart; because lastly where he saw anything wrong he was too honest to dissemble it.

Tuesday, 27th August

From the windows of our apartment on the left we see a part of the town situated at the foot of a high mountain which puts out rocks in several places in a singular way; on the right we have the Khan's Garden, a Mausoleum built in honour of some favourite relation, a Tartar burial ground consisting of a large garden and a high hill by way of termination to the whole: in front are the mosque and two mausoleums which served as places of interment to the Royal Family; over these the most romantic part of the rocks present themselves, and upon the hill at a distance the Jew Town. . . .

Two officers who had come as Courriers to announce M. Zeuboff as Governor General* dined with us in their travelling dress. They at the same time brought word of [his] having received the order of St. Andrew together with her Majesty's pourtrait, which last honour has never been conferred before, except on Prince Orloff and Prince Potemkin.

The Admiral reminds me of Pallas. . . . What surprised me was to see such a man making so great a distinction [*i.e. between Bootle and him*]. This is what begins to give me a perfect surfeit of my situation. Of all the men I ever conversed with he is the most dispassionate. His coolness has the effect to render his conversation, at least it did so at first, rather inanimate. As we proposed to set off in the morning we took our leave of him, and left our compliments to the ladies whom we did not see.

15 Kiev

Monday, 14th October

We arrived in the evening at Kieff, the splendid towers of which seen in a long line from the time of our being within fifteen versts of it might have induced us to expect a large and magnificent city. We entered at the highest part of the Town, that which goes under the name of Pitcherska where Peter the great made the fortress and where the Catacombs are. But instead of taking up our abode with a Tractyr here, we were prevailed upon to go down to the Podol or lower town, which is situated on a flat at the foot of the mountain and by the side of the river at the distance of four or five versts. We had five pretty large apartments at this place, but it was with the utmost difficulty that we could procure either a fire or a dinner.

Tuesday, 15th October

We got a Droosky and called this morning after breakfast on Prince Dashkoff* whose house is in the upper Town. He kept us to dinner and conducted us in the afternoon to the palace where we walked for some time about the gardens. . . . The Empress resided here. Our view from the Gardens down to the Podol and across the river was very agreeable. The Sovereigns have generally made a point of visiting Kieff from a principle of devotion; this being as it were Mecca of the Greek Religion. Her Majesty visited the Catacombs* with great parade and all the appearances of great piety.

The Prince was so obliging as to send us down in his carriage where we drove up and down the streets for at least two hours before we were able to find our lodgings.

Wednesday, 16th October

After dinner the Prince accompanied us to the Catacombs. . . .*
There are two Catacombs, one called the Catacombs of St. Anthony, because the relicts of St. Anthony are there, and the other those

of St. Theodosius for a similar reason. Their entrance is on the declivity of the hill from the fortress to the river, and consists of a labirinth of Galleries about seven feet high and three broad cut in a sort of earth, coved at the top, and now become rather black though at some time or other they have either been washed or plastered white. At every turn there are benches cut out of the sides or little recesses surrounded with benches of this kind on which the coffins of the Saints are deposited. There are also a great number of little windows not a foot square looking into little cells which had been excavated by pious Men and inhabited by them ever after while they lived (for they shut themselves up in them) and made the place of their burial when they died.

The history of these Catacombs, as well as I have been able to collect it, is that at a very early period soon after the introduction of Christianity into Russia, these Catacombs were two Monasteries, which in process of time being transferred to residence above ground, they were converted into repositories for the dead; especially for such as distinguished themselves by the virtues of a monastic life. The recesses which I have mentioned above were, while the monks resided here, Cells. There are two or three Churches, the Screens of which are embellished with paintings and gilding. The paintings are in the style of those from which we date the revival of the art in Italy. They even shewed the apartment which had been used for the Kitchen (I am speaking of St. Anthony's Catacombs), which apartment is now surrounded like the rest with benches supporting the Coffins of Saints.

There is one recess in which sick persons and particularly madmen, for whose use there is a chain for confining them, frequently request to pass a night in hopes of a miraculous restoration to health. A Madman, the Monk told us, not long ago remained five days in this recess, and in a month entirely recovered the use of his senses. We saw these Catacombs to great advantage because notice having been given of our coming, every thing was open for our inspection and we were conducted by persons capable of answering all our interrogations. The bodies of the Saints, having I suppose been well embalmed, are in perfect preservation. They were all dressed in embroidered silk or satin and over that in a robe of plain silk of different colours. In St. Anthony's Catacombs their dress was only a month old having been given or left them by some pious Merchant. The Empress presented them with a very rich apparel, which is preserved for great occasions, particularly holy week. I understood that they had a wardrobe very amply furnished. Our guide shewed us two of the Saints who have the thumb and fingers in the orthodox position for crossing themselves, which our guide said had frequently had the happiest effects on the Roscolnicks,* who seeing this had often with tears acknowledged their errors and returned to the right faith.

I forget whether it was in St. Anthony or St. Theodosius's Catacombs that we saw the body of a Saint up to above the middle in the ground* exactly as he had passed the latter part of his life. The whole number in St. Anthony's Catacombs is 73 or 4: in St. Theodosius's they are not so many, but we did not learn what the number is. We descended to those of Theodosius as we had done to St. Anthony's by a long wooden Gallery, which as well as everything else is kept in uncommon good order.

The two Catacombs are within the Precincts of the Monastery of Pitcherski and the two Convents which superintend them are under its jurisdiction. There are a hundred Monks in the Monastery of Pitcherski. The other two Convents have each a superior. Formerly they had an Archimandrite resident with them; but at present the Archbishop fills that place. The demand for Masses or Oraisons is so great that the annual sum put on this account into the Crusca has amounted to 5,000 roubles, which is divided among a small number. The Governor himself told Madame —— that last year, or in some one year, no less than 40,000 Pilgrims came hither from Poland only. Prince Potemkin resided in the Archimandrite's house which he polluted with all sorts of Debauchery.

The Prince Dashkoff is of Opinion that the dissolution of the Monasteries* was impolitic. These Monasteries superintended their estates with great care, maintained Schools, and were very charitable not only to the poor in general but particularly to many poor Officers. At present the villages or estates which were before under the management of the monks, are under that of agents with whom they do not fare so well. I think that the Pitcherski convent, though still permitted to subsist, maintains a school now of fifty instead of eight hundred students. Besides which they are no longer able as formerly to send their Brethren out of the country in order to accomplish themselves for the business of Education.

Wissenski near Gluchow four hundred Versts from Kiev was the residence of Count Romanzoff* when the Empress was here. He entertained her here and from thence accompanied her to Kief where he charmed her and all the Court by his amiable manners. Mamonoff who had come with a resolution not to be fascinated could not resist the fascination. Upon the arrival of Potemkin means were presently found to disgust [?] him. Upon which according to his usual way he feigned sickness and did not appear again out till he came to take leave of her Majesty. After resigning the Command in Moldavia he still continued to reside there in a small house near Jassy, the Prince says, in order that he might not seem to run out of the way of Prince Potemkin. The Empress wrote to him while there in the following terms—I have received the news of your being still in Moldavia. It will be for the benefit of the service that you should return into Russia. To which the Count replied 'The only news your Majesty can have of me is either that I am dying or dead. You may be assured wherever I am, that I am incapable of doing anything that can be injurious to your service.'

Thursday, 17th October

The Prince conducted us to see the Cathedral.* We paid a visit first to the Archbishop, a very venerable old prelate who received us with great politeness. He is the second in the Empire. His dress was a black silk gown lined with purple silk: a green robe under that fastened round with a rich cincture; a mitre on his head with a diamond cross in front; a label of some kind hanging from his neck: a stick in his hand. The Prince on entering kissed his hand. In the Cathedral we remarked first the ancient Mosaics in the principal dome and behind the Screen. The upper part of the ceiling, or rather the dome, is occupied by a long figure of the Virgin Mary. . . . Below is a range of twelve Metropolitans.

We were afterwards carried to see the Tomb (something in the way of a Sarcofagus) of the Great Duke Yaroslaf, who was a convert from Paganism to Christianity. . . . It was embellished in a very rude tasteless way and does no credit to the artists of the 12th Century.

Sunday, 20th October

The Prince accompanied us this morning in his carriage to . . . the Bratschi Monastery.* We were conducted about by the superior who understood German and another monk who spoke French; and the former treated us before we came away with bread and butter and a glass of brandy. The Monk who spoke French, upon my remarking the beauty of the Situation of St. Andrew's, tripped round and with a most significant style observed, il faut qu'elle soit belle, parceque elle a été batie au depens de l'Imperatrice. It was difficult to know whether he meant to make his court or to speak sneeringly by this stupid observation. The Prince however assured me that the former was his intention, though he as well as his whole order held her in abhorrence.

Tuesday, 22nd October

We dined again with Prince Dashkoff. . . . In the course of the afternoon there fell some snow and a heavy shower of hail which made us tremble at the thoughts of the long journey we had still to perform before the beginning of winter. . . . The Prince took a most affectionate leave of us and sent us away as much charmed with the goodness of his heart as the excellence of his understanding.

16 Kiev to Moscow

Wednesday, 23rd October

We set off this morning for Count Romanzoff's accompanied by
a young gentleman, though only a Serjeant, whom the Prince
supplied us with, under an idea as he was no stranger at the Count's
house that he might be of some use to us. Tippet saw us safe over
the floating bridge by which the Nieper, whose breadth is three or
four times as great as that of the Thames at London, is passed
at this season of the Year. In descending the vale which leads
down from Kieff to the river, we were very pleased with its picturesque Scenery. The view of Kieff when seen on this side from
below had been represented to us as very fine, but it exceeded our
expectations. The gilded domes of the Convents in the Pitcherski*
intermingled with the rich autumnal foliage of the trees presented
them selves from above in the first place. Presently the Podol or lower
town situated on a flat at the foot of the eminence . . . came in view.
Last of all the towers and domes of the old Town standing on
the height above the Podol was added to the scene. . . . Taken all
together, it struck me as one of the most enchanting views of a
town I ever saw, and wonderfully calculated at first to make a
strong impression on the mind of an enthusiastic Pilgrim.

The first part of the road to Barispol, i.e. for about twenty Versts,
was sandy and chiefly overgrown with Firs, trees to which we
have been long strangers. The latter part as it continued ever after
to Periaslaf, to the Count's and throughout the whole government
of Kieff was open, level, fertile, wholly cultivated and diversified
with patches or tracts of woodland often appearing at a great distance. From the chillness of the air in the morning we had reason
to expect [snow] and accordingly it snowed a little several times in
this first stage.

The most remarkable thing in the second [stage] was that we
performed it in one hour and ten minutes, from which it may be
inferred that the roads were very fine. In the room where we ate
our dinner [some women] were drinking brandy and finished a
bottle in a very short time. The Men who were present were plied
with the glass in their turn till they declined the offer. These

Amazons had on a headdress resembling that of the Polish, boots and an outer Garment like the men's.

It was quite dark for some time before we reached Periaslaf. The inhabitants of Little Russia are remarkable for their musical talents, and I was much entertained [by some] who sang in a variety of Keys. We took up our Quarters in Periaslaf at a Tractyr's and spent the evening in the Billiard room, which being also the bar, was open of course to every body. In comparison with what our accommodations have often been we found ourselves comfortable here. After drinking tea we retired to bed. Our young fellow traveller laid himself down wrapped round with a great coat on three chairs close to the stove. Coindet, Bootle and I slept on the floor round about the Billiard Table. Whether the Master occupied or no his bed which was also in this room I do not know.

Thursday, 24th October

We breakfasted and dressed before we set out. It had been a hard frost and I was very sensible this morning of the cold. Not far from Periaslaf we passed by a gap through a rampart lined with an intrenchment, both extending apparently a great way on both hands. Can they have been made at the time when this country was the borders of Poland and Russia?

The Count's Castle at Tachane is twenty seven Versts from Periaslaf, was erected on a plan of his own about twelve Years ago, and is an irregular pile of building in no particular style, though it approaches nearest to the Gothic. As [it] stands however high and occupies a large space of ground it has an imposing aspect at a distance, to which in my opinion its very irregularity (which disables the spectator from assessing its part and comprehending its form) in no small degree contributes. That regularity is not necessary to Magnificence is abundantly testified by all the finest monuments of Gothic Architecture.

We sent the young gentleman who had come with us from the Tractyrs with Prince Dashkoff's letter to the Count, who sent us an invitation immediately to the Castle. As the distance is small, we left our Equipage behind and went on foot. Three or four Officers, chiefly Aid de Camps I believe, received us at the door and conducted [us] into a little room almost adjoining where the Count was sitting. He expressed great satisfaction at seeing us; we conversed with [him] about quarter of an hour, and at the end of that time he asked us whether it would not be agreeable to dine, prendre de la soupe, apologizing at the same time for not [being] able to sit down with us. We adjourned into a very neat

P

but very cold apartment where we got one of the best dinners I ever partook of in my life in company with seven officers, only *one of whom* was able to talk with us and that in German.

After dinner when we had drunk our Coffee, we were again invited to go in to the Count, with whom we remained perhaps near an hour. We then accompanied the Aid de Camp who spoke German to his apartment and afterwards about the grounds. On our return we were shewn into the rooms set apart for ourselves and not long after we received a third invitation to visit the Count: with whom we remained longer than we ought to have done, till half past nine. During all this time he kept up the conversation with great spirit, giving manifest tokens during the whole of it of [a] memory the most retentive, and a clear judgement. A little but not much of that caustic humour, which we had heard so much [of], betrayed itself now and then. Upon retiring from him, we found a small table set out in the dining room, where we sat down with the Aid de Camp our friend, to a supper in no wise inferior to our dinner.

When we took leave of him he embraced us both very kindly and said that he was very much obliged to Prince Dashkoff for having introduced him to the pleasure of our acquaintance. Being indisposed he was in dishabille; yet even the dishabille of such a man is worth remembering. It consisted of a white cotton Nightcap, a brown old great coat, a green silk quilted waistcoat, dark casimir breeches and boots. In his stature he is tall and lusty, though his tallness is concealed by his being so bad of foot. His face is large and protuberant so as to remind me, as his person likewise did, of old Mr. Boucherett and Lord North. When I say this however, I do not speak of his size but of his general figure; for he is not only taller than the former was but also considerably taller I think than my Lord North. In speaking of his person I forgot to mention his thin grey locks which looked so venerable under his white Nightcap.

His manners were polite but perfectly easy and unaffected. In his conversation he was calm, cheerful and disposed to laugh at whatever struck him as ridiculous. He did not engross the conversation, he was not at all dictatorial, not at all flighty but sufficiently animated and never once suffering a pause, though we staid with him too long and towards the latter [end] of [the] time I have reason to believe that he was weary. Cheerful and lively as he appeared to us, his Aide de Camp assured us that when in perfect good health, he is a great deal more so.

The following were the instances which he gave of his caustic humour. . . . He amused himself with the idea that his Prussian

Majesty found a prodigious difference between the Polish Republicans and the French. He gave a smile and uttered an exclamation of astonishment, of contemptuous astonishment for the pride of courts, on hearing that neither the Dutchess of Cumberland nor the Dutchess of D.* had ever been received at court. He laughed aloud, it was a laugh of Pity for a person obliged to undergo a ridiculous and fatiguing ceremony out of complaisance, at the circumstance of their Majesties being expected to speak to every person who attended a drawing room; adding that on those days there was not he believed a subject in their dominions so fatigued as they were. He spoke rather sneeringly of the sacred or divine things which we had seen at Kieff: the Monks' dresses he imagined must have afforded us matter for ridicule; even the poor Archbishop's mitre did not escape his merriment. The distress and indignation of a German Prince seemed to divert him when he mentioned the presumption of a Swedish Senator for considering himself on a footing with so exalted a personage. He ridiculed the Chinese dress and the sublime ideas they entertained in comparison with the rest of the world to themselves.

Friday, 25th October

The Count was so obliging as to furnish us with horses to Kapustina the first post town. Tea and Coffee were sent up stairs to us before we set off, as well as a large provision of good things for the road such as liqueur, cold meat and wine; of the two latter several different kinds. It is a piece of old Russian hospitality to do this for the traveller and it is particularly acceptable in a country where the accommodations are so bad. We left Tachane with the deepest sentiment of veneration and gratitude for our noble host.

I observed in this stage what I had occasion to observe repeatedly afterwards, that the number of villages and the apparent population did not seem adequate to the quantity of labour required by a country entirely under the plough. . . . We made our dinner [between] Yegothan and Izgouzouk in a neat house plaistered within and without of a stone colour as the houses in this Country generally are. The materials underneath are sometimes wood and sometimes only wicker work.

In the way to Bikowa we met a great number of people coming from the Fair there in their carts. Instead of stopping here as we ought we were directed by some drunken information to proceed to a village a verst farther, where we passed the night. I preferred some straw on the floor of the cottage, which was very neat, to the bed in my Kibitka. Coindet, John and a Peasant lay on the floor in the same manner. A broad Bench and the Stove was crowded by the family, which consisted of Men, women and Children. The good woman of the house, though she went to bed late, was at her needle work by the light of a lamp an hour or two before day. I observed that several of the young women dressed out for the fair, had their heads adorned with flowers as in Poland. The great number of Mills which one sees in every village leads one to suppose that the peasants grind all their corn before they carry it to the Market. It was not in this day's journey only, but everywhere throughout the whole of Little Russia that we found this abundance of Mills. In the cottage to night I remarked that while within doors they cloathe themselves very slightly, but very warmly when they go out. The good woman above mentioned was at her Needle work in her shift.

Sunday, 27th October

In this stage between Kamarofka and Bourousna we saw a great number of young girls in their Sunday dress. Their heads were wrapped round with a fillet and the fillet adorned with berries of some kind, besides which a ribband hangs down behind. In other respects their apparel was not elegant. They wore large boots like the Men and a white coarse outward garment fastened round them in the same manner also as the men. This gave them a Masculine air, which has always a worse effect than the meere want of elegance.

Tuesday, 29th October

The moon rose at two and we got off at three, so that we performed the first stage before day. A little before we reached Gluchow some small unneveness in the face of the country announced the termination of the Ukraine, on the frontiers of which Gluchow is situated.

17   Return to Moscow

Monday, 11th November

We arrived at Moscow last night. . . .

Thursday, 14th November

We rose late and had time to do very little after breakfast before
it was time to dress ourselves for Count Razomofsky's with whom
we were determined to go and dine in the country at Petrofsky,
where he was waiting for the coming of winter. Petrofsky is ten
Versts from Moscow, and we passed on our way to it through the
Petersburgh gate. On the left we got a view in going of the imperial
palace at Petrofsky* built in the Gothic style. The Count's House*
is brick plaistered white and consists of a corps situated on one
side of a square which on the other sides is surrounded by lower
buildings. We found him playing at backgammon with a brother
of M. Goudovitch. He was in a white nightcap and a red great
coat with a black collar; the rest of his dress was of the same
colour as the cap of his coat. The principal enjoyment of a Russian
in the country is to go in perfect deshabille. Accordingly all the
difference which he made in his dress for dinner was to pull off
his nightcap and put on a wig, which he did in an instant. We
dined about sixteen persons who seemed to be chiefly of the family,
Aide de Camps, etc. The dinner was accompanied by Music in a
room adjoining. Not to mention other things we had Pontac,*
Champagne and white Burgundy, the latter of which I admired
exceedingly. We conversed a great deal and very pleasantly with
the Count both before and during dinner, on the subject chiefly
of our late expedition. As night and the roads were exceedingly
bad, we took our leave very [soon after] drinking coffee. I forgot
to mention that Count Razomofsky's house looks out onto a garden
in the French style, beyond which there is another according to the
English taste.

Sunday, 17th November

. . . To Prince Viazemsky's, head of the College of war at Moscow who has married an English Lady. We remained with him almost two hours engaged in a political conversation, and he pressed us exceedingly to dinner either to day or at any other time. He is a lively, thinking, agreeable, well informed man, but he seems to me too full of Speculation and too much attached to his own ideas, which are often exceedingly chimerical.

The Prince gave an account of M. Mordvinof's plan for attacking Constantinople, which he thinks could hardly have failed of success. As the war was foreseen for certain, it [*the plan*] was to prepair a number of floating batteries something like those employed against Gibraltar, and as soon as ever hostilities began to have sent this fleet with 10,000 chosen men to Constantinople. The enterprise would have been more easy then than it is now, because the passage was not . . . defended by Artillery à fleur de l'eau. The Turks would have been surprised, besides which some reliance might be placed on a part of the inhabitants in a place where so many of them are Christians. The Plan was offered for consideration but not put in execution.

We dined afterwards with Mr. Fine. . . . I was surprised to find that the lady whom I had taken in entering the room for Mr. Fine's daughter was his mistress. We concluded the day at the Masquerade given in honour of the Young Grand Duke's marriage* by the Merchants. On the preceding [Sunday] and on the Sunday preceding that, a similar entertainment had been given first by the Governor General and afterwards by the Nobility. I heard that there [were] five, six or seven hundred persons present this evening. It was given at the Nobles Club, where the great room being well lighted up, appeared most completely beautiful and handsome. . . . There were some few characters, for instance a Warrior, a Sorcerer, etc. etc. but I saw none of them attempting to support what their figure announced them. What amused me more was the great number of women in the National dress. The ornaments of their heads were particularly curious, being loaded with a profusion of Pearls and many of them undoubtedly of great value. The Arch Angel Dress, which consisted of a thick cloak thrown over the head, appeared rather too warm for so crowded [a] Masquerade. We staid I believe till three o'clock and were excessively weary, for we had been upon our legs the greatest part of the time, it being almost impossible to have a seat. The band of Music was fine and particularly the horns.

Monday, 18th November

We dined very comfortably with Maddox and met a M. Bogharet and a M. —— [?], the former of whom is a Swiss and lives with the Countess Golofkin,* the latter was formerly vice-Governor of Irkutsk and has now the management of the above-mentioned Countess's estates. [Bogharet] has been twenty-seven years in the country, had the Education of the Countess Golowkin's Children and lives with her now in the quality of friend or Paramour. He has an estate he told me on the borders of Savoy where he received last year the French Officers when they came to possess themselves of the country. They were very polite he said and did not commit the smallest outrages.

This man [M. ——], being a remarkably fine athletic figure and very handsome, went to Petersburgh seventeen years ago in hopes of meriting the Empress's notice and favour. It was thought advisable to send him out of the way, and therefore they appointed him Vice-Governor of Irkutsk. He has now quitted that situation but still continues to receive the stipend, which is 1,200 a year. N.B. Maddox twenty-seven years [ago] when he called on the Empress found her with Prince Orlow. They both of them struck him at that time as fine figures. They did not forbear their Caresses for his presence.

Tuesday, 19th November

It had been settled ever since we arrived almost to visit Zaritzina* on horseback, but all at once last night by the sage advice of Dr. Cayley, it was determined to go in a carriage; besides which in the morning he sent word that important business prevented him from accompanying us. The roads having been exceedingly deep before, were rendered in consequence of a hard frost, as rough and bad as is possible to conceive; while for a horse, as the country is all open, we could perceive to our mortification that a very tolerable way might have been picked out. We ascended in going to Zaritzina a continuation of the Sparrow hills, and enjoyed so fine a view of Moscow whose edifices were made very conspicuous by the reflection of a bright sun, that we were ready to prefer it to every other we had yet had. The winding Moscva, and the Convents of Novo Sarska and Simonof stood as the principal figures in the foreground. But the various colours of the Domes and houses is not, either on the Sparrow hills or here, to be perceived.

Zaritzina is an imperial palace in the Gothic Style which has been building ten years. The Country about it is well wooded and the ground lies exactly as the Gardener could wish. In the particular situation of Zaritzina, a deep valley, very bold on one side and formed by gentle slopes on the other but well wooded on both, winds along, watered formerly by a small stream, which they have now by damming it converted, as at Blenheim, into a broad lake or river. The palace is situated on the side of the water where the ground rises the most abruptly. It consists of several detached buildings dispersed about without forming one general whole which it is by any means possible to analyze, and built in a taste meant to be gothic, but fantastical and quaint beyond any thing of that kind that I ever saw. The Materials are brick and stone, the stone being used for the decorations of all kinds, such as columns, corniches, frames of windows, frames of doors and other embellishments, which are stuck all over in such profusion that we compared the ground on which they were stuck to a larded chicken. These buildings are also crowded together in such manner, that one could fancy it the object of the Architect to shut out as much as possible the beauties of the situation.

The most elaborate and gaudy structure, intended one may suppose to contain the state rooms, has indeed one end towards the water on the brow of the eminence, but it has close to it in the principal front one of those fantastic buildings and on the other a wood. A kind of Colonnade or Screen with a fine triumphal arch in the middle unites the palace with a very large and ugly pile of building round a small court. It was natural to suppose that this would have served for a passage between them. Upon examining it however, though there was an opening, it did not appear wide enough to answer the purpose of a passage. . . . A. M. Ismailoff, the Gentleman I believe whom we saw at Mr. Dickenson's, has the direction of this imperial bauble, which will not hand down to posterity, if it is as they say her own plan, any very favourable idea of her Majesty's taste. Perhaps if they proceed according to any Model and not altogether according to the whim of some fanciful Architect, the style may be at least as much Moorish as Gothic, the former being often mistaken and substituted for the latter, according to Mr. Walpole. . . . I grudged the labour and particularly the fine stone which has been thrown away in this motley and tasteless undertaking.

Thursday, 21st November

We set off this morning to visit Kaskovo, Count Scheremetew's Villa,* . . . in common great coats, though as we were informed afterwards, there were at an early hour not less than fifteen degrees

of cold. Of course we found ourselves exceedingly incommoded. . . .
Our approach was announced by a handsome arch which turned
out when we came up to it to be of wood covered with canvass. . . .
We set off from the Orangery in which we found a great number
of remarkably fine trees. We then were carried through a most
wretched specimen of an English garden, in which they had put,
not to mention the Canal which went wriggling along in the most
ridiculous way imaginable, a Diogenes's tub, a Chinese banqueting
room, and two grottos, one inhabited by a dragon and the other
surrounded with Spouts for wetting the cloathes of those whose
curiosity induced them to approach it. We came afterwards to the
theatre, a very neat structure capable of containing a thousand
spectators but built of wood and plaistered or I believe white-
washed only. In our way from hence to the house we were shewn
a theatre of earth in the open air, which had been honoured by the
presence of her Majesty.

Near the house are a pretty little building called the Italian
house, a Grotto ornamented on the inside . . . with a variety of
Shells, the Kitchen which is always detached from the body of
the house, a Church and . . . a building appropriated for the ladies.
The house consists of one floor, has a Colonnade in front and a
broad formal piece of water before it. . . . On our return from
thence to where we set off, an Area surrounded by miserable
statues in marble, a building called the Flemish house because
the Gabel end is like that of a Flemish house . . . and lastly the
Hermitage.

Here in imitation of that in the Palace at Petersburg, a small
party, to the number of sixteen, can dine without the waiting of
Servants. We saw the Apparatus for that purpose through the
windows in the Room below. The table I imagine rose set out first;
and afterwards whatever was required upon ringing the proper bell
was sent up one by one.

At this season of the year every place is seen to disadvantage, but
after allowing for that, I must say, that even as a specimen of the
Dutch or French style, Kuskovo appears to be totally destitute
of taste and beauty. Suppose all these buildings, the names of which
I have mentioned, scattered up and down a garden divided into
plots of various figures by cut hedges and stuck full on all sides
of miserable statues without either grace or meaning, and it is
easy to conceive that the place cannot be very agreeable. I forgot
to mention the Draw bridges opposite to each other, which among
other heterogeneous ideas, are intended to give it the appearance
of a fortress. To the credit however of the Count's taste, we were
assured that he took no delight in it.*

We saw one of the favourites, a M. Yermonhoff, at the [Nobles']
Club this evening. He has married a Princess Golitzin, a very
pretty woman who was hanging on his arm. Though now so mild
and gentle in his demeanor, he behaved with great insolence during
his short reign which lasted only a year.

Sunday, 24th November

Before dinner we received a visit from Prince Gagarin,* who
surprised me by saluting me in my dressing gown all powdery
as it was, and not prepared any more than myself for such an
embrace. We dined at Count Batourlin's* and after dinner I had
a very political conversation with a M. Satrapassof, in the course
of which I inveighed exceedingly against the seditious, restless,
innovating temper of our Manufacturers in England without knowing till afterwards that M. Satrapassof is a manufacturer himself. . . .

Monday, 25th November

We dined at Prince Viazemsky's* where we met Prince Bieloselskoi* the Russian Minister at the court of Turin, a man of wit,
who tells a bawdy story with great humour and amuses the ladies
with composing jeux d'esprit.

Yermonhoff bought two carriages in Petersburgh and sent orders
from Tsarskoe Zelo for one to have horses put into it and to wait
at an appointed place where a gentleman would appear and make
use of it. It came as ordered, Yermonhoff disguised got into it and
was driven to some house in Petersburgh where after remaining
for some time he went back to Tsarskoe Zelo without being absent
more than four hours. About three weeks after, the same orders
were given to the other carriage. It came as appointed but no
person appearing, after waiting till twelve o'clock the next day
it quitted its station and on the same day Yermonhoff was disgraced.

Had Pugatcheff come to Moscow all the nobility and all the
foreigners would undoubtedly have been put to death, and nothing
could have prevented him from being Emperor. Dickenson went
to see him in prison; he was asleep; his guard made him get up
as if he had been a wild beast in order to shew himself; he was
a little black man; 'I am, said he, the Impostor Pugatcheff, pray
for me I entreat you.'

Friday, 29th November

We dined at Prince Gagarin's. . . . After dinner Mops, Pol and the Monkeys chiefly employed our attention. . . . Gagarin having been grand Master of the Free Masons at Moscow pretends to know for certain that the Jacobin Principles had their origin in the meetings of that society. Cagliostro had been by this means enabled he thought to fortell the fall of the Bastille. The Duke of Orleans was Grand Master at Paris and the Duke of Sodermania at Stockholm. Gagarin unites the employments of a departmental Procureur with that [of] Procureur General . . . Zeuboff's father was a departmental Procureur sometime ago at Petersburgh, but was so corrupt that the Empress by the request of his son made him a Senator and sent him to Moscow. The son observed at the same time that his father disgraced him in every instance.

Sunday, 8th December

We set off about ten o'clock both in one Kibitki for the Troitskoi convent,* sixty four versts distant from Moscow and as the road was bad for want of snow, we did not arrive there till eight o'clock in the evening. . . . We passed the night at Troitskoi in a Peasant's Cottage where we found another traveller arrived before us. Bootle was desirous of having some boiled milk, but he could not on account of a prohibition to light a fire after a certain hour. We therefore made our supper on the cold things we had brought with us which were all, bread beef and wine, frozen, had our beds taken out of the Kibitka and slept on the benches. The night was so cold that neither Bootle nor I had the courage to put [off] our fur great coats. Our fellow traveller lay on another part of the Benches, and some old infirm person of the family at Bootle's feet on another. A young man and woman, perhaps a new-married [couple], had a bed inclosed with curtains, and the rest of the family took their night's repose on the perch [?]. We were indulged with a candle, but pieces of split fir which they fixed to the top of a staff knocked down into the ground served them for lights.

Monday, 9th December

The family was stirring very early. It amused me to see the operation of heating the perch, the ceremony first of washing themselves and then of paying their devotions to the sacred picture in the corner which happened to be over my head. . . . I was much entertained with the manner in which a woman from another house took her leave when she went away. She first crossed herself to the saint, and then bowed with the greatest composure to all the family; which, having once done it, though she had occasion to speak to them again, she did not repeat.

After breakfast we repaired to the Monastery. While John was looking about for a person to act as our conductor, we stepped into one of the Churches where Mass was saying. Several Monks were placed in a Seat opposite to the sacred doors and a number of Men stood immediately before them whom I took for 'Freres'. We were led from hence by our guide to the Refectory,* a long oblong room, at the extremity of which the service was performing in another Church. A Monk into whose hands we were put here, asked us then whether we chose to wait upon the Archbishop,* which offer we readily embraced. He received us with great complaisance and good humour; and after having sat conversing with him for at least an hour and a half and drunk a dish of tea, he was so obliging as to conduct us himself to see the Curiosities of the Convent, viz. the principal Church and the apartments where the dresses and plate belonging to it are kept. We found him dressed in a purple silk robe lined with white fur and a red mitre over his grey locks. But when he went out he put on a larger mitre covered with a sort of white veil which hung down behind and was embellished before with a cross of Amethysts. This looked very venerable. Over his silk robe he wore another much thicker and longer and he walked with a staff.

In this church the Relicts of St. Sergius, the founder of the Convent, repose in a silver shrine or Coffin which was opened for our inspection. He pointed out the precious stones which embellished [it] as well as the case of gold which covered in part some of the holy pictures. This Church has a gilt cupola in the middle and four domes round it of tin painted green. The Apartments where the sacerdotal dresses and Utensils belonging to the Convent are deposited are a suite of four handsome rooms fitted with Cabinets all round, in which these Articles are laid up and arranged with great good order. They become more and more costly as one advances and of course the most costly things are in the last apartment, in the midst of which stands a large table covered with Bibles and Gospels. The Epitrachilion which Sophia the wife of Vassili Ivanovitch brought from Greece was shewn as a curious piece of antiquity. There were two or three things, epitrachilia I think, worked by the Empress Anne which however the Prelate observed did more credit to her devotion than her skill. . . . The Epitrachilia is a long, narrow, oblong [vestment], is fixed round the neck and hangs before. . . . The Panagea is a picture of our

Saviour's head set round with brilliants in the form of a star. He shewed us one prodigiously rich which he said he used to wear constantly, but not of late, his taste for such things having much abated. The Crosses are often very precious. There were several very rich mitres. He put one, given and in part worked by the Empress Elizabeth, on Bootle's head. . . . The Metropolitan was exceedingly communicative and not the least in a hurry.

When we returned to the house we were presented with a glass of brandy and found a tray set out as usual with dried fish which we were partaking largely, under an idea that nothing more was to follow (Bootle observed, I suppose this is the whole of his dinner), when to our surprise we were invited, if we could make a meagre dinner, to go into the next room and dine. A most excellent meagre dinner it proved, for we had two courses and besides caviare, fish soup, Kissel and stewed barley, we had a variety of fishes dressed in a great variety of ways. Our liquors were Russian Ale, a Levant Wine which was placed on the table, and at the conclusion two glasses of different sweet wines. Thus it is, he said, with great good humour, that we mortify. The Bishops in the Greek Church are never permitted to eat flesh meat. If we do it, said he, we must do it in private. In public it cannot be done without giving great offence. A pretty Turkish Boy, who was taken at Ismail and whom he seemed to treat with great tenderness, waited at table.

When we adjourned back to his sitting room to take our Coffee, You must however, said he, see my Convent at Bethany.* Upon our consenting he ordered his Carriage, and excusing himself on account of the weather, sent the Professor of French in the Academy and his Maitre d'hotel to accompany us. Bethany is about two Versts from Troitskoi in a charming situation and consists of a Church, a house for himself, a house for his visitants and habitations over the Gateway for the fraternity, which I think are but three in number; the whole surrounded I think by a wall. It was so dark when we arrived that we were obliged to see both the house and the Church by candlelight. Notwithstanding the offense which he told us the People took at Italian Prints I observed some in that style in this church, the walls of which are ornamented [in] fresco with views and plans of subjects suitable to the place, such as the Pitcherski convent at Kief, the catacombs there, the Troitskoi convent, Mount Athos, Mount Sinai, and what surprised us much, after knowing his antipathy to the Pope, St. Peter's in Rome.

In a recess on one side of the Choir he has deposited the old brass coffin in which the relicts of St. Sergius were deposited and which serves to sanctify in the eyes of the people this new establishment. There is also a little Chapel in the house where the Screen is open work with a Curtain behind it, as it was formerly every-where. The apartments are neat, prettily fitted up and furnished with Prints. I observed particularly Volpati's Prints of Raphael's Stanze [in the Vatican]. After seeing the house we were carried into a little apartment inhabited by the Monk who takes care of the house and found tea ready, I imagine by order of the good Archbishop.

When we came back he [*the Archbishop*] treated us again with a dish of tea and we had another long conversation upon a variety of subjects, political, moral and religious. . . . Diderot paid him a visit at Petersburgh without any previous introduction. Yet he burst into his room in a loud fit of laughter and the first word he said was 'Non est Deus'. To which the Archbishop replied 'There is nothing new in that; as long since as the time of David, 'Stultus dixit in corde suo, non est Deus'. . . . Voltaire is the man whom he charges with having induced the Empress to pursue the measures which she has done in regard to the Church. For some time what-ever was French has been admired in this country.

He seems to have a great antipathy to the Pope and was sorry that we had begun to relax in England in regard to the Roman Catholics. The Pope he said had made repeated attempts to establish his authority in Russia. . . . When Peter the Great was at Paris, the Proposal was made to him for uniting the two Churches, to which he answered that being only a warrior he did not understand these matters, but that he would communicate the thing to his Bishops, who he supposed would be able to give the proper answer.

He himself, in conversation with some Romish Ecclesiastic upon the conformity of their two religions, had charmed him by making every concession he could wish with regard to Ceremonies and Doctrine. But when they came to the Pope's authority, he denied that he had any more than himself, being Bishop of Rome in the same manner as he was Bishop of Moscow and no otherwise. This threw the Ecclesiastic into a greater rage than if he had disputed all the Doctrines and all the Ceremonies of the Romish Church.

Alexei Czarovitch [son of Peter the Great] was knouted he said by order of his father and died of the Chagrin which this indignity excited in him. . . . Ivan the 1st had six wives, though it is con-trary to the Canon Law to have more than three. He obtained the consent of the Clergy under a pretext that he wished to have children. Upon the death of the fourth wife and again of the fifth, he took a new wife without asking their consent, saying that if it was lawful to marry a fourth it must be equally so to marry a fifth and a sixth.

The Peasants who have been taken away from the Clergy dread above all things becoming the Property of Individuals. By the change which has been made, we have the advantage of being relieved from the trouble of managing our estates which, as they were dispersed up and down the Empire, it was very difficult to do in a country where the Governors etc. are so exceedingly corrupt.

We had agreed on coming away to kiss his hand, but on Bootle's making an offering to do it, he drew it hastily away and very positively refused to suffer it. The old woman at the Cottage where we slept upon our giving her rather more than she expected could not be withheld from repeatedly kneeling down and out of gratitude and respect touching the ground with her head. We set out at eight o'clock in the evening. The cold was so intense that the Postillion was almost frozen from head to foot when we arrived at the first station, which obliged us to halt there for some hours. . . . It was ten o'clock on Tuesday morning when we got back.

Saturday, 14th December

. . . I made the circuit of the Vassili Vlascheni Church* which in its way is a most sumptuous piece of Architecture. In surveying it, as often on other occasions, I stood in astonishment at the vast effects which the religious principle in man has made, I convinced myself of the utility and necessity of such a principle, I made myself certain that it never can be extinguished. I also persuade myself that it is not agreeable to the character of the deity to qualify us for society by means of a principle which is not founded in reason and truth.

We dined at the younger Poltaratski's whose house as usual was most uncomfortably cold. We then called upon Eaton's affair on Prince Gagarin, who received [us] in his Cabinet where he showed us Monkies, Parrots and bawdy pictures.

Monday, 16th December

We dined en famille at Prince Viasemsky's who is always very pleasant and whom I like better than the Princess. I find that he and the Princess were in Italy at the same time that I was. So likewise was the Minister Markoff. So likewise also was Prince B[obrinskoi], the Empress's son by Orloff. Markoff's answer to the Duke of Rohan when he asked him to shew him the Empress's son: 'Sir, if you look into the Almanach you will find that the Grand Duke is the only son the Empress has'. He [Bobrinskoi] was attended by a person recommended by Prince Potemkin very unfit for the charge. The Emperor [Joseph II] made him a Prince and his Mother conferred the order of St. Andrew on him. The Marble Palace was intended for him. The cause of his misunderstanding with his mother was his losing 500,000 roubles at Paris. All she desired of him was to acknowledge his fault, which he refused. He resides either at Narva or Riga and has an allowance of 1,000 roubles a month. N.B. Viazemsky has 18,000 roubles a year.

Tuesday, 17th December

John very unfortunately was taken ill this morning, which prevents us from setting off as proposed to morrow. I begin to despair of ever seeing England again.

Wednesday, 18th December

In the morning John complained to me of a pain only in his back, to Cayley he complained of his head and his throat. What is the meaning of this inconsistency? We are making here a most miserable waste of time!

Friday, 20th December

. . . I first to the theatre where I saw the School for Scandal translated from the English as they pretend by the Grand Duke.

Saturday, 21st December

I am come home to pay Kocho's bill. Bootle is at Madame Anthing's. We are going to drink some Punch at Dr. Cayley's and then set off.

18 Return to St. Petersburg

Saturday, 28th December

As soon as we arrived Bootle posted away to Mr. Whitworth's for our letters, from whence he sent for [me] in my dishabille as I was to come and breakfast there; and in that forlorn condition I [was] surprised by several visitors.

Monday, 30th December

We also paid a visit to the Princess Dashkoff whom as usual we found at Cards.

Catherine II to the Princess Dashkova: Though I enjoy the Crown I know I have no right to it; and you are as much to blame as I am.

A suspicion was intimated that the Princess was connected with R[adishev] who has been sent to Ilinsk for writing the Journey from Moscow to Petersburgh.

The Princess applied through Count Zeuboff for the order of the white Eagle which the father had had on behalf of her son. The Count wrote back that he had communicated her request to the Empress, who would speak to her about it herself. The Princess waited upon her Majesty the next day who expressing some surprise to see her 'I am come, she said, Madame in consequence of the note received from Count Zeuboff'. 'You don't know, the Empress said, for whom you apply. Your son is a drunkard and a fool and borrows money of his Officers without paying them again.'

Tuesday, 31st December

We dined at Whitworth's in Paget's Apartments . . . I had a great deal of conversation with Hinam. . . . We then went to Luff's where we staid to sup. A table was standing in the outer room covered with Music round which a Polish Nobleman and several others were amusing the company with a concert on the Violin. Old Luff came home from Court where he said that we had been the subject and where he had told the Empress that we had been as far as Okotsk.

Wednesday, 1st January, 1794

After paying two or three unsuccessful visits we determined to beat up the Princess Dashkoff's quarters with whom we remained to sup. The old lady was very pleasant.

Thursday, 2nd January

Having received an invitation from the Countess Soltikow I went with Sir Charles [Whitworth] about half past five to Count Chernichew's house* where the play of Racine's Iphigene was performed in the dining room converted into a very pretty theatre. . . . All the best company in Petersburgh were assembled here on this occasion. The Countess Prascovie Saltikof* who played Iphigene and the countess Shouvalow* had very much superiority over the rest: of the two I gave however the preference to the former as more chaste and correct than the other. It at the same time [must] be acknowledged that their style of acting as well as the Characters they had to personate were totally different. The leading features in Iphegenia's Character is sweetness and filial affection under great distress of mind, that of Eriphyle jealousy and disappointed love. For which reason I could fancy that the parts were well cast, for I can hardly conceive the Countess Prascovie succeeding in the Character of Eriphyle, in which one must own at least that Countess Shouvalow acquitted herself perfectly well.

We adjourned from the Theatre to Count Saltikoff's house where there was a ball and supper and where we as usual staid all the company out. The Countess Prascovie must have found some inconvenience from such a load of Jewels. Her girdle hardly less than three inches broad, the bracelets on her wrists and arms, her Necklace and her earings besides a prodigious quantity in her headdress were all of diamonds, which shed such a lustre as can hardly be conceived.

Friday, 3rd January

We had a visit this morning from our little friend Balikoff who had been so obliging to us at Tobolsk, and who distressed us now by desiring us to introduce him to Sir Charles Whitworth and by assuring us that he would do us the favour of his company every day.

Balikoff: The 'Maitre des ballets' at Tobolsk was an Italian Hairdresser, a servant formerly of the Neapolitan Minister whose pretensions to the employ were founded on his having a brother a dancing Master. Bactyr has undertaken the management of the theatre.

Sunday, 5th January

I could not accompany Bootle this morning to Court because I have nothing but mourning, all my cloaths through a blunder of Bayley's house being sent to London. It would have been particularly improper to have gone to day, as according to the old style it is Christmas and a great gala day on which every body makes a point of putting on fine cloaths. Bootle kissed the old lady's hand as usual and had the honour of being introduced to Count Zeubof.

In the evening we went to Madame Zagraiski's and staid for some time after supper. . . . Mordvinoff came from Court where he had been to join in the Christmas Gambols which always take place there on this day. They begin at seven and last till nine. It is what they call a moyen Hermitage; and the number of persons assembled on this occasion is about a hundred and fifty. The Empress takes a part in them. She caught hold of the band which Mordinoff was dragging along and was caught by him in return, that is had it twisted round her.

N.B. A French officer was remarked one day at Court by the Empress who observed to M. Choiseul* that she did not know him. Choiseul related a pitiful story of him. The Empress turned round immediately to Zeuboff and ordered that he should [be] provided for and placed. Zeuboff replied that it should be done immediately. Yes, let it be done she said, immediately and let that immediately be to morrow. Yet nothing has yet been done for him. The reason is that the application was not made by Esterhazy.

N.B. Is it but a few years ago that the ceremony of exposing the bloody shift was observed even among People of fashion? Is it true that in the Villages they hang it out the day after the marriage before the door? . . . Whitworth who mentioned these things was told last Sunday at the Countess S[altikov]'s by Count Golowin that this precious mark of his wife's Virginity was locked up in a box as a relict and kept somewhere in the house, he did not know where.

Tuesday, 14th January

Bootle spent the morning in singing old country dances to a Man who was sent from the countess Prascovie Saltikoff to copy them from his own voice. Balikoff I left to assist at this comedy.

Wednesday, 15th January

The Prince and Princess Radzivil, M. Sarti* the celebrated musician . . . etc. etc. dined at Sir Charles Whitworth's. The Princess Radzivil played and sang some charming things. She also accompanied Sarti on the Harpsichord. . . . Sarti gave us some of the airs from his composition for the Mass performed here on occasion of the King of France's death. The Princess Radzivil gave a very melancholy description of the state of Society at Warsaw. 'Ils ne font que gemir'. She gave at the same time a very agreeable one of the State of Society at Riga and especially of the Governor General, whom she represented as not having renounced the gaiety of a gallant man to make way for the gravity of a Philosopher but uniting the one with the other.

While we were at Luff's the Princess Radzivil paid her first visit and introduced herself there, as she does everything, with great dignity and grace.

Saturday, 18th January

We went from Warre's to a concert at Count Sheremetof's given out of compliment to Made Somoilow. All the first people in Petersburgh were assembled there. The Count performed himself and the rest of the band were his own slaves. He has a considerable number of young females in the house for this purpose.

Friday, 24th January

Bootle was presented, as I should have been if I had gone [to Court], to the young Grand Duke Alexander and the young Grand Dutchess his wife. The former mumbled something in English which he did not understand. N.B. The Empress does not like the black colour. She does not like either to be left alone. She must always have some living creature with her; at least a dog or something of that kind (Goltz).*

Mollendorf* is sixty-eight. He was connected at the age of twenty with a diseased woman and renounced all female connexions ever after. He rises every morning at four, writes and reads till eight, exercises the troops till twelve, dresses, sits down to dinner at one, continues at table till five during which time he drinks two or three bottles of wine, plays afterwards his game of cards and goes to bed at nine (Goltz).

Saturday, 1st February

Besborodko gave a ball this evening to all the Actresses of every description. The company who attended besides them were to pay. . . .

No person will give in proposals for supplying the Empress's table. One proposal indeed has been made but it is on condition of having a debt amounting to 100,000 roubles discharged first. Shairp* received some brilliants with instructions to dispose of them for goods or money, but not on trust. Shairp carried them to a Mr. Strekelow who shewed them to the Empress who ordered him to purchase them; Mr. Strekelow on having the Terms on which they were to be disposed of desired Shairp to purchase the goods, assuring him that he should be reimbursed immediately. Notwithstanding which assurance he remained without his Money three years and then was obliged to receive Cabinet Assignations which dropped thirty per cent the moment they were issued, and are payable only at the end of four years.

Wednesday, 5th February

Orders have certainly been given to neglect the Schools all over the Empire, with a view to continue the people in their ignorance, it being feared, if they become enlightened, that it may not be possible to govern them. A Book explaining the duties of man has been particularly prohibited, and the masters of Schools have been charged to say nothing concerning the judgement to which Kings and Princes will be subject hereinafter. Two Masters who have offended in this way have been taken up and sent into Siberia (Hynam).

Friday, 7th February

I called on M. Samborski and sat with him for a considerable time. He intimated that a check, as Hynam had told us, has been given lately to the diffusion of knowledge; even of that, I could infer from what he dropped, which concerns the duty of a man in Society.

The Courier who is just arrived from Nicolaef brings word (indeed he told it to Mr. Samborski) of a rising at that place of

10,000 Men partly of one description and partly of another, threatening if their wages were not paid to pull down the houses, for that they were in want of bread. A Brigadier had had the courage to go amongst them and the address to pacify them.

While I was with him a Greek Archimandrite, a native of Tenos, came in to take leave of him immediately before he set off for Nicolaef. This man who had been living in Samborski's house, employs himself, partly because he thinks it meritorious and partly in hopes by that means of getting preferment, in bringing colonists from Greece to Nicolaef. He came to Petersburgh to sue for money in their behalf, but he has not succeeded in his application.

Saturday, 15th February

. . . it was determined to go down to Strelna, where we dined a Pick Nick, in the carriage. . . . As it was a dinner for an English party the Landlord had endeavoured to hit our taste by a multiplicity of substantial dishes. When the dinner was almost over, Akin* and Tessaker dropped in from Cronstadt. There was at last a great deal of harmony and good humour, i.e. we were most of us half drunk.

Tuesday, 18th February

I breakfasted this morning with Gould who . . . walked with me once more through the Saloon and Winter Garden, with which I was again as much struck as I had been at the first sight. The Model for a bridge of one arch over the Neva which we went to see in the Vasili Ostrof is now removed hither and placed over a piece of water. Potemkin meant to have embellished the Ground in front of the palace with Colonnades. The work at present going on is an Ah Ah and iron railing to encompass the whole garden.

Gould says, though the Empress looks very well when made up, she appears very much otherwise in dishabille, indeed with strong symptoms of old age. She takes however, he says, all possible care of herself; and if she seldom or never comes here, it is because she does not like to come down stairs. She is very familiar and good in conversing with her Equals, but you must not prevaricate, or talk foolishly to her: she perceives it immediately and takes you up. She means to come here, as she did last year, in the month of March. The Young Grand Duke and his bride are to be in the house with her.

Paget and Eton being engaged in putting a long dispatch into cypher, Sir Charles, Bootle and myself formed the party at dinner.

Sir Charles was very pleasant and communicative and I hardly remember to have passed two or three hours more agreeably. Besborodko he said was particularly and chiefly useful for comprehending the Empress's ideas and conveying them in the language which she approves of. But he seemed to say that he was entirely destitute of all order and application.

Marcoff he allowed to be a man of talents but a man who, if he might have his choice, would be better pleased to overreach the person he treats with than to convince him. He is an indolent man and he's therefore fallen into a habit of deferring his business as long as possible. For he sits down to it in the evening at one, two or three o'clock after leaving his party. He goes into an undress, has his hair combed out, and perhaps continues writing till six, seven or eight o'clock in the morning. The consequence is that he does not rise till twelve or later.

Friday, 7th March

. . . in the evening we sat an hour with Hynam and then came home.

Three Kirghese Chieftains were very formidable to the Russians. On the advice of the Person who has the care of the State Prisoners, Schafosk or some such name, while a treaty was on foot with them, some dresses were sent them as presents which had previously been worn by people ill of the small pox; in hopes that these Chieftains would take the disease and, as it is very fatal to their Nation, die. The event turned out to their wishes for all three died. Mr. Hynam heard the son of the man who advised this piece of Villainy boast of it as a masterpiece of Policy.

Upon Zoritch's swooning the Empress observed that she should not have suspected that of so strong a man. After which speech he was thrown in her way and presently became the favourite (Hynam).

Thursday, 13th March

I called again upon Weitbrecht this morning and had a long conversation with him. Dr. Weikert told Weitbrecht that the Empress was subject whenever she caught any little cold to certain obstructions from which the vigour of her constitution had hitherto been able to relieve her by means of a looseness. This lasted two days or thereabouts; she took nothing for it, but when it began to abate, made use for her diet I think of rice and milk. His opinion was that whenever Nature should at last prove too weak to make these efforts, an Apoplexy or a dropsy capable of carrying her off in three days would be most probably the consequence. So that her death bids fair to be sudden.*

On our way home we stopped in at Mad^e Zagraiski's which reminded me very much of our Senior common room about eleven o'clock in the evening.

Old Sutherland* was very much attached to the Empress who when he died observed to Whitworth unfeelingly at Court that Oisters would now be cheaper: alluding to his great fondness for them.

Friday, 21st March

In the evening we paid a farewell visit to the Princess Dashkoff and Mad^e Zagraiski; at the latter's we met with Mr. Marcoff. . . . It snowed about eight this morning very hard.

19 Warsaw

The Account of the Massacre at Warsaw as far as he* was an eyewitness of it, together with the particulars of his own escape etc.

*M. Wladeck, Kronscreiber, Polizcy commissar, and Chambellan du Roi.

He had called on Gen. Igelstrom* on Wednesday evening and afterwards on Gen. Apraxin,* which last having learnt from him that the former was at home said that he should go to him. At five o'clock on Thursday morning his servant came into his room and told him that there was an alarm. He immediately sprang out of his bed and ran to the Window, where he heard the commandant of all the Polish troops in Warsaw, who lived in the opposite house, giving orders to some officers to assemble their men; for that the Russians were going to set fire to the Arsenal. Having slipped on his cloaths he ran to the Prussian Minister, M. Backholtz, whom he found totally at a loss what to do and his wife in tears and almost distracted.

While he was there the Saxon Charge d'affaires came and prevailed on M. Backholtz to take refuge in the house of the Saxon Minister which it was hoped that the revolters would respect. When he left the Prussian Minister's the street began to be full of people, and as he knew himself to be an obnoxious person he thought it time to provide for his own security: for which purpose he took refuge in a Lutheran Church, the Sacristan of which being his friend conducted him to a closet in the Belfry. He remained here all that day and till the evening of the following. During this whole time his ears were assailed with mixed and incessant din of alarm, bells tolling, dogs howling and cannon firing. The effect was aweful and tremendous and might have been considered as fine by a Person not in the same perilous circumstances.

One thing that seems to have rendered him particularly obnoxious, and he himself said had so, was his joining in a proposition to the Diet to compel all the French at Warsaw or in Poland to take the Oath of allegiance to Lewis the 17th. The Jacobin Party, he said, had never forgiven him that. It also appeared from his own account of himself that he was very much connected

229

with Igelstrom, Apraxin and Backholtz: and he acknowledged himself from the first as a friend of the Russian or Prussian System.

They [*the Poles*] had given out, but I don't know in what way, that they would particularly respect the houses of the Imperial and Saxon Ministers. They had also in certain Acts spoke with the highest contumely of the Empress and the King of Prussia, in the true Jacobin style calling the former Catherine Tyranne and the latter Guillaume Traitre.

Some women having observed him go into the Church suspected him to be a Pole in the Russian Interest. The Sacristan acquainted him with these suspicions of the women and at the same time brought him a cloak and a sabre in order that he might find an opportunity of stealing away and mixing with the mob. Upon receiving this alarming intelligence he fastened a cord to the Transom of the window, in order at the worst to let himself down. Not long after, the women having denounced him, a mob consisting of more than a hundred people beset the door of the Church which they were proceeding to force. He had recourse immediately to his rope, and mixing with the mob assembled on the other side, cried out 'My friends, why do you lose your time in hunting after a worthless Pole while there still remain Russians to my certain knowledge not yet destroyed. Follow me and I will lead you to where they are!' Being all intoxicated, they jumped at the proposal and he lead them from one street to another, joining in all their fury and extravagances, till at last he found an opportunity to separate himself from them and make his escape by sliding down the Fossé. During this Perambulation he passed by his own house in which he observed that all the windows were broken, he perceived his servant not five yards before him at one time armed with his own musket; and he stepped over the dead bodies of a great number of Russians stripped (depouillés) and already beginning to stink.

After making his escape out of the Town he took refuge in the house of a friend in the Suburbs who dissuaded him from returning to his house, as he wished to do in order to enquire for his wife. He made the best of his way therefore to the first Post stage on foot and proceeded from thence to Sukatchef, where he arrived about twelve o'clock on Saturday morning, with a pair of torn borrowed breeches, a beard that had not been shaved and a shirt that he had worn for three days. Though he forgot or had not time to take his breeches, he had the presence of Mind enough to take his purse.

Apprehensions had been entertained for some time of such a

revolt, for which reason Mad^{me} Apraxin* and Mad^e Sherbinin* had left the Place. These apprehensions had been communicated to General Igelstrom (I strongly suspect that our friend himself might be the informer; which perhaps his situation of Policy Commissary gave him an opportunity to be), but he did not conceive them to be well founded, and had ventured by the detachments to Cracow to reduce his force, which had been lately 12,000 Men, to 2,500. For some time past verses or inflamatory papers (or placards, i.e. Papers fixed up and down on the walls or elsewhere) had even been circulated, the object of which was to encourage the people, now that the strength of the Russians was so small, not to lose such an opportunity of revenging their wrongs.

The King himself was suspected of carrying on a correspondence with Koshiutsko* by the Vistula and information was given of it to Igelstrom. His answer was, is it not enough for me to be at the trouble of ferretting the Post, but must I also set a watch over all the boats that pass and repass on the Vistula. Besides who can believe that the King is capable, contrary to his own interests as a sovereign, of acting in concert with a set of Jacobins? The King in fact had cajoled and lulled him into security in regard to the intentions of certain Persons connected with himself whose conduct gave umbrage and excited suspicion; assuring him always and taking upon himself to answer for it that they had no such views as were imputed to them.

In a word Igelstrom, who had lost all the energy of his character, who was become an old woman, who was totally unfit for his situation, being neither a General nor a Statesman, had been most completely cajoled by the King and must be considered, either owing to his folly or want of attention, the sole cause of this calamity. The Soldiers were even dispersed all over the Town. So that they were massacred one by one in small Parties.

Many threw down their arms and begged in vain for Mercy. If they took refuge in a house, cannon was immediately planted against it until they were driven out or destroyed. The Palace of the Republic and perhaps that of the Castellan of Cracow was in this manner burnt down and destroyed, the former with all the Archives. Wladeck could not help exclaiming when we first saw him that there never was so merciless a Massacre, and that the Russians no doubt in revenge would not leave one stone on another in Warsaw.

The bloody business, he said, began at five and the greatest part of the Russians were destroyed by eleven. If the Firing and tumult continued, it was he imagined in order to search out and destroy one by one all those that had concealed themselves. If they presented themselves anywhere in the Streets it was the amusement of a drunken Mob to discharge the Cannon at them.

That the King was privy to the Conspiracy he concludes from the leaders at Warsaw and elsewhere being all such persons as are known to enjoy his confidence. When General Volki sent to ask him whether he wished to be succoured and what his sentiments were under the present circumstances, he returned for answer that he should certainly be glad in case of necessity to be succoured; and that as to his sentiments, they were he must confess with the Nation. Je me tiens a la Nation.

General Volki the Prussian General, who lay with five or six thousand Men within three miles had offered M. Igelstrom to march thither and strengthen his hands, but the offer was declined out of jealousy, for fear if the Prussians once got a footing in that place, it might not be so easy to get rid of them; or at least without agreeing to some further pretensions of theirs, such I believe as the extending of their frontier to the Vistula.

In order to save the King, to encourage the People, or because it really was so, the cry of their leaders (among these were several of his friends) to the Mob was, the King is worth the Nation, everything which he has done having an appearance to the contrary he has done by constraint. They brought the Empress's Picture down into the street out of the Embassador's house, insulted it, stamped upon it, treated it with every indignity and tore it to pieces.

Notes

The system of transliteration used in the Notes is that employed and recommended by *The Slavonic and East European Review*, as set out in volume XXX, No. 75, June 1952, 'The Latinisation of Cyrillic Characters', by W. K. Matthews.

JOHN PARKINSON was born in 1754 at West Ravendale, Lincolnshire, of a family established in the county as small landowners since 1592.

Educated at Brigg and Louth Grammar Schools, he matriculated at Corpus Christi College, Oxford, in 1770, receiving his B.A. at Magdalen College, Oxford, in 1774. Fellow of Magdalen College from 1775 to 1798, becoming a Junior Doctor of Arts there in 1786, Bursar 1787. Contested the Presidency of Magdalen in April, 1791, but defeated by Dr. Routh. Doctor of Divinity 1797.

Rector of Brocklesby, Lincolnshire, 1785–1840, and of Fittleton, Wiltshire, 1797–1840. Patron of Healing, 1793, when he presented his cousin, John Parkinson, to the living.

Married, 1805, Mary daughter of William Gilliatt of Wold Newton, Lincolnshire, and by her had two sons and a daughter.

His diaries comprise: the English Diary (1790 onwards with many gaps), Swiss Tour (June to November, 1780), West of England Tour (June to August, 1781), Italian Tour (August, 1783 to July, 1784), Dutch Tour (June to July, 1790) and the Northern Tour (Spring, 1792 to October, 1794).

Died 1840. Commemorated by a monument in Riby Church, Lincolnshire.

EDWARD WILBRAHAM-BOOTLE, to whom John Parkinson acted as companion on the Northern Tour, was born in 1771, son and heir of Richard Wilbraham-Bootle, formerly Wilbraham, of Lathom House, Lancashire. Educated at Eton and Christchurch College, Oxford, matriculating 1788; M.A. December 1791.

M.P. (Tory) for Westbury, 1795–6; Newcastle-under-Lyme, 1796–1812; Clitheroe, 1812–18; Dover, 1818–28. Created, 1828, Baron Skelmersdale.

Married, 1796, Mary Elizabeth, daughter of the Reverend Edward Taylor, of Patrixbourne, Kent. Died 1853.

1 ELSINORE TO STOCKHOLM

Page
3 . . . *Admiral Modée.* . . . Carl Whilhelm Modée (1735–98), naval officer. Lieutenant 1755; served with the French navy as 'enseigne de vaisseau', 1757–59, and took part in the Seven Years War, afterwards returning to Sweden. After the naval actions of 1789 promoted Konteramiral. Commandant at Karlskrona, 1790. Married, 1772, Ebba Ulrika Sparre of Söfdeborg.

Page

3 . . . *Sir Sidney Smith.* . . . Sir William Sydney Smith (1764–1840), admiral, chiefly remembered for his defence of Acre against Napoleon, visited Sweden on six months leave of absence from the British Navy in the summer of 1789, returning to England in January, 1790, to obtain permission to join the Swedish fleet. A.D.C. to the Duke of Södermanland, 1790, on the outbreak of the Russo-Swedish War. Prevented the naval engagement of June 3rd to 4th from developing into a Swedish defeat; changed that of July 9th into a victory for the Swedes. Returned to England, August 1790, with the reward of a Swedish knighthood.

4 . . . *Maneurts or Mannablood.* Sambucus ebulus, the Danewort or Dwarf Elder, flowering in England from mid July to mid August.

2 STOCKHOLM

5 . . . *Gustavus III.* . . . King of Sweden (1746–92), eldest son of King Adolphus Frederick and Louisa Ulrica sister of Frederick the Great. Married, 1766, Sofia Magdalena, daughter of Frederick V of Denmark. Succeeded his father 1771, obtaining greater control of government by a *coup d'état* 1772. Visited France and Italy 1783–4. Established virtual absolute monarchy 1789. Conducted an indecisive war with Russia 1788–90. Allied with Russia in return for subsidies 1791. Shot and wounded 16th March, 1792; died of the wounds 29th March. Author of plays and essays of considerable merit.

5 . . . *Gustavus IV.* . . . King of Sweden (1778–1837), son of Gustavus III. Married, 1797, Frederica Dorothea of Baden. Took control of government 1796. Involved Sweden in the coalition against France, 1805–7, resulting in the loss of Swedish Pomerania. Increasing violence merging into insanity led to his deposition by army officers, 1809. Exiled, died in poverty at St. Gall, Switzerland.

5 . . . *Mr. Liston.* . . . Mr., later Sir Robert, Liston (1742–1836) was tutor to the sons of Sir Gilbert Elliot; then private secretary to Hugh Elliot when Minister to Munich, Ratisbon and Berlin. Minister to Madrid and Stockholm, 1783–8 and 1788–93. Ambassador to Constantinople twice, 1793–6 and 1812–21; in the interval Minister to Washington and The Hague. Spoke ten languages.

5 . . . *Westley.* . . . Henry Wesley, later Wellesley (1773–1847), created 1828 Baron Cowley, younger brother of the first Duke of Wellington. Appointed Secretary of Legation at Stockholm, January, 1792. Afterwards Ambassador to Spain 1811–22, Vienna 1823–31, Paris 1841–7.

5 . . . *Ankeström's head.* . . . Jacob Johan Anckarström (1762–92) was executed 29th April for the assassination of King Gustavus III at a masked ball in the Stockholm opera house. A former court page and guards ensign, embittered by a lost law suite in which the King had intervened. Drawn into the plot against Gustavus towards the end of 1791.

6 . . . *Major Pechlin.* . . . Karl Frederik Pechlin, Baron von Löwenbach (1720–96), Swedish politician, Holsteiner by descent, nicknamed General of the Riksdag from his leadership of the parliamentary Cap party. After the royal *coup d'état* of 1772, went to rally provincial regiments against Gustavus and on the strength of his commission from the

Senate threatened to arrest Lieut. Hjerta, sent to arrest him with only verbal instructions. Pardoned 1773, but imprisoned again with other opposition leaders 1779. Absented himself from the masked ball but imprisoned when it was discovered that the conspirators had met at his house the following day. Died in custody at Varberg.

7   . . . *Ribbing.* . . . Adolf Ludvig Count Ribbing (1765–1843), entered the French army and served in America during the War of Independence. Returned to Sweden and became a member of the Riksdag opposition, 1786. Exiled for complicity in the King's assassination. In Paris took the name of de Leuven. Known as *le beau regicide*, befriended by Barras, Mme de Stael and Benjamin Constant.

8   . . . *unable to get the Queen with child.* . . . Sofia Magdalena, Queen Consort of Sweden (1746–1813), daughter of Frederick V of Denmark and Louisa, daughter of George II of England. Married Gustavus III in 1766; marriage consummated 1771; pregnancy and miscarriage 1775. Accused 1778 by the Queen Mother of adultery with equerry Munck. Gustavus forced the Queen Mother to make a public written apology and disavowal.

8   . . . *Monk* . . . Adolf Frederik Count Munck (1749–1831), court equerry, chosen to reconcile Gustavus III and Queen Sofia, 1771, because engaged to Frukken Ramström, one of the Queen's maids of honour. Subsequently accused of adultery with the Queen by the Queen Mother. Member of the Board of War during the Russo-Swedish War of 1788–90.

9   . . . *Count de Taube.* . . . ? Evert Vilhelm Baron Taube (1737–99), political confidant and secret agent of Gustavus III, accompanied him round Europe 1783–4. On Gustavus's death appointed Minister of Foreign Affairs.

9   . . . *the Duke of Ostrogothia.* . . . Frederik Adolf Duke of Ostrogothland (1750–1803), youngest brother Gustavus III. Helped to secure the loyalty of the army to Gustavus in 1772, forestalling Pechlin. Loyal to the Queen Mother after her break with Gustavus, 1778.

9   . . . *Birnsdorff.* . . . Andreas Peter Count von Bernstorff (1735–97), Danish Minister of Foreign Affairs, 1773–80 and '84–97.

12   . . . *the Miss Berries.* . . . Mary and Agnes Berry (1763–1852 and 1764–1852), friends of Horace Walpole, who left them Little Strawberry Hill. Parkinson had met them in 1784 in Rome, where he had also been presented to Gustavus III. On the 19th March, 1784, Parkinson noted in his diary: 'In the Evening we went to Cardinal Berni's where there was a Concert. . . . The King of Sweden had received some disagreeable news which occasioned him to observe that all the unhappy Events of his life had happened to Him in the Month of March.'

13   . . . *Sir Robert Ainslie.* . . . (?1730–1804), youngest son of George Ainslie, merchant at Bordeaux. First public appointment, September 1775, Ambassador to Constantinople with a knighthood. Remained there 1776–92, making an important collection of drawings of the Near East and a large, valuable collection of ancient coins, recorded in book form by Domenico Sestini, who describes him first as a Maecenas, in a later work as 'a malignant speculator and trader in antiquities'. M.P. for Milbourne Port, Somerset, 1798–1802. Created a Baronet 1804.

Page

15 . . . *Horn.* . . . Frederik Count Horn (1763–1823), son of Lieut.-General Count Horn (supporter of Gustavus III in the *coup d'état* of 1772 but deprived of command of the guards 1790). The conspirators are said to have met at his country house of Hufvudsta to plan the assassination of the King. Exiled, lived in Denmark, fought in the Napoleonic Wars against England.

15 . . . *Armfeldt.* . . . Gustav Mauritz Count Armfelt (1757–1814), a native of Finland. Defended southern Sweden from the Danes 1788. Employed on diplomatic negotiations, notably the Peace of Verela with Russia 1790. By Gustavus III's will a member of the Council of Regency, but soon sent away as Swedish envoy to Naples. Forced to fly to Germany and Russia. Reinstated by Gustavus IV, 1799, and sent as envoy to Vienna 1802–4. Fought in Pomerania 1805–7 and Norway 1808. Retired to Finland and made President of the Council of Finland by Alexander I of Russia. Married, 1785, Hedvig Ulrica, daughter of Count de la Gardie.

16 *Madame Piper.* Countess Piper, mistress of Count Armfelt and daughter of Frederik Axel Count von Fersen, a leader of the opposition to Gustavus III. Sister of Hans Axel Count von Fersen (1755–1810), friend of Marie Antoinette and organizer of the French royal family's flight to Varennes.

16 *The Duke of Sodermania.* . . . Karl Duke of Södermanland (1748–1818), younger brother of Gustavus III and later, 1809, chosen King as Charles XIII. Gave valuable support to Gustavus in 1772 and 1789. Married his cousin Hedvig, Princess of Holstein-Entin, 1773. Abjured by Gustavus to conceal the names of his assassins from his young son and to remit the death penalty on all except Anckarström.

18 *An old woman at Stockholm who passes for a prophetess.* . . . She appears as the witch in Verdi's *Ballo in Maschera* and had been well known for many years before the assassination. Parkinson mentions her in his Italian diary in 1784.

3 ST. PETERSBURG

20 . . . *Mr. Gould.* . . . In a letter from St. Petersburg to his brother, Parkinson refers to 'A Mr. Gould formerly gardiner to Prince Potemkin and now to the Empress'.

20 *The Taurida.* . . . Built by Ivan Starov (1743–1808) in 1783 and given by Catherine II to Prince Potemkin, conqueror of the Crimea or Taurida. Returned to the Crown on his death, 1791.

20 . . . *Couvent des Demoiselles nobles.* . . . Begun 1748 by Bartolommeo Rastrelli (1700–71) on the site of an earlier building; enlarged 1765.

20 . . . *the Nobles' Club.* . . . On the Nevski Prospect, not far from the Winter Palace. Founded by Prince Dolgoruky in 1783.

20 . . . *Lord Granville Leveson.* . . . (1773–1846), younger son of the first Marquis of Stafford, had matriculated at Christchurch, Oxford, in 1789. On his return from Russia entered politics, becoming M.P. for Lichfield 1795, for Staffordshire 1799. Ambassador to St. Petersburg 1804–5, to Paris 1824–7 and 1830–41. Viscount Granville 1815, Earl Granville 1833. His *Private Correspondence*, 1916, I, p. 56, in a letter of 5 Nov., 1792, mentions that 'There is arrived here Booth [*i.e. Bootle*]

NOTES   237

Page

and Sir W. Wynn; they both look in high beauty and as alike each
other as two peas. I understand that the latter is entertaining from his
translations of English into French, and from his imagining himself
to be an object much admired by the Fair Sex.'

20 . . . *Mr. Paget.* . . . Hon. Arthur Paget (1771–1840), younger son of
the Earl of Anglesea and brother of the Lord Uxbridge who fought
at Waterloo. Secretary of Legation at St. Petersburg, 1791. Ambassador
to Vienna, 1801–6; to Constantinople 1807–9. Married 1809 Lady
Augusta Vane two days after she had been divorced by Lord Borringdon, to whom Paget paid £10,000 in damages.

20 . . . *Mr. Whitworth the English minister.* . . . Charles Whitworth
(1752–1825), guards officer 1772–83, lt. col. 104th regiment 1783–5.
Minister to Warsaw 1785–91; to St. Petersburg 1791–1800 where his
liaison with Madame Gerepzova, sister of the favourite Platon Zubov,
made him influential. Negotiated an Anglo-Russian alliance with
Catherine 1795, and with Paul 1798. Married the dowager Duchess of
Dorset 1801 and made Ambassador to Paris 1802–3. Through his
wife's relationship to the Prime Minister, Lord Liverpool, appointed
Lord Lieut. of Ireland 1813–17. Baron Whitworth 1800, Viscount 1813,
Earl 1815. According to Napoleon *abile, adroit* and *fort bel homme.*

20 . . . *Lord Borringdon.* . . . John Parker 2nd Baron Borringdon (1772–
1840), created Earl of Morley 1815. Supported Pitt and Canning in
Parliament. Married 1804 Lady Augusta Vane, who in 1809 after
bearing him a son eloped with Sir Arthur Paget. The courts awarded
him £10,000 damages from Paget and he divorced her by Act of
Parliament. Her return ten years later to nurse her dying son provided
Mrs. Henry Wood with the plot for her melodrama *East Lynne.*

21 . . . *Lord Dalkeith.* . . . Charles William Henry Montagu Scott (1772–
1819) eldest son of the 3rd Duke of Buccleuch. Tory M.P. 1793–1807,
Baron Tynedale 1807, succeeded as 4th Duke of Buccleuch and 6th
Duke of Queensberry 1812. Friend of Sir Walter Scott, who dedicated
to him *The Lay of the Last Minstrel.* Died at Lisbon of consumption
aged 47.

21 . . . *Count Osterman's* . . . Ivan Andreyevich Count Osterman (1724–
1811), grandson of the chief minister to the Regent Anna Leopol-
dovna; minister to Stockholm before being placed in charge of foreign
affairs; made Grand Chancellor by the Emperor Paul, dismissed by
Alexander I.

21 . . . *the Empress.* Catherine II of Russia (1729–96), daughter of
Prince Christian Augustus of Anhalt-Zerbst and Princess Johanna.
Married at the age of fifteen to her cousin Peter of Holstein-Gottorp,
nephew and heir to the Empress Elizabeth. By the *coup d'état* of
June, 1762, proclaimed Empress in succession to her husband, who
was shortly afterwards murdered. Her reign was marked by Russian
territorial gains from Turkey and Poland; by Pugachov's peasant
revolt; by intelligent patronage of letters, arts and sciences; and by a
brilliant, extravagant and corrupt court life revolving round Catherine
and her succession of lovers.

21 . . . *Lord Westcote* . . . William Henry Lyttleton (1724–1808), a Lord
of the Treasury in Lord North's government; created 1776 Lord
Westcote of Ballymore in the peerage of Ireland.

22 . . . *Prince Gallitzin's* . . . Probably either Prince Mikhail Galitsin

R

Page

or Prince Sergey. Prince Mikhail was a lieutenant-general married to Countess Praskovya Shuvalova; Prince Sergey Fyodorovich (1749–1810) a general married in 1779 to Varvara Vasil'yevna Engelhardt, niece and mistress of Potemkin.

22 *The second grandson Constantine* . . . The Grand Duke Constantine Pavlovich (1779–1831), was at this time being educated by the French writer César La Harpe. Soon afterwards in 1795, aged sixteen, he was married to Princess Juliana of Coburg. Fought bravely but usually unsuccessfully in the Napoleonic campaigns. Made Commander-in-chief in Poland, 1815; married the Polish Johanna Grudzinska, 1820. Refused the Russian crown on the death of his elder brother Alexander I, 1825; killed after his Polish troops rose against him in 1830.

22 . . . *the Grand Duke* . . . Catherine II's son, the Grand Duke Paul (1754–1801), later the Emperor Paul I, had been proclaimed heir to the throne after the revolution of 1762 but had long been alienated from his mother. She mistrusted him as the natural rallying figure for all who opposed her; he resented her monopoly of power and connivance at the murder of his putative father, Peter III. Catherine's refusal to compromise with the French revolutionary movement, which by the end of 1792 had started to spread outside France, left Paul as the one hope of reforming, constitutional elements among the nobility. Parkinson was right in supposing that those in power under Catherine would not acquiesce in losing it, for the favourite Zubov and his brothers played a leading part in Paul's assassination in 1801.

23 . . . *Markoff* . . . Count Arkady Ivanovich Markov son of an impoverished nobleman of Moscow, rose through the protection of the favourite Zubov to be first counsellor of the department of foreign affairs. Dismissed by Paul I and forced to sell his palace in St. Petersburg. Re-employed by Alexander I as envoy to Paris, 1801–3.

23 . . . *Bezborodko* . . . Aleksandr Andreyevich Bezborodko, (1747–99), created Count and Prince. As secretary to Marshal Rumyantsev was brought to court at the end of the Russo-Turkish War of 1768–74 and recommended to Catherine II. Appointed Secretary of Petitions, soon transferred to department of Foreign Affairs. Negotiated Peace of Jassy with Turkey, 1792. Made Imperial Chancellor by the Emperor Paul. Parkinson notes: 'Counseiller privé actuel & maitre de la cour. He was not possessed originally of 500 roubles. . . . His income at present is about 27,000 roubles a year.'

23 *Potemkin* . . . Grigory Aleksandrovich Potemkin (1739–91), guards officer, helped Catherine at the *coup d'état* of 1762 and rose to be imperial favourite, 1774–76, subsequently appointing favourites until Catherine herself chose Platon Zubov in 1789. Helped to negotiate the Peace of Kuchuk-Kainardje with Turkey, 1774; Governor-General of the Southern Provinces, which he pacified and settled, 1776–87. Carried out army reforms 1783–84 and commanded an army during the second Russo-Turkish War, 1787–91.

23 . . . *the Polish Business.* The Russian intervention in the quarrels of the Polish constitutionalists and oligarchs which led to the second partition of Poland in 1793.

24 . . . *the Sister of the Princess D[ashkova]* . . . Countess Yelizaveta

Romanovna Vorontsova (1739–92), mistress of the Emperor Peter III,
1754–62. Banished to Moscow after the deposition of Peter and
accession of his wife as the Empress Catherine II. She bore two
children after her marriage, 1765, to Colonel Aleksandr Ivanovich
Polyansky, but had none by Peter, a fact adduced to suggest that
Peter was impotent and that the Emperor Paul was Catherine II's
son by Count Sergey Saltykov, as Catherine's *Memoirs* imply.

24   . . . *Gershore* . . . William Garthshore (1764–1806), tutor at Christ-
church College, Oxford, companion to Lord Dalkeith on a tour of
Europe. Later a Tory M.P. and a Lord of the Admiralty, 1801–4.
Went mad on the death of his wife and only child.

24   . . . *Sir Watkin Williams Wynn* . . . Fifth baronet (1772–1840),
landowner in north Wales, later M.P. for Denbighshire and Lord
Lieutenant of Merionethshire. Married, 1817, Lady Henrietta Clive,
daughter of the first Earl of Powis.

24   . . . *the favourite's sister.* Madame Gerepzova, only sister of the
four Zubov brothers, of whom the second, Platon, was Catherine II's
favourite, 1789–96. *Catherine II* by the Reverend W. Tooke, chaplain
to the English factory at St. Petersburg, states in so many words that
the British Minister, Charles Whitworth, was Madame Gerepzova's
lover.

24   . . . *Tasa* . . . ? from *chas*, the Russian word for time or hour,
genetive case *chasa*; hence 'Of the hour or time'.

25   . . . *Princess Dolgorucki* . . . Parkinson notes: 'The Prince is the
son of the Dolgorucki Crimski, who is dead. This gentleman is very
lusty and served with reputation in the 2nd Turkish war. The Princess
has a very majestic air but is acclaimed one of the prettiest women
here. Potemkin could not succeed with her.' Prince Vasily Vasil'yevsky
Dolgoruky (1750–1812), son of Prince Vasily Mikhailovich Dolgoruky (1722–82), the victor of the siege of Perekop in 1771 which
resulted in the surrender of much of the Crimea. Joined the Gardes
à Cheval 1752, rose to major general 1774, having accompanied his
father in campaigns. A.D.C. General to the Empress 1783. Took part
in the capture of Ochakov, for which decorated and made a Privy
Councillor. Married 1786 Princess Yekaterina Fyodorovna Baryatinsky
(1769–1863).

25   *The Young Princess Galitzin* . . . Parkinson notes: 'Le Prince
Michel de Galitzin & Mad^me. Gentilhomme de la chambre en fonction.
The Princess is a pretty woman and is said to have been a favourite
of Potemkin's. At present with child.'

25   *The Countess Tolstoi* . . . Princess Anna Ivanovna Baryatinsky
(–1825) married Count Nikolay Aleksandrovich Tolstoy (1761–
1816), in charge of the household of the Grand Duke Aleksandr,
becoming Grand Master of the latter's court 1796–1801. Grand
Master of the Imperial Court 1801. Elder brother of General Count
Pyotr Aleksandrovich Tolstoy, army commander in the Napoleonic
wars, and of the same family as the celebrated writer.

25   *Zeuboff, the present favourite* . . . Platon Aleksandrovich Zubov
(1767–1818), guards lieutenant before becoming imperial favourite
from 1789 until Catherine's death in 1796. Second of four brothers
in a family distantly connected with Count Leon Saltykov, who may
have recommended him to Catherine's notice. Politically influential

after Potemkin's death in 1791. Exiled by the Emperor Paul and deprived of his estates, but allowed later to return. One of the band of conspirators who assassinated Paul in 1801.

25 ... *whose name I think was Manhoff* ... Aleksandr Matveyevich Count Dmitriyev-Mamonov (1761–1803), imperial favourite 1786–9. Extravagant, fond of the arts, especially music. The maid of honour whom he married was the Princess Dar'ya Sherbatova.

26 ... *Orloff.* Grigory Grigor'yevich Orlov (1734–83), second of five brothers who all entered the imperial guards. Played a leading role in helping Catherine to dethrone her husband, the Emperor Peter III in 1762 and became her favourite, 1762–71. Created a Count and lieutenant general 1762; Prince of the Holy Roman Empire 1763. Took little part in government but advocated partial emancipation of the serfs to the commission of 1767 and restored order in Moscow during the bubonic plague of 1771. Married his niece Yekaterina Nikolayevna Zinov'yeva. Left no legitimate children but at least six illegitimate, including, by Catherine II, Count Aleksey Grigor'yevich Bobrinskoy, known as Prince Sitsky (see note to p. 54). Went mad some years before his death.

27 ... *Count Cobenzl.* Ludwig Graf von Cobenzl (1753–1808), son of a governor of the Austrian Netherlands, ambassador to St. Petersburg 1779–97. Won the friendship of Catherine by writing, producing and acting in plays performed before her. Concluded with Whitworth and the Empress the tripartite Austro-Anglo-Russian alliance of 1795 against France. Austrian signatory of the treaties of Campo Formio and Lunéville with Napoleon; Austrian chancellor and foreign minister 1801–8.

27 ... *forty V[ersts].* ... One verst, the Russian measurement of distance, is 0·663 or almost exactly two-thirds of a mile.

28 ... *the Empress having no sword.* ... A version of a story current in several forms. In a letter to Poniatowski about the *coup d'état*, Catherine mentions that he acted with courage and expeditiousness; other accounts elaborate on this and state that he offered her the plume from his hat or the sword knot from his own sword.

28 ... *affecting madness.* ... About 1774, having quarrelled with the favourite Vasilchikov, Potemkin became moody and taciturn and eventually retired to the Aleksandr Nevsky monastery, from which he was fetched with promises of imperial favour by the Countess Bruce.

28 ... *old Zeuboff.* ... Aleksandr Nikolayevich Count Zutov (1727–95), a provincial governor suspected of more than usual corruption. Resigned from state service to manage the estates of General Count Nikolay Saltykov. Made a Senator after his son became imperial favourite.

28 ... *suffered to appoint his successor.* ... Pyotr Vasil'yevich Count Zavadovsky (1739–1812), private secretary to Marshal Rumyantsev, who recommended him with Bezborodko to Catherine for similar work. Chosen shortly afterwards as favourite, having been passed as suitable by the Countess Bruce and Dr. Rogerson. Dismissed after quarrelling with Potemkin. As a capable administrator, given various posts: Senator 1780, a director of the State Bank, in charge of the Chancery 1786, Minister of Public Instruction 1802–10. Married, 1787, with imperial approval, Countess Vera Apraksina, niece and heiress

Page

of Count Kiril Razumovsky, who had inherited the immense fortune of his brother Aleksey, morganatic husband of the Empress Elizabeth.

29 ... *north of the Amoy.* ... The Amur province was only acquired from China in 1858. At Tobolsk, Parkinson was told by a Dr. Peterson: 'If Potemkin had lived, Russia would have had a war with China. The number of troops was augmented with this view in this Government and [that] of Kolyvan [by] 30,000 troops.'

29 ... *her 'élève'.* Catherine II often referred to her favourites as such, but it was to the Empress Elizabeth that Potemkin was presented when a student at Moscow University.

29 ... *a cataract.* ... Potemkin lost the sight of an eye about 1763 and retired from court for eighteen months. It was rumoured that the Orlovs had bruised his eye in a quarrel, but a more probable explanation is that an eye infection was wrongly treated.

29 ... *he would have turned Priest.* ... There are several accounts of occasions in his later years when Potemkin talked of retiring from the world to a monastery; on a visit to Mogilev, and at Jassy shortly before his death in 1791. At Kiev during Catherine's visit in 1787 he took residence in the Pecherskaya monastery (see p. 201).

30 ... *a composer in Music.* Potemkin worked closely with the Italian composer Sarti in determining the form of a *Te Deum* to celebrate the capture of Ochakov in 1788. He maintained an orchestra of 200 musicians.

30 ... *Potocki.* ... Stanislas Felix Potocki (1752–1805), palatine of Polish Russia 1782, lieut.-general 1784, general 1789. Opposed the Polish liberals, retired first to Vienna, then to St. Petersburg, 1792, to form the pro-Russian Confederation of Targowica. After the liberals had been overthrown appointed Polish envoy to Russia, March 1793. Retired to his estates after the second partition. For his appeals to Zubov not to withdraw Russian troops from Poland see Lord, *The Second Partition of Poland*, pp. 384-5.

30 ... *either July twelvemonth or July two years ago.* This was the great 'Potemkin Feast' of April 28, 1791, at the Taurida Palace.

30 *The Princess [Dashkova].* ... Yekaterina Romanovna née Vorontsova (1744–1810), younger sister of Peter III's mistress, married 1759 Prince Mikhail Dashkov. Took part in the *coup d'état* of 1762, but on quarrelling with the favourite Prince Orlov was ordered to travel abroad, 1768–82. On her return made Director of the Academy of Arts and Sciences, which she replaced in 1784 by the Russian Academy, becoming its first President. Edited the Academy's Russian Dictionary, wrote two plays and edited a monthly magazine. Banished from St. Petersburg by the Emperor Paul for her part in overthrowing his father. Her *Memoirs*, written in English, first published 1840 in London.

30 ... *Eaton.* ... William Eton, traveller and promoter of British trade to the Black Sea. Early in his career became Dutch Consul in Basra; formed with a Russian partner a trading venture at Constantinople 1776. Whitworth in a letter to Greville, March 29, 1794, mentions 'a plan for attacking Constantinople by sea which was drawn up by order of Prince Potemkin some years ago by Mr. Eton, a very ingenious man who is now with me. ...' Wrote a widely read

Page

Survey of the Turkish Empire, 1798; also *Materials for a History of the People of Malta*, 1802–7; *Commerce and Navigation of the Black Sea*, 1806; *Letter on the Political Relations of Russia*, 1807.

30   . . . *Catherinehoff*. . . . Yekaterinoslav, now Dnepropetrovsk.

30   . . . *Mad^{me} Potemkin*. . . . Tat'yana Vasil'yevna Engelhardt, one of the five daughters of Potemkin's sister Maria; married first her distant cousin General Mikhail Potemkin, secondly Prince Nikolay Yusupov.

30   . . . *Princess Michel Galitzin*. ? a mistake for the second of Potemkin's five nieces, Varvara Engelhardt (1757–1815) who married Prince Sergey Galitsin in 1779.

31   . . . *Dr. Pallas*. . . . Peter Simon Pallas (1741–1811), German naturalist and traveller, studied medicine at German universities. Made a geographical survey of the English coastline 1761; F.R.S. 1764, aged 23. Professor of Natural History at St. Petersburg 1768. Travelled to China via Persia and Turkestan 1769; in the Ukraine, Crimea and Caucasus 1793–94. Given 10,000 roubles and an estate at Simpheropol in the Crimea to carry out botanical researches. On the death of his second wife, 1810, retired to Berlin.

32   . . . *Democrite*. . . . A verse comedy in five acts, *Démocrite amoureux* by Jean François Regnard (1655–1709). First performed 12th January 1700. Repeated throughout the 18th century in France, e.g. in 1789 at the Comédie Française.

32   . . . *Count Saltikoff's*. . . . According to a later note by Parkinson: 'M. le Comte de Saltikoff, General en chef, & Mad^{me}. He commanded in Finland after Moussin-Pouchkin. He remained all the time at Wyborg and gave no specimens of his military talents. . . . The eldest countess is one of my great favourites.' Count Ivan Petrovich Saltykov (1739–1805) was appointed, 1790, General-in-chief commanding the army which stopped the Swedish advance on Bjorno. Married to Countess Dar'ya Petrovna Chernicheva (1739–1802).

32   *Dr. Rogerson*. . . . John Samuel Rogerson (1741–1843), Scottish physician, went to Russia 1766. Appointed court doctor 1769, retired 1804. Employed by Catherine II to vet the health of prospective favourites, particularly in case they should have venereal disease, which she was much afraid of catching. Returned to Scotland, 1816.

32   . . . *the Duke of Sodermania*. . . . See note to p. 16.

32   . . . *the Duke of Sierra Capriola's*. . . . Antonio Maresca, duca di Serra Capriola (1750–1822), Neapolitan minister to St. Petersburg since 1783. Married firstly Maria Adelaide del Carretto di Camerano; secondly, 1788, Princess Anna Aleksandrovna Vyazemskaya. Employed by Catherine as confidential agent in peace negotiations with Turkey and Sweden 1790. Induced Paul to sign a treaty of alliance with Naples and send Russian troops there against the French. Through his friendship with Princess M. A. Naryshkina, favourite of Alexander I, influenced the Emperor in favour of the Bourbons.

34   *One of them, Branicki*. . . . Count Francis-Xavier Branicki (1730–1819), married Aleksandra Engelhardt (1754–1838), eldest niece of Potemkin, and inherited most of his wealth. On behalf of the Polish Confederation of Targowica had come to thank Catherine for the Russian 'liberation' of Poland that summer and to warn her of the possibility of a revolution if the Russian troops were withdrawn.

34   . . . *the grand Ecuyer Narishkin*. Prince Lev Aleksandrovich Narysh-

kin (1733–99) had been appointed a gentleman of the bedchamber to the Grand Duke Peter in September 1751 and according to the *Memoirs* of Catherine II was suggested to her as a lover when it seemed that she would have no children by her husband; but she had already chosen another courtier, Sergey Saltykov.

34 *. . . the four eldest Princesses. . . .* Daughters of Karl Friedrich Margrave of Baden-Durlach and his first wife Louise, a Princess of Hesse-Darmstadt, related to Wilhelmina of Darmstadt, first wife of the Grand Duke Paul, later Emperor. They came to Russia in 1783 soon after the early death of their mother. Princess Maria Louisa married the Grand Duke Alexander, later Alexander I, in 1793.

34 *The first Grand Dutchess. . . .* Princess Wilhelmina of Hesse-Darmstadt married the Grand Duke Paul in 1773 and died in 1775.

35 *Rasomovski. . . .* Prince Andrey Kirilovich Razumovsky (1752–1836), friend of the Grand Duke Paul. Minister to Naples 1777–84, subsequently to Stockholm and Vienna, representing Russia at the Congress of Vienna in 1814. Friend of Haydn, Mozart and Beethoven; famous for the concerts and picture gallery at his house.

35 *The present Grand Dutchess. . . .* Maria Fyodorovna (1759–1828), née Princess Sophia Dorothea of Würtemberg, married the Grand Duke Paul as his second wife in 1776. One of nine children, her father was Prince Friedrich-Eugen of Würtemberg, General in the Prussian army, married to a niece of Frederick the Great. He was governor of Montbéliard, 1769–95, Duke of Würtemberg 1795–97. Although his daughter was brought up to sympathize with the Enlightenment, she became a patroness of Russian conservatives during the reign of her son, the Emperor Alexander I. Her eldest brother, Friedrich-Ludwig, became the first King of Würtemberg in 1806.

35 *. . . Alexander. . . .* Aleksandr Pavlovich (1777–1825), succeeded to the throne as Alexander I after the death of his father Paul, 1801.

35 *The Theatre. . . .* 1783–87 by Giacomo Quarenghi with a semicircular auditorium, the back wall decorated with scagliola columns, niches and plaques in a Neo-Classical manner. The Empress was seated in front in a central space below the curved benches. Although the design derives from Palladio's Teatro Olimpico at Vicenza and Scamozzi's theatre at Sabbioneta, the stage, larger than the auditorium, is suitable for elaborate moveable scenery. A deep proscenium arch of pine acts as a form of sounding board, for enhancing resonance.

36 *. . . Partie de chasse d'Henri IV. . . .* By Charles Colle (1709–83), who became secretary to the Duke of Orleans, 1739, for whom the play was first performed privately, 1762, as *Le roi et le meunier*. Refused a public performance by Louis XV because it treated a king too familiarly; first publicly performed 1774 at the Comédie Française.

36 *. . . le Pique. . . .* Le Picq, pupil of J. G. Noverre (author of *Lettres sur la dance et sur les ballets*, 1760), succeeded Gasparo Angiolini, 1789, as choreographer of Catherine's Court Ballet. Employed also by Count Sheremet'yev.

36 *. . . M. Anikoff. . . . ?* Ivan Ivanovich (1743–1821), officer in the Preobrazhensky regiment; on retirement endowed a monastery and entered it as a monk.

Page

36 . . . *Prince Repnin's Embassy.* . . . Nikolay Vasil'yevich Prince Repnin (1734–1801), diplomatist and general, commanded Russian armies in the Turkish wars. Ambassador to Constantinople 1775–76 during the reign of Mustafa III; viewed by the Turks with suspicion. Governor General of the new Lithuanian provinces, 1794.

36 . . . *a sort of fraternity.* . . . These bands of dogs were a well known feature of Constantinople until modern times. See Reader Bullard, *The Camels must Go*, p. 54.

36 . . . *the Count d'Artois.* . . . Charles, comte d'Artois, younger brother of Louis XVI and XVIII and later Charles X of France, had fled to Hamm in Westphalia where, on news of Louis XVI's death, January 21st 1793, he was proclaimed lieutenant general of the armies of the kingdom of France. Set out in February for Russia; met at Riga by Repnin, received at St. Petersburg by Catherine.

37 . . . *Shubin.* . . . Fyodor Ivanovich Shubin (1740–1805), one of the best Russian sculptors of his time; pupil of Pigalle and Nollekens. Worked mainly at portrait busts in a graceful style between Rococo and Neo-Classical.

38 . . . *the* éloignement *of her son.* . . . Pavel Mikhailovich, Prince Dashkov (1763–1807), in command of Russian troops at Kiev. Educated at Edinburgh University. Military adviser to the Emperor Paul, 1796–1800. Married without issue Anna Semenovna Alferoya but left several natural children, including a son, Senator and Privy Councillor Mikhail Pavlovich Sherbinin, and two daughters brought up by his sister. One married Count Ivan Ilarionovich Vorontsov, authorized by Alexander I in 1807 to add the surname Dashkov.

39 *The Free Masons.* . . . Mistrusted by Catherine as a possible nucleus of aristocratic opposition, idealistic and humanitarian. Led since the early 1780s by the journalist and publisher Novikov, imprisoned 1792–96 at the fortress of Schlüsselburg.

39 . . . *General S[uvorov].* . . . Aleksandr Vasil'yevich, Count Suvorov-Rymniksky, Prince Italisky (1729–1800), entered the army as a boy, rose during the Seven Years War and Turkish wars to the rank of general. For victory over the Turks at Rymnik, created Count with the added name of Rymniksky, 1789. Stormed and sacked the Turkish fortress of Ismail, December, 1791. His later brilliant campaigns as Russian supreme commander against the French Republican armies, 1798–1800, were arbitrarily ended when the Emperor Paul recalled him.

40 *Golofkin.* . . . Probably Count Fyodor Gavrilovich Golovkin (1766–1823). Served in the Semyonovsky regiment 1783–85; A.D.C. general to Ivan Saltykov in the Swedish war. Appointed minister to Naples, 1794–95. Married 1790, Natal'ya Ismailova.

41 . . . *the Yekaterinehof.* . . . The park of the Yekaterinhov Palace, built for Peter the Great in 1703 and named after his wife, the Empress Catherine I.

41 . . . *Mr. Raikes.* . . . Timothy Raikes, a prosperous merchant, admitted to the Russian Company 1759, married 1776 Mary Cavanaugh, the daughter of a merchant of the Company.

41 . . . *Count Romanzoff.* . . . Count Sergey Petrovich Rumyantsev (1755–1838), studied at Leyden, travelled in Poland and Germany, returning to Russia 1776. Stayed a year in England 1780–81 (see

Page

the *Pembroke Papers*, I, p. 294). Russian envoy to Berlin and Stockholm; appointed by the Emperor Paul a member of the Board of Foreign Affairs; by Alexander I a member of the State Council. Father of three natural daughters by the Countess Anastasya Golovina. For his father see op. cit., pp. 228, 233-35.

42   . . . *Quarenghi*. . . . Giacomo Quarenghi (1747–1817), Italian Neo-Classical architect, born at Bergamo, studied painting with Pozzi and Mengs, architecture with Derizet and Paolo Posi. Called to Russia by Catherine II, 1780. Designed some thirty major buildings, mainly in and around St. Petersburg. They included: the Nevskaya Rooms and St. George's Hall (1785–96) of the Winter Palace; much of the Hermitage, with its Raphael Gallery (1783–92) and Theatre (1783–7); park temples and follies at Tsarskoye Selo, together with the Alexander Palace there (1792–6); some private palaces in St. Petersburg, such as the Bezborodko Palace (1780–90), for which see p. 43; and several government buildings. Also designed stage scenery. Parkinson notes: 'Quarenghi's Pension is 4,000 roubles a Year.'

43   . . . *Falconet*. . . . Etienne-Maurice Falconet (1716–91), born in Paris, achieved fame there as a sculptor before coming to St. Petersburg, 1776, to execute for Catherine II his great equestrian statue of Peter the Great beside the Admiralty.

43   . . . *At Laff's this evening*. . . . ? L'vov. Nikolay Aleksandrovich L'vov (1751–1803), well known writer and architect, and his wife, Maria Alekseyevna née D'yakova (1755–1807), daughter of an Ober-Procuror of the Senate, were hosts to those interested in art and literature.

43   . . . *Potocki*. . . . See note 241

43   . . . *Ogenski*. . . . ? member of the Polish princely family of Oginski. Prince Michal Casimir Oginski (1731–1803) built the Oginski canal joining tributaries of the Niemen and Dnieper and maintained at his estate of Slonim a small private opera and orchestra.

44   . . . *Orgeat and Ratafia*. . . . Orgeat, pronounced orjaw, from the French *orgeat* (Latin *hordenin*, barley), a syrup or cooling drink made originally from barley, for which almonds are sometimes later substituted, and orange-flower water. Ratafia, a cordial or liqueur flavoured either with almonds or the kernels of peaches, apricots or cherries.

44   . . . *the Hermitage*. . . . Catherine II's private palace, adjoining the Winter Palace and used for gatherings of the inner court, contained the Empress's private apartments, a small theatre and a picture gallery with the splendid collection which she had amassed.

44   . . . *the Count Stackleberg*. . . . Otto Magnus Stackelberg (1736–1800), created Count 1775. Russian ambassador to Poland, took part in the negotiations for the second Partition of Poland. Had been the main power behind the Polish throne from the first Partition until the overthrow of Russian influence by the Patriot party, 1788.

45   . . . *Zeuboff's brother*. . . . The two elder brothers, Nikolay and Dmitry, were of less importance than the younger, Valerian Aleksandrovich Zubov (1771–1804), probably the subject of the portrait. Created A.D.C. General to Catherine II, 1792. Served under Potemkin in the second Turkish War, 1790–92; in Poland, 1794; in Persia as Lieutenant-General, 1796, capturing Derbent. Dismissed by the Emperor Paul, whom he and his brothers helped to assassinate, 1801.

Page

45 ... *en sa place*. ... Aleksandr Dmitriyevich Lanskoy (1758–84), of the provincial nobility, officer in the Chevalier Guards, appointed A.D.C. to Potemkin 1779. Shortly afterwards became imperial favourite; with Catherine II patronized artists and architects, notably Quarenghi. Took no part in politics. Died suddenly, probably of diphtheria. Left a large fortune of 7–8 million roubles (7–8 roubles equalled £1).

46 ... *fourteen en titre*. ... Estimates vary between twelve (Polovtsoff, *The Favourites of Catherine the Great*) and twenty-one (Soloveytchik, *Potemkin*). In rough chronological order, those not accepted by Polovtsoff in brackets, they were: 1752–8, Sergey Saltykov, Stanislas Poniatowski; 1761–72, Grigory Orlov; 1772–9, Vasilchikov, Potemkin, Zavadovsky, Zorich, Rimsky-Korsakov (Stakhiev, Strakhov, Levashov, Rantzov); 1779–90, (Visotsky, Mordvinov) Lanskoy, Yermolov, Dmitriyev-Mamonov (Stoyanov, Miloradovich, Miklashevsky); 1790–96, Platon Zubov.

47 *The Empress Elizabeth*. ... Elizabeth (1709–62), daughter of Peter the Great and Empress of Russia from 1741, had one lover before her accession, Aleksey Shubin, sergeant in the Semyonovsky Guards, who for this offence was banished, minus his tongue, to Siberia by the Empress Anne; afterwards only two known favourites, Ivan Shøuvalov and Aleksey Razumovsky (whom she secretly married).

47 *Her Valet de Chambre*. ... Zachary Zotov.

47 ... *Esterhazy*. ... Count Valentin Ladislas Esterhazy (1740–1806), Colonel of the Esterhazy hussar regiment, 1764. Brigadier-General, 1780. Sent as special envoy to Catherine II by the Counts of Provence and Artois, brothers of Louis XVI.

47 ... *the Prince Sapieha*. ... ? son of Prince Kasimir Nestor Sapieha, a leader of the Polish Patriotic party and marshal for Lithuania in the Polish Diet of 1788–92.

49 ... *The late Emperor*. ... *strangled*. Cf. p. 85. Carried out by Aleksey Orlov and Fyodor Baryatinsky, at Ropsha, 1762.

49 *Alexei is still living in Moscow*. Aleksey Grigoryevich Orlov (1737–1808), guards officer, elder brother of Grigory. Created Count, 1762, by Catherine II for helping to depose her husband Peter III. Won the sea battle of Chesme in the Aegean against the Turks, 1770. Resigned official posts, 1776, retiring to Moscow to devote himself to horse breeding.

51 ... *her Majesty's innoculation*. ... 1768 by Dr. Thomas Dimsdale (1712–1800), who also innoculated her son Paul. Rewarded with the title of Baron, £10,000 and an annuity of £500. Returned to Russia, 1784, to innoculate her grandsons Alexander and Constantine.

51 ... *a London Tippy Bob*. ... Slang for a man dressed in the height of fashion. 'Tippy' had roughly the meaning of tip-top.

53 ... *M. Masson*. ... Probably Massot, senior surgeon of the French royal bodyguard, lent to Potemkin during the second Russo-Turkish War at the request of Count Roger de Damas, serving as a volunteer with the Russian army.

53 ... *Nassau*. ... Prince Charles of Nassau-Siegen (1745–c. 1804), son of a putative Prince of Nassau-Siegen. Entered the French army at fifteen; left to go round the world with Admiral Bougainville, 1766–9. Rejoined as an infantry colonel, distinguished himself at the siege of

Page

Gibraltar, 1779–80. Commanded a Black Sea squadron of the Russian navy in the second Russo-Turkish War. In the Russo-Swedish War commanded a squadron of galleys and gunboats; heavily defeated at the second battle of Svensksund, 1790. Made a rich marriage with Charlotte Godza, divorced wife of Prince Sangusko.

53 *The Duke de Richelieu.* . . . Armand-Emmanuel-Sofie-Septimanie du Plessis, duc de Richelieu (1766–1822), grandson of the Maréchal de Richelieu (1696–1788). Married at fifteen to Rosalie de Rochechouart, a deformed child of twelve. Left Paris to go with Prince Charles de Ligne as a volunteer with the Russian army fighting the Turks, 1790. Recalled to Paris by Louis XVI, but allowed to return to Russia 1791. Governor of Odessa 1803–5; Governor-General of New Russia 1805–14. Prime Minister of France 1816–18 and 1821.

54 *. . . a Prince.* . . . Count Aleksey Grigoryevich Bobrinskoy (1762–1813), natural son of Catherine II and Grigory Orlov. Said to have owed his surname to the beaver (Russian *bobr*) skin rug in which he was smuggled after birth from the palace. Known as Prince Sitsky, brought up abroad. Entered the imperial guards as a cadet, 1774, rose to brigadier on retirement, 1790. Travelled round Europe, 1782–7; afterwards sent to live at Reval. Created a Count by Paul and allowed to marry Anna Dorotea, daughter of the Estonian Baron Waldemar Konrad von Ungern-Sternberg, 1796. Left, besides legitimate offspring (from whom descends the present Count Bobrinskoy), two natural sons surnamed Raiko.

54 *. . . find another Empress.* . . . This story is known in outline from other sources. Simon Gavrilovich Zorich (1745–99), a Serb by birth, uneducated, at one time a Turkish galley slave, became an officer in a Russian hussar regiment. Chosen by Potemkin for Catherine, 1777. She found his physique magnificent but conversation boring and readily agreed, when he quarelled with Potemkin, to his retirement to an estate near Mogilev with an annuity of 200,000 roubles. Founded an officer cadet school. Returned to St. Petersburg after Catherine's death.

54 *. . . the Baron in the haunted Tower.* . . . A character in J. Cobb's play, *The Haunted Tower*, first performed in 1789.

55 *. . . the figure of Belisarius.* The name part in *Belisarius or Injured Innocence*, a tragedy by John Philip Kemble (1757–1823), performed at Liverpool and Hull in 1778.

57 *. . . Ribas.* . . . Giuseppe de Ribas (1749–1800), born in Naples of a Spanish father. Met Aleksey Orlov in Livorno, helped him to kidnap a daughter of the Empress Elizabeth, rewarded with a post of officer-instructor in a cadet corps. Married Natalya, daughter of Ivan Betskoy (reputedly Catherine II's father). Accompanied her natural son Bobrinskoy on his travels, rewarded with the rank of brigadier and command of a regiment of caribineers. Made an admiral by Potemkin, commanded a Black Sea galley flotilla, gaining several victories in the 2nd Turkish War. One of the three Russian plenipotentiaries at the Peace of Jassy, 1792. Dismissed by Paul but reinstated through the friendship of his wife with Paul's mistress Mlle Nelidova.

57 *. . . Mollendorf.* . . . Richard-Joachim-Heinrich Count von Möllendorf (1725–1816), Prussian general. Commanded the Prussian army during the occupation of Poland preparatory to the second partition,

Page

1793, for which made Field Marshal and Governor of South Prussia. Had previously served with distinction in the Seven Years War and War of Bavarian Succession. Fought the French republican armies, winning the battle of Kaiserslautern, and helped negotiate the Treaty of Basle, 1797. For details of his character and daily life, see p. 224.

59   . . . *M. de Tchitchagow.* . . . Admiral Vasily Yakovlevich Chichagov (1726–1809), trained partly in England. Led a fleet to the Mediterranean, 1782. Naval Commander-in-Chief in the Russo-Swedish War, 1788–90. Rewarded with 3,805 serfs, though more credit was really due to his subordinates, Admirals Sir Samuel Grieg (note p. 79) and Aleksandr von Kruze (note p. 88). Married Elizabeth Proby, daughter of Captain Charles Proby.

59   *Trevannion.* . . . James Trevenen (1760–90), English naval officer. Sailed with Captain Cook on his third voyage to the Pacific, 1776–80. Transferred to the Russian navy, 1787, as a Captain-Lieutenant. During the Russo-Swedish War took part in the battles of Hogland, 1788, and Öland, 1789. Promoted full Captain 1789. Mortally wounded at the battle of Viborg, 1790.

59   . . . *Marshall.* . . . Son of a Commissioner of the British Navy, in which he had served as a Lieutenant. Captain in the Russian Navy. Died in the second battle of Svensksund, 1790.

59   . . . *Denniston.* . . . Francis Dennison, British naval officer serving with the Russian Navy. Promoted Captain-Lieutenant 1777; by 1787 full Captain. Brought a Russian ship from Archangel to Kronstadt, 1787. Took part in the battles of Hogland, 1788, and Öland, 1789, where he was in command of the rowing frigates and described as Brigadier. Killed at the second battle of Svensksund, 1790.

60   . . . *took off Aiken's leg.* . . . See not p. 226.

60   . . . *'le jaloux'.* Probably, of a number of plays of this name, the five act comedy in free verse by Rochon de Chabannes, performed at the Comédie Française in 1784.

61   *Madame Protassov.* . . . Countess Anna Stepanovna Protasova (1745–1826), cousin of Prince Orlov, who obtained for her a place in Catherine's entourage. Maid of honour, 1762–84; lady in waiting, 1784–96. Known as *L'Eprouveuse*, employed as a close friend of the Empress to test the amatory skill of prospective favourites. Byron in *Don Juan*, canto IX, mentions 'her mystic office'.

62   . . . *some ugly little girl.* . . . Yekaterina Ivanovna Nelidova (1756–1836), maid of honour to the Grand Duchess Maria Fyodorovna from 1777. The Grand Duke's friendship with her caused a rift with the Grand Duchess, 1792, when she retired to the Convent of Smolny. Later returned to court. Superseded in Paul's favour by Anna Lapukhina, 1798.

62   . . . *a hat* à la étui. . . . A *chapeau à étui*, the narrow folded hat of the time.

63   . . . *Potemkin's soup.* . . . Another source mentions Potemkin's sterlet soup, made from the small sturgeon, *Acipenser ruthenus*, found in the Black and Caspian seas. Reputed to have cost three thousand roubles, it was served from a large silver tub.

63   . . . *the Duke of Choiseul.* . . . Louis XV's foreign minister 1758–61 and 66–70. Minister of war, 1761–70, of marine 1761–66.

63   *Lord Carysfort.* . . . John Joshua Proby, Earl of Carysfort (1751–

Page

1828), politician and author, in Italy between 1770 and 1773, when he took his seat in the Irish House of Lords.

63   *Whitbread.* . . . Samuel Whitbread (1758–1815), brewer and Whig politician.

64   *The present Grand Signior.* . . . The Turkish Sultan Selim III (1761–1808), son of Mustafa III and a Circassian. Succeeded his father 1789. His reforms, including a new model army on western lines, eventually provoked his assassination by the Janissaries, who were given religious sanction by the Grand Mufti's decision that a sultan who had reigned more than seven years without offspring was unworthy of the throne.

64   . . . *Aqua Tofana.* . . . Acqua Tofana, also known as *Acqua di Perugia* or *acquetta*, a slow arsenic-based poison used in Italy in the 17th century.

64   *Baratinski.* . . . Prince Fyodor Sergeyevich Baryatinsky (1742–1814), one of the officers at Ropsha, where Peter III was imprisoned in 1762. A note to Catherine II from Aleksey Orlov explained that Peter had been accidentally killed in a fight with Baryatinsky. Exiled to his native village by Paul after Catherine's funeral.

64   . . . *Siberia.* . . . Population in parts of northern Siberia declined during the 17th century owing to excessive hunting and trapping for furs, which reduced the supply and caused hunters to move farther east. Russian exploitation of the natives, to whom they bequeathed drunkenness and syphilis, increased their wretchedness but in general did not diminish their numbers; though some of the small groups, e.g. the Kamchadal, seemed to have suffered an absolute decrease, even taking into account assimilation into other groups. See T. Armstrong, *Russian Settlement in the North*, 1965.

65   *Young Baratinski.* . . . Prince Ivan Ivanovich Baryatinsky (1772–1825), appointed a gentleman of the court 1790. Counsellor of embassy in London 1804–8. Married Frances Dutton daughter of the first Lord Sherborn.

65   . . . *the princess's of the same name née Holstenbeck.* . . . Princess Yekaterina Petrovna von Holstein-Beck married 1767 to Prince Ivan Sergeyevich Baryatinsky (1740–1811), minister to Stockholm 1763, to France 1773–86. By Count Fyodor Grigor'yevich Orlov, younger brother of the favourite Prince Orlov, she had a son surnamed Silverbrick (1750–1811).

66   *His father's name was Saltikoff.* Count Sergey Vasil'yevich Saltykov (1726–?), married 1749 Matryona, daughter of Pavel Balk-Polev and lady in waiting to the Empress Elizabeth. In 1752 he became the lover of the Grand Duchess Catherine, later Catherine II, who in December that year, after a rough journey to Moscow, had a miscarriage. Another followed in the summer of 1753, but in 1754 she gave birth to a son, the Grand Duke, later Emperor, Paul, whom she half admitted in her *Memoirs* was Saltykov's. He went as Russian minister to Hamburg and Paris, 1754–60, and was replaced in her affections by Stanislas Poniatowski.

66   . . . *Yermonhoff.* . . . Aleksandr Petrovich Yermolov (1754–1834), A.D.C. to Prince Potemkin, accepted as imperial favourite 1785. Dismissed 1786 for quarrelling with Potemkin over diversion of public money by the Prince. Sent abroad for five years, 1786–91. On his

Page

return to Russia settled in Moscow and married a Princess Galitsina. Went abroad again, 1800, eventually settling at the Styrian castle of Frohsdorf, later residence of the comte de Chambord.

66 *Sir James Harris.* . . . diplomatist and courtier (1746–1820), created Earl of Malmesbury 1800. British minister to St. Petersburg 1777–82. Attempted via Potemkin to arrange an Anglo-Russian alliance; failed through the opposition of Count Panin, in charge of foreign affairs.

66 *. . . Count Panin.* . . . Count Nikita Ivanovich Panin (1718–83) placed by Catherine II in charge of foreign affairs, 1762–82. Favoured a policy of friendship with other northern powers, principally Prussia, with which he arranged the first partition of Poland. Parkinson's account of the formation of the Armed Neutrality is interesting and probably reliable as to details, though the project was already envisaged by Panin as an extension of his general policy and was not simply a counter to Harris's proposals.

67 *St. Priest.* . . . François-Emmanuel Guignard, comte de Saint-Priest (1735–1821), younger son of an Intendant of Languedoc, became a Knight of Malta at the age of four, at fifteen entered the royal Garde du Corps, made a colonel at twenty-seven. Represented France at Lisbon (1762–9), Constantinople (1769–84) and The Hague (1787). In Necker's first government advocated a Franco-Russian alliance. Went, after Louis XVI left Versailles, to Sweden and on to St. Petersburg, August, 1791. Catherine refused his plea for troops to aid Louis but offered him employment in Russia. Returned to Sweden on Esterhazy's arrival (as agent of the emigrant princes), leaving two sons in Russian service.

68 *. . . Quass.* . . . Kvass, a popular drink made from malt, water and various sorts of bread.

69 *The Consul.* . . . John Cayley, formerly a merchant of the Russia Company in the firm of Thornton, Cayley and Co.; British Consul-General in St. Petersburg and Agent of the Russia Company, 1787–95.

70 *. . . Sherematof.* . . . Count Sheremet'yev, see note p. 264.

70 *. . . Korkassof.* . . . ? Korsakov, Russian general.

70 *. . . Mary Luffofna.* . . . See note p. 43, daughter of Maria Alekseyevna L'vova, née D'yakova.

70 *La Baronne Stroganoff.* . . . Princess Anna Sergeyevna Trubetskoy, married 1791 to Baron Grigory Aleksandrovich Stroganov (1770–1857), appointed a Gentleman of the Court 1790. Later Russian minister to Stockholm and Constantinople, ambassador extraordinary at the coronation of Queen Victoria.

71 *. . . Calmuc.* . . . The Kalmyk or western branch of the Mongols (from the Turkic *kalmac*, separated, remaining behind) inhabited the Kalmyk steppe, an area on the right bank of the Volga plus a wedge shaped area on the left bank bordering on Kirghiz territory. In 1771 about 169,000 Kalmyks—those on the left bank—set off for China. Tibetan Buddhists since the 16th–17th centuries, keeping much of their earlier Shamanism.

71 *. . . Kirghese Tartars.* Inhabitants of the mountainous area bordering Sinkiang on the north west. Turkic speaking Sunnite Moslems conquered by the Russians in the later 19th century.

Page

72 . . . *Cranberry Postilla.* From the Latin *postilla,* afterwards; hence a kind of dessert after the main dish.

72 . . . *the Golitzin family.* . . . Russian princes since 1560, descended from the Guedemine Grand Princes of Lithuania.

72 . . . *Sir Joshua* . . . *his perishing colours.* . . . Sir Joshua Reynolds experimented with various techniques after his return from Italy from 1753 onwards. Instead of vermilion for flesh colouring he often used a carmine which faded within his lifetime. His pictures also suffered from the use over the paint of waxes mixed with pigment on which were superimposed glazes incorporating tinted varnish. In his last years the employment of too much bitumen caused surface cracks.

72 . . . *Moushkin-Poushkin's.* Count Valentin Platonovich Mushkin-Pushkin (1735–1804), Field Marshal, commanded the Russian army in the Russo-Swedish war of 1788–90; began his military career in 1758 in the Gardes à Cheval. Married Princess Praskovya Vasil'yevna, daughter of Prince Vasily Dolgorukov-Krimsky.

73 . . . *Prince Viazemskoi.* . . . Prince Aleksandr Alekseyevich Vyazemsky (1727–96), sent by the Empress to pacify ironworks in the Urals, 1762–3. In charge of government finance, 1764–92, beginning the differentiation of financial from general administration in the provinces and increasing central control. On his retirement Catherine took personal charge of finance with the help of a subordinate official.

73 . . . *the English Church.* . . . Visited by Parkinson for the first time for a Christmas service according to the Russian calendar.

73 . . . *Alfieri.* . . . Count Vittorio Alfieri (1749–1803), poet and dramatist, lover of the Countess of Albany, wife of the Young Pretender.

73 . . . *Count Starenberg.* . . . ? serving under Count von Cobenzl, Austrian ambassador to St. Petersburg.

74 . . . *Madame Zagraski's.* . . . Natal'ya Kirilovna (1747–1837), daughter of Count Kiril Rasumovsky. Married to Nikolay Aleksandrovich Zagraysky (1743–1821), court chamberlain.

74 *Somoilow.* . . . ? General Count Aleksandr Nikolayevich Samoilov (1744–1814), nephew of Potemkin. Commanded the left wing in the assault at Ochakov, 1790. Wrote a life of Potemkin.

75 . . . *the Marble Palace.* . . . Built 1768–72 in the early Neo-Classical style by Antonio Rinaldi (*c.* 1709–after 1790) for Grigory Orlov. So called from the grey marble external walling, interspersed with red granite. The interior has since been remodelled except for the staircase.

75 *The Duc de Montmorency Laval.* . . . See note p. 82.

76 . . . *Zavadovsky.* . . . See note p. 28.

76 *Woronzoff.* . . . Count Aleksandr Romanovich Vorontsov (1741–1805), Russian minister to London, 1762. President of the Trade Department to 1791. With Bezborodko advocated the second partition of Poland. Alexander I's Imperial Chancellor 1802. Brother of Princess Dashkova and of Count Semen Romanovich Vorontsov (1744–1822), Russian minister to London, 1785–96, ambassador 1796–1800.

76 . . . *Count Stroganoff's.* . . . Aleksandr Sergeyevich Count Stroganov (1733–1811), former confidant of the Empress Elizabeth, member of Catherine's inner court circle. Immensely wealthy with perhaps the finest art collection in Russia after that of the Empress. His second wife, née Princess Yekaterina Petrovna Trubetskaya, went to Moscow

in 1778 to live with the recently disgraced imperial favourite Ivan
Nikolayevich Rimsky-Korsakov. Her son Pavel Aleksandrovich
Stroganov (1772–1817), brought up with her three children by Rimsky-
Korsakov, became an officer in the Preobrazhensky Guards. He was
recalled from a visit to France, for taking too sympathetic an interest
in the French Revolution, and married to Princess Sof'ya Vladimirovich
Golitsin.

77 . . . *the Empress's son by Prince Orloff*. . . . See note p. 54.

77 . . . *Koutousoff*. . . . ? Kutuzov or Kutaisov. For Kutuzov see note
p. 89. Kutaisov (1759–1834), a captive Turkish child given by Catherine
to the Grand Duke Paul. Created Baron and Count 1799; given estates
in Courland 1801.

78 . . . *a veil over his bust*. . . . Catherine's bust of Charles James Fox
by Nollekens was seen by Parkinson at Tsarskoye Selo placed between
those of Cicero and Demosthenes (see p. 83). Fox's support of Poland
and of the French revolutionaries had changed her approval to
dislike.

79 . . . *Dr. Guthrie*. . . . Matthew Guthrie (died 1807), Scottish physician
at the Russian court, published medical papers, wrote *Dissertation sur
les Antiquités de Russie*, 1795, *Noctes Rossicae* on Russian music
and *A Supplementary Tour through the Countries on the Black Sea*
to go with his edition of *A Tour . . . through the Taurida or Crimea*
by his wife, Maria Guthrie, 1802.

79 . . . *Admiral Grieg*. . . . Admiral Sir Samuel Greig (1735–88) transferred from the British to the Russian navy, 1764. Served under
Aleksey Orlov in the Mediterranean, 1770–74. In the Russo-Swedish
War fought an indecisive action off Hogland, July 1788, sending
seventeen Russian officers back to St. Petersburg for neglect of duty.
Kept the Swedish fleet shut up in Sveaborg until his death, October
1788, after which it broke the blockade.

82 *The Duke de Laval*. . . . Anne-Adrien-Pierre de Montmorency,
duc de Laval (1768–1837), French emigré, befriended when in England
by the Prince Regent. Allowed to return to France by Napoleon.
After the Restoration ambassador to Madrid, Rome and Vienna.

82 . . . *Dumourier*. . . . Charles-François Dumouriez (1739–1823), French
general, Girondist minister for Foreign Affairs. Defeated the Prussians
at Valmy and the Austrians at Jemappes, 1792. Deserted after defeat
at Neerwinden to avoid the guillotine. Lived in exile, finally settling
in England.

82 *Custine*. . . . Adam-Philippe, comte de Custine (1740–93), French
general. Fought in the Seven Years War and the War of American
Independence. Appointed 1791 Lt. General commanding the army of
the Vosges; took, 1792, Spires, Worms, Mainz and Frankfurt. Forced
to retreat during the winter of 1792–93 by the Prussian army; guillo-
tined August 1793.

82 . . . *Valence*. . . . Cyrus-Marie-Alexandre, comte de Timbrune-
Valence (1757–1819), French general, nephew of Timbrune, governor
of the École Militaire. A member of the Palais Royale circle. Commanded the reserve at the battle of Valmy, 1792. Deserted with
Dumouriez, 1793. Allowed to return to France 1801; Senator 1805.
Fought for Napoleon in Spain, Germany and Russia, 1805–13. Peer
of France at the first Restoration and during the Hundred Days.

Page

After Waterloo a commissioner of the provincial government negotiating with Wellington and Blücher.

82 *Montesquieu.* . . . Baron de, grandson and last descendant of the famous writer. Served with the rank of Colonel in the American War of Independence. Emigrated 1792, joined the staff first of the duc de Laval, then of Lord Moira. Died in England 1822.

82 *The Baron Sternberg.* . . . Baron von Ungern-Sternberg, German Balt with estates in Estonia; married to a sister of General Samoilov. His daughter Anna married Catherine II's natural son by Grigory Orlov, Count Bobrinskoy, in 1796.

82 . . . *the palace of Tsarskoe Zelo.* . . . The Great Imperial Palace at Tsarskoye Selo (now Pushkin), built *c.* 1750 for the Empress Elizabeth by Bartolommeo Rastrelli (1700–71), partly redecorated for Catherine II by Charles Cameron (*c.* 1740–1812), who added the 270 feet long Kamerovna Gallereya for sculpture, 1783–85. The main façade of the palace, at right angles to the gallery, is 858 feet long, i.e. slightly more than the combined length of the centre and one of the wings of Versailles. Rastrelli's building is exuberantly Baroque, Cameron's wing Neo-Classical, not unlike the later work of the brothers Adam.

83 . . . *Mr. Bush's.* . . . John or Joseph Bush published in 1790 an engraved *Plan du Jardin et Vue des Differents Batimens de Czarskoe Selo,* dedicated to Catherine II. Her project for a museum and colonnade by Cameron, described on pp. 83–84 is of interest.

84 *Several buildings.* . . . Quarenghi is known to have designed the following: Music Pavilion (here called *Chambre de Musique,* also known as the Temple of Friendship), commissioned 1782 when Lanskoy was favourite, built 1784–88; two cast iron Bridges, 1782–86; the Ruin (serving as a kitchen), 1785–86; the Baths, in wood, 1791. Later, 1795, he built a Temple for an island in the lake. Outside the park, his Alexander Palace, for Catherine's grandson, was under construction in the years 1792–96. For the Princesses of Baden he designed a wooden villa built within the grounds of the imperial palace. Catherine also commissioned from him a design (now in the Museo Civico at Vicenza) for a Pavilion to contain a cast of the statue of the Apollo Belvedere.

84 . . . *a favourite* . . . *who was turned off for incapacity.* . . . See note p. 66 on Aleksandr Yermolov giving the real reasons for his dismissal.

85 . . . *an Imperial Villa called Tchesme.* . . . Named after the naval victory of Chesme, 1770, in the Aegean over the Turks. Built 1770–73 by Y. M. Velten (1730–1801), architect son of Peter the Great's Danzig-born head chef. The villa was converted under Nicolas I into a hospital for old soldiers.

85 . . . *the Chinese Town.* . . . More generally known as the Chinese Village, built 1782–6 from designs by Charles Cameron.

85 . . . *Kiachta.* The trading settlement of Kyakhta was established on the borders of Outer Mongolia in 1728.

85 . . . *the Empress was married to Potemkin.* . . . A rumour current at the time which has never been proved. The marriage was said to have taken place late in 1774 in great secrecy at the Church of St. Samsonyevsky, St. Petersburg.

S

Page

85   *. . . the unhappy Prince dropped down dead. . . .* This account of Peter III's death agrees with the state of the corpse at the lying in state. His face was bandaged and nearly black, presupposing strangling.

86   *The Count D'Anhalt.* . . . Son of Prince Victor Amadeus of Anhalt-Bernbourg-Schaumbourg (1744–90), General in the Russian service, killed fighting in Finland.

87   *. . . Necker's timid counsels.* . . . The conciliatory policy as adviser to Louis XVI of Jacques Necker (1732–1804) during the early stages of the French Revolution, 1789–90.

87   *. . . the sending away of Mr. Chauvelin.* . . . François-Bernard, marquis de Chauvelin (1766–1832), French ambassador to London since April, 1792, with the task of keeping England neutral, was ordered on the 23rd January, 1793, to leave, following William Pitt's rejection on the 31st December of the French Convention's decree opening the Scheldt to commerce. Chauvelin's dismissal presaged war, declared by the French government against England and Holland on the 1st February, 1793.

88   *. . . Admiral Creuse.* . . . Aleksandr von Kruze, born 1726 in Moscow, his father, also a Russian naval officer, being apparently of Danish ancestry. Served seven years in the British navy. Captain at the battle of Chesme, 1770. Vice-Admiral, 1783. Took a leading part in the war with Sweden in the Baltic, 1788–90.

89   *Orloff, a general of the Cossacs.* . . . ? Count Fyodor Grigor'yevich Orlov (1741–96), younger brother of the favourite Prince Orlov. Commanded Russian troops landed in the Morea during the Russo-Turkish war of 1768–74 which failed to take the fortresses of Coron, Modon and Tripolitza. Unmarried, fathered seven natural children by three mistresses, including by Princess Baryatinsky a son surnamed Silverbrick.

89   *. . . Mad^{selle} Poljanski.* . . . Anna Aleksandrovna Poliansky, daughter of a court chamberlain married to Yelisaveta Romanovna Voronzova, mistress of Peter III and sister of Princess Dashkova. Married Baron D'Hoggier, Dutch minister to St. Petersburg.

89   *His other mistress.* . . . Yekaterina Ivanovna Nelidova. See note to p. 62.

89   *General Kakhouski.* . . . Commanded the Russian army in Moldavia which helped to conquer Poland in the summer of 1792, nominally on behalf of the Confederation of Targowica.

89   *. . . General Koutousow.* . . . Mikhail Ilarionovich, Prince Golen-ishchev-Kutuzov-Smolensky (1745–1813), sent as ambassador to Constantinople, 1793; had served in the Russian army in Poland, 1764–69, and against Turkey, 1770–74. In command of an army in the Russo-Turkish war of 1778–91. Served under the Emperor Alexander I at Austerlitz, 1805. Commanded Russian forces in the Turkish war of 1811–12. Commander-in-chief against Napoleon, 1812–13.

90   *. . . the armed Neutrality.* Formed 1780, challenged British claims to block neutral ships from trading with an enemy, in this case the American colonies. Russian withdrawal from the armed Neutrality was an empty concession in 1793, when trade with America was no longer at stake. In return Russia required British acceptance of the second partition of Poland according to the terms jointly agreed by Russia and Prussia, January 23, 1793. Whitworth's protests about

Page

the partition were reported by him to London on January 25, 27 and 29 and February 12, 1793.

90 *The King of Prussia has been the principal mover.* . . . An impression the Russians wanted to convey, though it is very doubtful whether they were any less eager than the Prussians.

91 . . . *Baron de la Turbie's.* . . . Sardinian minister to St. Petersburg.

91 . . . *two toises.* . . . Twelve feet. One toise equals a fathom or six feet.

93 . . . *Count Tchernichev.* . . . Count Ivan Grigor'yevich Chernishev (1726–97), President of the Admiralty.

93 . . . *the Print of Gholtzius.* . . . Hendrik Goltzius of Harlem, engraver and painter (1558–1616).

94 . . . *Stedingk the Ambassador's brother.* . . . The Swedish ambassador to St. Petersburg from 1790 to 1808 and 1809–11 was Curt Bogislaus Ludvig Christoffer, Count von Stedingk (1746–1837), army officer and diplomatist. Second in command of the Swedish army in Germany, 1813–14, under Bernadotte.

94 *Bentham.* . . . Sir Samuel Bentham (1757–1831), engineer, inventor and naval architect, only brother of Jeremy Bentham. Went to Russia in 1779, travelled widely, notably in Siberia, where he reached Kiakhta and Irkutsk. Employed by Potemkin to found an industrial centre on his estates at Krichev in White Russia, 1782–7. Fitted out at Kherson a flotilla which won the battle of Balta Liman against the Turks, 1788. In command of a Siberian regiment, 1788–91. Returned to England, 1791; technical adviser to the Admiralty, 1795–1807, returning to Russia 1805–7 to try to build ships for the British navy. See M. S. Anderson, 'Samuel Bentham in Russia' in *American Slavic and East European Review*, 1956.

95 *Radiskef.* . . . Aleksandr Nicolayevich Radishchev (1749–1802), reforming writer. Studied at Leipzig, 1767–71. Employed as a customs official. Wrote, 1790, *A Journey from Petersburg to Moscow* describing social evils, for which he was sentenced to death, commuted to exile in Siberia. Recalled by Paul I, 1796. Committed suicide when there seemed no hope of reforming Russian society, 1802.

4 ST. PETERSBURG TO MOSCOW

98 . . . ad modum jaculabuntur. Parkinson's dream has been left in the Latin of his MS as far as this can be made out.

5 MOSCOW

99 . . . *Dickenson.* . . . Head of the manufacturing firm of Tamez. See also pp. 102, 103.

99 . . . *Count Razomofsky.* . . . Count Kiril Grigor'yevich Razumovsky 1718–1803), younger brother of the Empress Elisabeth's favourite and (?) husband. Hetman of Little Russia and a Field Marshal at the age of twenty-two. Refused Aleksey Orlov help in the *coup d'état* of 1762, subsequently deprived of his Cossack command, remaining a Senator. Inherited vast wealth from his brother; owned over 100,000 serfs. Had eleven children by his wife, Yekaterina Naryshkina, who died 1771. His niece, Countess Sof'ya Apraksina, then became his mistress and estranged him from his children.

Page

100 . . . *the Samoyede, the Kamtschadale.* . . . The Samoyed peoples, speaking a Finno-Ugrian language, inhabit the extreme north of Russia and north west Siberia from the White Sea to the Taymyr peninsula. The Kamchadal, aboriginal inhabitants of Kamchatka, speak a language of the Paleosiberian group. Their name was sometimes applied in the 18th century to the descendants of early Russian settlers in Kamchatka.

100 . . . *Prince Gagarin.* . . . Probably Prince Ivan Sergeyevich Gagarin (1754–1810), naval captain and free mason; participated in the naval battle of Chesme and at Leghorn helped Count Aleksey Orlov to capture the Princess Tarakanova, reputed daughter of the Empress Elizabeth. See also p. 219, refering to a message from William Eton, whom he may have encountered in connection with his Mediterranean voyages.

104 . . . *Guldenstaed.* Johann Anton Guldenstaedt (1745–81), naturalist and physician, born in Riga; published 1787–91 his *Voyage en Russie et dans les montagnes du Caucase.*

104 . . . *two country houses.* . . . Kuskovo and Ostankino, see note p. 213.

6 MOSCOW TO KAZAN

108 . . . *Nijni Novgorod.* . . . Founded 1221 by the Grand Princes of Vladimir, whose capital it became in the 14th century. The Kremlin was rebuilt in 1508–11, with thirteen towers and walls 65–100 feet high, by the Italian architect Pietro Francesco.

108 . . . *Casan.* . . . Kazan, capital of a Tatar khanate in the fifteenth century, captured by Ivan the Terrible in 1552, had been destroyed by Pugachov in 1774. Soon rebuilt, it retained the walls and some towers of the Kremlin constructed for Ivan the Terrible.

110 . . . *Prince Baratiew.* . . . Prince Pyotr Mel'khizidekovich Barataev, later Governor of Simbirsk, which became a provincial capital in 1796.

110 . . . *Bolghari.* . . . Medieval capital of the kingdom of the Bolghars, a Finno-Ugrian people converted to Islam in the mid tenth century. The deserted ruins were rediscovered in the reign of Peter the Great.

110 . . . *Pugatcheff.* . . . Emelyan Pugachov, Don Cossack, served in the Seven Years War and against Turkey, 1769, when he deserted to Siberia. Returned May, 1773, to the southern Ural mountains, claiming to be the Emperor Peter III and raising the Yaik Cossacks in revolt. Joined by the Bashkirs and other Asiatic tribes, by serfs from the Ural mines and foundries, and by peasants, the revolt spread to the west bank of the Volga. Deterred from marching on Moscow, July, 1774, by Russian peace negotiations with Turkey. Defeated by Count Pyotr Panin at Chernoyarsk, betrayed by supporters to Suvorov. Executed in Moscow, January, 1775.

7 KAZAN TO PERM

115 . . . *M. Sokolof a lieutenant in the Guards.* . . . Pavel Apollonovich Sokolov (1774—before 1854), lieutenant 1792 in the Semyonovsky regiment, rising to Major General, 1848. Married Aleksandra, daughter of Prince Yakov Aleksandrovich Kozlovsky.

8 PERM TO TOBOLSK

Page

117 *... the Bachkirs. ...* A people of disputed origin, the Bashkirs speak
a Turkic language and live mainly on the west slopes of the Urals.
Numbered about 200,000 in 1760. Russian controlled since the capture
of Kazan, 1552. The first Russian settlement in Bashkiria was Ufa,
founded 1586.

119 *... Catherinenbourgh. ...* Yekaterinburg, founded 1721, named after
the Empress Catherine I. Initially a mining town fortified against
the Bashkirs. Mint established 1735. Now renamed Sverdlovsk.

119 *... the inspector of the mint. ...* Parkinson's notes on the mint,
headed 'The Monnoie. 1ˢᵗ The house were they heat the Pigs of
Copper & draw them out to a proper thickness for stamping. The
pieces are drawn through a rolling press 3 times; the 2 first heated,
the last cold. 2ᵈˡʸ the house where pieces of a proper size for stamping
are cut out of the plates. 16 people employed and capable of cutting
out 16,000 pieces in 24 hours. The engines for this purpose are worked
by means of an overshot water wheel. A man was employed in separat-
ing the imperfect pieces from the good. 3ᵈˡʸ the house for cleaning,
polishing & reducing the edges of the cut copper pieces. First they
were heated in a furnace, then put into water, then shaken in a sieve
with sawdust. 4ᵗʰˡʸ the milling house, where boys were employed in
milling the Coin by means of horizontal steel wheels. 5ᵗʰˡʸ The stamping house where there were 12 Engines. A boy sitting in a hole in
the ground supplies each of his stamps with Pieces of Copper. A chain
went from each to the waterwheel & from each to the roof. Its weight
drew it down & gave the blow; the water wheel drew it up & the Chain
to the roof prevented it from going too far. Here they were employed
in weighing the Copper. 16 ——— to make a pood [*36 pounds avoir-
dupois*]. They could stamp 12,000 roubles. 6ᵗʰ the house where the
dies were engraven. They are stamped first by means of a similar
engine to those in the last house; with this difference that Men were
employed instead of the water wheel to raise the weight. 9 Men
employed here. After the impression was made they proceeded to cut
it deeper. 7ᵗʰˡʸ the house where the imperfect pieces & the plates out
of which the Coin was cut, were fused & reduced to the form of pigs.
'The Mines belonging to the Crown furnish annually 100,000 Poods;
those of individuals 70,000. Every individual is obliged to furnish half
of his produce at the rate of 5 R [*roubles*] & 50 C [*copecs*] a Pood:
and a tenth part of the whole for nothing; so that he retains only
4 Parts which he disposes of for 12 or 13 or at present 15 roubles a
pood. As each pood is coined into 16 roubles, & the Crown pays
Proprietors 5R., 50 Copecs a pood & the other expenses amount to
40 Copecs a pood, the Crown gains on each of the 70,000 poods
furnished by Individuals a profit of more than 10 roubles.
'The Profit upon a million of roubles he said was 600,000. If therefore, as he said was the case, a million & ½ is coined here & ½ a
million in the Government of Perm, the profit of Government ought
to be 12,00,000 roubles. The whole coinage is sent partly to the Bank
at Moscow & partly to the Bank at Petersburgh.
'400 workmen employed in the Monoye. The workmen receive from
30 to 100 Roubles a Year. The Boys receive a rouble a month.'

Page

120 . . . *the Forges*. Parkinson's notes were less systematic than for the Mint and have been re-arranged as follows: 'The 1st step is to burn the Ore. The Rader [?] obtained from this is mixed with Charcoal, Sand & Lime. The Airon obtained by this Process is beat out into Bars by means of Hammers worked by Water Wheels. There are in all nine but for want of water two only were going. For the same reason the Saw Mill was not going.

'We found in one room a Peasant belonging to the Family painting pictures for the Church. In another a Manufactory of Guns &c for the use of the house.

'In all there are about 3,300 employed. They fuse about 500 Poods in a day. The quantity of Iron manufactured here 100,000 pood in a Year. The Iron sells for 1 Rouble 3 a Pood.'

9 TOBOLSK

124 . . . *Mr Baktyr*. . . . Afterwards Governor of Khar'kov.

124 . . . *M. Tchoglikoff*. . . . Naum Nikolayevich Choglokov (1743–98), son of the Empress Elizabeth's Grand Master of Ceremonies and grandson in the female line of a sister of Catherine I. Officer in the Horse Guards. Sent, 1770, to Transcaucasia to wage guerilla war on the Turks. Cashiered for insubordination, 1771, and deported to Siberia, first to Berezov, then to Tobolsk. The charge against him was probably fabricated to get a possible claimant to the throne out of the way. His brother Samuil was accused in 1767 of attempting to assassinate Catherine II and deported to Siberia, while his brother Nikolay was imprisoned for fifteen years at Schlusselburg for an alleged attempt on the life of Baron von Ungern-Sternberg, but allowed to return to Reval, 1796.

125 . . . *Andrew Razoumofski*. . . . Son of Count Kiril Razumovsky, see note, p. 99.

125 *M. Derzhavin*. . . . Gavril Romanovich Derzhavin (1743–1816), lyric poet. Went as an army officer to Kazan during the Pugachov rising. Entered the civil service, 1777. Later became a state secretary and Senator.

125 . . . *Felista*. . . . *Felitsya*, i.e. Felicity, an ode to Catherine II by Derzhavin, 1782.

125 . . . *Glaboff* . . . ? Aleksandr Ivanovich Glebov (1722–90), General-Procurator under Peter III and Catherine II. Dismissed for irregular conduct, 1764. Removed from all posts and banned from the capital, 1782.

125 *Count Skavronski*. . . . Count Pavel Martynovich Skavronsky (1757–93) married 1780 Yekaterina Engelhardt, youngest niece of Potemkin. Russian minister to Naples.

126 . . . *a second day's ague*. Parkinson may have meant a secondary ague.

128 . . . *Prince Heraclius*. . . . Heraclius II, King of Georgia (*c*. 1720–98), son of Teymouraz II. United the provinces of Karthli and Kakhetli, defeated the Persian Asad Khan, 1752, and annexed land up to the Araxes. Joined Count Todleben's Russian army helping Solomon, King of Imeretia, 1772. Recognised Russian suzerainty 1783. His grandson David ceded Georgia to Russia, 1801.

Page

128   ... *Prince Dolgorucki.* ... Prince Aleksey Grigoryevich Dolgoruky (–1734), made a Senator with the support of Menshikov. Member of Peter II's Supreme Privy Council, in control of government after the banishment of Menshikov to Siberia. Opposed the accession and autocratic rule of the Empress Anne, who exiled him.

128   ... *Prince Menchikof.* ... Prince Aleksandr Danilovich Menshikov (1670–1729), soldier, general and statesman. Made a Field Marshal for his part in the battle of Poltava, 1709. On the death of Peter the Great, 1725, proclaimed Peter's widow Catherine I. Controlled the empire for her. Dismissed by Peter II, 1727, exiled to Siberia 1728.

128   ... *Count Osterman.* ... Heinrich Johann Count Osterman (1686–1747), born in Westphalia, went to Russia in 1704. One of Peter the Great's principal advisers, tutor to Peter II. Minister under the Empress Anne, 1730–40, and Ivan VI, 1740–41. Arrested and exiled on the accession of Elizabeth.

130   ... *Iverdan.* ? the estate of the marquis de Girardin, where Rousseau lived in the year of his death, 1778.

130   ... *great nephew of the Poet.* I.e. of Aleksandr Petrovich Sumarokov (1717–77), the renowned playwright and poet, admirer and imitator of French literature; politically an enlightened advocate for his own class, the nobility, opposed both to despotism and to arbitrary serfdom.

131   ... *Beverley.* ... First produced 1768, a tragedy in free verse in five acts by Bernard-Joseph Saurin (1706–81) in imitation of English plays.

131   ... *Radiskef.* ... See note to p. 96.

136   *Somoilow.* ... See note to p. 74.

136   ... *the Brigadier.* ... The popular comedy, a satire on half-educated Francophil Russian nobles, written 1766 by Denis Ivanovich Fonvizin (1744–92).

140   ... *a war with China.* This agrees with other signs of Russian official interest in the Far East in the last ten years of Catherine's reign. In 1786 she had approved Bezborodko's scheme for claiming the Aleutian and Kuril islands and the Alaskan coast. In 1794 Whitworth brought to Lord Grenville's attention 'a new chart of the Russian Empire, in which a considerable tract of the North West Coast of America, to the Northward of Nootka Sound is found to be part of Her Imperial Majesty's Dominions.' If the additional troops in Siberia were destined ultimately for the Amur basin, they might have anticipated the annexations of Count Muravyov-Amursky in 1858–60.

10   SAREPTA

142   ... *the Brethren.* ... German speaking brethren of the Evangelical Society from Bohemia, generally called Moravian Brethren. The settlement, in Saratov *guberniya* or province, was founded by about 120 people in 1765. There were said to be 200 families in 1793.

147   *Dr. Sedler.* ... Pallas refers to a Dr. Seydel at Sarepta.

147   ... *Eimer.* ... A measure of capacity equivalent to 12·806 litres.

148   ... *the Cuban Tartars.* ... Inhabiting the area round the River Kuban east of the Sea of Azov.

150   ... *a Dictionary.* ... *The Comparative Dictionary of all Languages and Dialects, compiled by a Most Illustrious Personage,* 1787–89.

Page

Compiled under the direction of Catherine II; of very little use compared with the Russian Academy's Dictionary supervised by its President, Princess Dashkova, and published 1788–95.

11 SAREPTA TO ASTRAKHAN

152 *... the stags at Lime.* ... Lime Park in Cheshire.

153 *... the first Stanitza.* ... Stanitsa, Russian term for a Cossack settlement. A farming village with military links, usually in regions with few Russian inhabitants. There were many stanitsy in southern Siberia.

153 *The Dolmetcher of the Calmucs.* ... Russian official with special responsibility for relations with the Kalmyks.

155 *... in Tangut.* The language of north eastern Tibet, in the region of Koko-nor, where the Tibetans of the early middle ages united to form a kingdom sufficiently important to menace China.

156 *... the primitie.* ... *Primitiae*, first fruits.

159 *... the Calmucs who made their escape out of Russia.* ... See note to p. 71.

12 ASTRAKHAN

162 *... Tent.* From the Spanish *tinto*; a deep red wine, mainly from Spain.

163 *... Astrabad.* ... Town and frontier province in north-east Persia, which had been ruled by Murtasa-Kuli, defeated by his eunuch half-brother, Agha Mohammed, later Shah, in 1780.

164 *... The Indians.* ... They are described by Pallas as coming from Multanistan, i.e. the Punjab.

164 *Astracan not being paved.* ... The town grew rapidly in the early 18th century at the time of Peter the Great's war with Persia. It had been the capital of a Tatar khanate before its capture by Ivan the Terrible in 1557.

165 *... M. De Ligne.* ... Younger son of the courtier, writer and general, Charles-Joseph, prince de Ligne (1735–1814). The elder son, Charles-Joseph-Emmanuel du Plessis de Ligne was killed fighting the French Revolutionaries in 1792; the younger, Louis-Lamoral (1766–1813), became a Colonel in the Austrian service, married 1803 comtesse Louise-Josephine van der Noot de Duras.

165 *... our crazy countryman.* ... ? Captain Kelly, described on p. 168 as 'an American Englishman' and 'a wild impetuous man'. Dr. Pallas, in Astrakhan the same year, met a 'M. Digbye, architecte d'Astracan'.

166 *... Bruce.* ... James Bruce (1730–94), traveller. Sketched ruins in north Africa, 1765, and Syria, 1768. Explored Abyssinia 1769–71, finding the source of the Blue Nile. Wrote *Travels*, 5 volumes, 1790.

166 *... the Queen.* ... ? Ozoro Esther, young and beautiful wife of King Tecla Haimanout, whose favour Bruce won by curing some important subjects of smallpox.

166 *... Worthley Montague.* ... Edward Wortley Montagu (1713–76) author and traveller, son of Lady Mary Wortley Montagu. Wintered

Page

in Egypt 1762. Went via Sinai to Jerusalem; on to Venice, 1765. At Smyrna 1769; then settled at Rosetta; back at Venice 1774. Translated Veneroni's *Dialogues* into Arabic.

167 . . . *some such name as Setleek.* . . . ? Sutlej river, which runs through the Punjab south east of Kashmir. In its upper basin the Sikhs first established themselves in the early 17th century, forming a theocratic confederacy in the 18th.

172 . . . *the Cathedral.* . . . The Uspensky Cathedral, built 1700–10, with five green cupolas, stands within the Kremlin, founded in the late 16th century.

174 . . . *a learned Persian of Sallian.* . . . ? a corruption of Enzeli-Kazian, one of the main Persian ports on the southern shore of the Caspian.

177 . . . *Non eadem aetas non eadem mens. 'Non eadem est aetas, non mens':* My age is not the same, nor my inclination. (Horace, first Epistle, line 4.)

178 . . . *the Bielogorod.* . . . The old town immediately south east of the Kremlin. Literally White Town.

13 GEORGIEVSK

180 . . . *Goudovitch.* . . . Ivan Vasil'yevich, Count Gudovich (1741–1820), army officer. Sent by Peter III to Frederick the Great to announce his accession and conclude peace, 1762. Fought in Poland, 1764, and in the Turkish wars. Sent after the conclusion of the second Turkish war to act as military Governor-General of the north Caucasus. Given 1800 serfs in Podolia by Catherine II; by Paul given a further 3,000 serfs and made Governor-General of Kamenetz-Podolsk. For Alexander I commanded an army in Georgia and Daghestan; created a Field Marshal, 1807, after defeat of Yousouf Pasha. Retired 1809 to his estates to pursue his hobbies of hunting and music.

181 . . . *the Club.* . . . The Nobles Club in St. Petersburg. See note, p. 20.

183 . . . *Anapa.* . . . Turkish fortress town on the north-east shore of the Black Sea, unsuccessfully attacked September, 1787, and March, 1790, taken 1791.

183 . . . *the five Mountains.* Lysaya Gora, Mashuk, Zmeinaya, Beshtau and Zhelyeznaya Gora. All of volcanic origin; and the highest, Beshtau, 4,593 feet above sea level. Near them lies the modern town of Pyatigorsk (literally, five mountains).

185 . . . *the Princes and the Usdens.* . . . Circassian princes and nobles (uzden) were in control of land and herds. Below them was a complex patriarchal hierarchy based on extended families within tribes.

186 . . . *the Eaux aigres.* . . . A carbonic spring called by the Circassians the 'drink of heroes'. The spa of Kislovodsk grew up round the spring during the 19th century.

186 . . . *Abbaizas.* . . . Abkhasians, one of the ancient peoples of Caucasia, inhabiting the coastline north west of Georgia until 1864, when most joined the mass emigration of the Circassians to Turkey.

189 . . . *whether Erdburus is nearer than the rest.* . . . Mount Elbrus stands north of the main Caucasian range, but as Georgievsk lies north east of it, the difference in distances from Georgievsk of Elbrus and the adjoining peaks is not more than a few miles. Elbrus at

18,470 feet above sea level is 1,415 feet higher than the next highest point, the Duikh-Tau, some forty-five miles south east.

190 ... *some Turkoman Tartars.* ... Nomadic tribes, Sunni Moslems of the Turkic linguistic group, living mostly between the Caspian and the river Oxus. Traditional enemies of Persia and probably cultivated by Russia for this reason.

14 BAKCHISERAI

193 ... *Bakchiserai.* ... In Tatar, 'court surrounded by gardens'. Former capital of the Tatar Khans of the Crimea, which was annexed by Russia in 1783.

193 ... *the palace.* ... The Khan Sarai, built 1518 for Khan Abdul Sahel-Girai, largely destroyed 1736 and rebuilt 1786–88 by Charles Cameron, aided by William Hastie. With its mosque and mausolea it surrounds a rectangular court about 425 feet by 125. Contains many springs, the most famous the Spring of Tears, where water falls into ten shells sunk into a marble table.

193 ... *Mordvinoff.* ... Nikolay Semyonovich, Count Mordvinov (1754–1845), naval officer, younger son of an admiral. His elder brother Aleksandr was considered by Catherine II in 1781 for the post of favourite. Spent three years in England, 1774–6. Rear-Admiral commanding the Kherson squadron at the beginning of the Russo-Turkish War of 1787–92; placed in command of all Black Sea naval forces in 1789, superceding Nassau-Siegen and John Paul Jones.

194 ... *Jew village on an eminence.* ... Tchufut-Kale, or 'Fortress of the Jews', inhabited by the Karites, Jewish disciples of the letter of the Mosaic law. Deserted by its inhabitants in the mid 19th century.

196 ... *a Greek Church cut out of a rock.* ... One of five churches belonging to the Uspensky Monastery founded in the 15th century.

198 ... *Zeuboff as Governor General.* ... Count, later Prince, Platon Aleksandrovich Zubov, imperial favourite, was made Governor General of Yekaterinoslav and Tauris in succession to Prince Potemkin.

15 KIEV

199 ... *Prince Dashkoff.* ... See note to p. 38.

199 ... *the Catacombs.* ... The catacombs of St. Anthony and St. Theodosius date largely from the 12th century and consist of narrow passages off which open burial niches and former cells of hermits. The clay soil in which they were excavated is lined with masonry.

201 ... *the dissolution of the Monasteries.* ... Of more than a thousand monasteries in Russia in 1764, over half were closed after the secularization of church lands in that year. Over one million male serfs were transferred to state ownership in the process. They are generally thought to have benefited from better conditions as a result, but the many state serfs granted by Catherine to favoured subjects were worse off.

201 ... *a Saint up to above the middle in the ground.* ... Ivan the Longsuffering (12th century) is reputed to have lived thus for thirty

Page

years and is so buried, wearing a mitre, in the Catacombs of St. Anthony.

201 . . . *the Roscolnicks.* . . . From *roskol*, schism, in the Russian Orthodox Church during the 17th century, when the Old Believers, led by Avakum, left the church rather than accept changes in the forms of religious service instituted by Patriarch Nikon.

201 . . . *Count Romanzoff.* . . . Pyotr Aleksandrovich, Count Rumyantsev-Zadonayskoy (1730–96), Field Marshal. Served in the Seven Years War and in both Russian wars against Turkey. For his victories in the first Turkish war made a Field Marshal and given the additional name Zadonayskoy, the Transdanubian. Resigned his command in the second Turkish war in disgust at Potemkin's inaction. Father of Count Sergey Petrovich Rumyantsev, for whom see p. 41.

202 . . . *the Cathedral.* The Cathedral of St. Sophia, built 1037–49 by order of Grand Prince Yaroslav after his victory over the Pechenegs. Five aisled plan, 180 feet long with apses and transepts. Crowned by fifteen gilded domes. Inside two mosaics, of the Virgin and the Last Supper, and the monument of Yaroslav I (died 1054) date from the 11th century.

202 . . . *the Bratschi Monastery.* Stands in the Podol, or lower town, and contains the Cathedral of the Epiphany dating from 1693.

16 KIEV TO MOSCOW

204 . . . *the Pitcherski.* . . . Pecherskaya, the south-east quarter of Kiev, on high ground near the river Dnieper, contains several monasteries and many churches.

207 . . . *neither the Dutchess of Cumberland nor the Dutchess of D.* . . . Anne née Luttrell, widow of Christopher Horton, married 1771 Henry Frederick, Duke of Cumberland, fourth son of Frederick, Prince of Wales. George III disapproved and instigated the Royal Marriage Act of 1772. The Duchess of D.: probably Georgiana née Spencer, wife of the fifth Duke of Devonshire, who canvassed for Fox at the Westminster election of 1784.

17 RETURN TO MOSCOW

209 . . . *the imperial palace at Petrofsky.* . . . Built by the Russian architect Kazakov, 1776; occupied by Napoleon, September 1812. Destroyed by fire when the French left Moscow. Rebuilt 1840 in a North Italian Gothic style.

209 *The Count's House.* . . . Commissioned by Kiril Naryshkin for his grandson, the future Emperor Peter the Great. Given to Count Razumovsky, 1763, by Catherine II. Bought by the state, 1861, demolished and replaced by an agricultural institute.

209 . . . *Pontac.* . . . A sweet wine from the Basses Pyrénées.

210 . . . *the Young Grand Duke's marriage.* . . . The Grand Duke Aleksandr Pavlovich, later Alexander I of Russia, married 1793 Princess Maria Louisa of Baden, who adopted the Russian names of Yelisaveta Fyodorovna.

Page

211   . . . *the Countess Golofkin.* . . . Countess Yekaterina Aleksandrovna
Golovkina (1733–1821), lady in waiting, daughter of Field Marshal
Count Aleksandr Ivanovich Shuvalov and wife of Count Vavrila
Ivanovich Golovkin, privy councillor.

211   . . . *Zaritzina.* . . . Tsaritsina, begun for Catherine II by the architect
Bazhenov, unfinished because she thought its towers looked like
candelabra surrounding a coffin.

212   . . . *Kaskovo, Count Scheremetew's Villa.* . . . Kuskovo, a Sheremet'yev
possession since the early 16th century, soon to be superceded as the
main family seat by Ostankino, stands eight miles east of Moscow.
Count Nikolay Petrovich Sheremet'yev (1751–1809), studied at Leyden
university, succeeded to his vast estates 1788. Kept a serf orchestra,
in which he sometimes played double bass (see p. 224), and an opera
and ballet company whose *prima donna* Praskovya Kovaleva (stage
name *Zhemchugova* or Pearly) he married, 1801.

213   . . . *he took no delight in it.* Count Sheremet'yev seems to have preferred Neo-Classical architecture, concerning himself closely with the
designs for Ostankino, where Bazhenov was probably responsible for
the theatre and Francesco Camporese for the wings. Quarenghi
designed a palace for him in Moscow which was never completed;
it was to have had a theatre similar to that at the Hermitage and an
English garden with winding paths.

214   . . . *Prince Gagarin.* . . . See note to p. 100.

214   . . . *Count Batourlin's.* . . . The Counts Baturin, of Translyvanian
origin, came to Russia in the 15th century and were nobles of Tula
province.

214   . . . *Prince Viazemsky's.* . . . Prince Yakov Yakovlevich Vyazemsky
(1741–1833), aulic councillor.

214   . . . *Prince Bieloselskoi.* . . . Prince Aleksandr Mikhailovich Belosyelsky
(1752–1809), guards officer appointed 1779 Russian minister to Dresden,
1780–93 to Turin. Senator 1796.

215   . . . *the Troitskoi convent.* . . . The Troitsa-Sergeyevskaya Lavra,
famous monastery of the Holy Trinity, founded in the fourteenth
century by St. Sergey of Radonezh, lies about 44 miles north of
Moscow. The second oldest and richest monastery in Russia (after
the Kiev Lavra). The buildings, including thirteen churches, are enclosed by a tall wall, two-thirds of a mile round, pinnacled, with
nine towers.

216   . . . *the Refectory.* . . . Completed 1692, 240 feet long, painted with
Biblical scenes.

216   . . . *the Archbishop.* . . . Archbishop Platon of Moscow, born Pyotr
Yegorovich Levshin. Completed his religious education at the Slav-
Greek-Latin Academy in Moscow. Entered the Troitsa-Sergeyevskaya
Lavra, 1758. Went to St. Petersburg, 1763, where he gained fame as a
preacher. Returned to the monastery as Archimandrite, 1766. Appointed Archbishop of Moscow, 1775; took steps to reform the diocese.
Prepared for himself a hermitage at Bethany, 1783, which later became a monastery. Entered Moscow, 1812, after Napoleon's invasion,
but feeble and paralysed was carried back to Bethany where he died.

217   . . . *my Convent at Bethany.* . . . Founded 1783, includes, besides
Platon's residence, the Church of the Transfiguration with a fine
interior.

Page

219   . . . *the Vassili Vlascheni Church.* . . . The cathedral known as of St. Basil the Blessed, but dedicated to the Virgin Protectress and Intercessor. Built 1555–60 by Postnik and Barma for Ivan IV as a thank-offering for his conquest of Kazan and Astrakhan. Polychromatic decoration and a combination of towers, spires and onion domes give it a more fantastic appearance than any other Russian church of its type.

18   RETURN TO ST. PETERSBURG

222   . . . *Count Chernichew's house.* . . . The town house of the Chernishev family would have been inhabited at this time by Count Ivan Grigor'yevich, for whom see note to page 93, and Count Grigory Ivanovich (1762–1831), a captain in the Gardes à Cheval who married in 1796 Princess Yelisaveta Petrovna Kvachnina-Samarina. Their son Zakhar was one of the Decembrist revolutionaries of 1825.

222   . . . *Countess Prascovie Soltikow.* . . . Countess Praskovya Ivanovna Saltykova (1771–1859), lady in waiting to the Empress, married 1795 Count Pyotr Vasil'yevich Myatlev (1758–1833), Senator.

222   . . . *the Countess Shouvalow.* . . . ? Countess Yekaterina Petrovna née Saltykova (1743–1816), married to Count Andrey Petrovich Shuvalov (1743–89), Senator, Director of the Credit Bank.

223   . . . *M. Choiseul.* . . . Marie-Gabriel-Florent-Auguste, comte de Choiseul-Gouffier (1752–1817), archaeologist and traveller wrote, 1782, *Voyage pittoresque en Grèce*, which led to his admission to the Académie Française in succession to d'Alembert. Acted as intermediary between Turkey and Russia in the Russo-Turkish war of 1787–92; from Constantinople sent artists to Syria and Egypt to record monuments there. On the French government's order of arrest, November 22, 1792, sought refuge in Russia. Appointed by the Emperor Paul a Privy Councillor and Director of the Academy of Fine Arts and of the imperial libraries. Returned to France 1802 and published further books on archaeology. Nominated a Minister of State by Louis XVIII.

224   . . . *M. Sarti.* . . . Giuseppe Sarti (1729–1802) from Faenza, composer, chiefly of operas. Invited by Catherine II to Russia, 1784, to succeeed Paisiello in charge of court music. Wrote music to Catherine's libretto *The Early Reign of Oleg. (Nachal'noye upravlenie)* in imitation of ancient Greek music; a *Te Deum* for the capture of Ochakhov employing fireworks and cannon; and a *Requiem* for Louis XVI. Made Director of the St. Petersburg Conservatory 1793.

224   . . . *(Goltz)* Lieut. Gen. Leopold Heinrich von der Goltz (1745–1816), Prussian minister to the court of St. Petersburg, 1789–94. Created Count 1789.

224   *Mollendorf.* . . . See note to page 57.

225   *Shairp.* . . . Mr. Shairp, merchant of the Russia Company, son of the British Consul-General before Cayley.

226   . . . *Akin.* . . . Captain James Aiken, second in command to Captain Trevenen during the Swedish war, seriously wounded in the action off Viborg on June 22, 1790.

227   . . . *her death bids fair to be sudden.* It was in fact so sudden that she

Page

had no time to put into execution any plan to substitute Alexander for Paul as her successor. See *Ruskaya Starina*, xxxvii, pp. 471-2.

227 *Old Sutherland.* . . . Baron Richard Sutherland (1739–91), counsellor of state, banker to the imperial court.

19 WARSAW

229 . . . *Gen. Igelstrom.* . . . Count Joseph Igelstrom (–1817), Russian general from Livonia. Served in Poland, 1764, seizing Gaetan Soltyk, Archbishop of Cracow. Fought under Prince Galitsin against Turkey, helping to take Akerman in 1770. Governor of Simbirsk 1784, of Pskov 1792, Kiev 1793. Escaped from Warsaw with 300 men 1794. Governor of Orenburg 1796–8.

229 . . . *Gen. Apraxin.* . . . Count Stepan Stepanovich Apraksin (1757–1827), said to have been made a captain in the army as an infant, began military service at fifteen as colonel of the Kievsky regiment. Brigadier 1788, took part in capture of Ochakov, December 1788, and promoted lieutenant general. General of cavalry 1798. Military governor of Smolensk 1801–9. Owned 27,000 serfs.

231 . . . *Mad^me Apraxin.* . . . Princess Yekaterina Vladimirovna Golitsina (1768–1854), married General Apraksin 1793.

231 . . . *Mad^e Sherbinin.* . . . Anastasya Mikhailovna Dashkova (1760–1831) daughter of the famous Princess Dashkova, married Brigadier Prince Andrey Evdokimovich Sherbinin. After her brother's death in 1807 brought up his three natural children, who took the name Sherbinin. Strongly opposed her mother's friendship with the Wilmot sisters. See *The Russian Journals of Martha and Catherine Wilmot*, ed. Londonderry & Hyde, 1934.

231 . . . *Koshiutsko.* . . . Tadeusz Kosciusko (1746–1817), Polish patriot. Fought for the colonists in the American War of Independence. Defended Dubienka in Poland against the Russians 1792. Headed the national resistance movement 1794. Died in exile.

INDEX

References in the Notes appear in Italics; bold print indicates a main reference. Modern spellings of names are given in brackets after those used by Parkinson.

267

T

274INDEX

Mordvans (Mordvins), inhabiting the middle Volga provinces, 144.
Mordvinoff (Mordvinov), Admiral Count Nikolay Semyonovich, 193, 197–8, 210, 223, **262**.
Mordvinoff (Mordvinov), Madame, 193–4.
Moscow, xii, xiii, 23, 26, 39, 41, 49, 57, 61, 63, 65, 69, 84, 95, 99–106 (chapter 5), 121, 150, 209–20 (chapter 17), *238, 241, 246, 250, 256, 263–4*;
— appearance of, 99;
— clubs, 106, 210, 214;
— market, 102;
— plague, 105;
— Vassili Vlascheni Church, 219, **265**.
Moushkin-Poushkin (Mushkin-Pushkin), Count Valentin Platonovich, 72, **251**.
Munich (Münnich), Christine Lucretia née von Wizleben, Countess von, 129.

Naples, 30.
Nargekin, 29.
Nariskin, Narischin (Naryshkin), Count, later Prince, Lev Aleksandrovich, 34, 47, 50, 88–9, 181, **242–3**;
— family of, 33.
Nariskin (Naryshkin), son of above, 71.
Narva, Ingria, 49, 54, 220.
Nassau (Nassau-Siegen), Prince Charles of, 53, **246**, **262**.
Necker, Jacques, 87, *250, 254*.
Nelidova, Yekaterina Ivanovna, *247, 248, 254*.
Nerva, see Narva.
Neva, river, 20, 38, 91, 226.
Nicholson, General, 150.
Nicholson, Margaret, 14.
Nicolaef, Black Sea port, 225–6.
Nielson, 19.
Nieper (Dniepr), river, 204.
Niester (Dniestr), river, 71, 104.
Nijni Novgorod, 108, **256**.
Nikita K., Armenian at Astrakhan, 176–7.
Noailles, Duke de, 53.
Nogai Tartars, 184.

Norje, 2.
North, Lord (Frederick, 2nd Earl of Guildford, 1732–92, prime minister as Lord North 1770–81), 206.
Novogorod (Novgorod), 96, 129.

Oby river, Siberia, 128.
Ogenski (Oginski), 42, **245**.
Okotsk, seaport, 222.
Oleg, 57, 67, *265*.
Olonetz, 68.
Opera, Italian, at St. Petersburg, 42.
Oranienburg, 86, 88.
Orenburgh (Orenburg, renamed Chkalov), southern Urals, 65, 126, 138.
Orgeat, 44, **245**.
Orleans, Duke of, 215
Orloff (Orlov) brothers, 49, 62, 77, 128–9, *241*.
Orloff (Orlov), Count Aleksey Grigor'yevich, 49, 64, 69, 77–9, 81, 85, **246**, *247, 249, 252, 255–6*;
— portrait of, 51.
Orloff (Orlov), Count Frederick, 84.
Orloff (Orlov), General Count Fyodor Grigor'yevich, 89, *249*, **254**.
Orloff (Orlov), Prince, Grigory Grigor'yevich, 26, 49, 84, 124, 127, 129, 143, 198, 211, 219, **240**, *241, 246–9, 251–3*;
— character and career of, 49, 51–2;
— children by Catherine II, 54, 77;
— portrait of, 51.
Ostankino, country house near Moscow, *256, 264*.
Osterman, Count, Heinrich Johann, 128, **259**.
Osterman, Count, Ivan Andreyevich, Vice Chancellor of Russia, 21–2, 27, 33–4, 38, 48, 55, 65, 89, 90, 93, **237**;
— appearance of, 55;
— trustee for Choglokov, 124.
Ostiacks (Ostyaks), natives of western Siberia, 132.
Ostrogothia (Ostrogothland), Frederik Adolf, Duke of, 9, 16, **235**.
Oswald, John (member of the *Club des Jacobins*, author of *Review of the Constitution of Great Britain*) 77.
Ozoro Esther, see Queen of Abyssinia.

276 INDEX

Potocki, Stanislas Felix, 30, 43, 70, **241**, *245*.
Poushkin (Pushkin), M., 131.
Poushkin (Pushkin), Madame, 131–4.
Poushkin (Pushkin), Mesdemoiselles, 136.
Poussin, Nicolas, 45.
Prétendante (Princess Louisa of Stolberg, married to the Young Pretender, Charles Edward), 73.
Protassov (Protasova), Countess Anna Stepanovna, 61, **248**.
Protassof (Protasova), Mesdemoiselles, 77.
Prussia, Frederick William III King of, 37, 73, 90, 206–7, 230, *255*.
Pskow (Pskov), White Russia, 54, *266*.
Pugatcheff (Pugachov), Emelyan, xv, 110, 128, 135, 144, 146, 214, **256**, *258*.
Puskof, M., 106.
Pyszma river, Siberia, 122.

Quarenghi, Giacomo, architect, 42–5, 50, 62, 64, 68, 84, *243*, **245**, *246, 253, 264*;
— his opinion of Reynolds, 46;
— income of, 47;
— on Catherine II, 48.
Quass (Kvass), 68, 138, **250**.
Queen of Abyssinia, Ozoro Esther, 166, **260**.
Queen of Sweden, see Sofia Magdalena

Racine, Jean, 222.
Radiskef, Radishev (Radishchev), Aleksandr Nikolayevich, xii, 95, 131, 221, **255**, *259*.
Radzivil, Prince, 224.
Radzivil, Princess, 224.
Raikes, Timothy, 41, **244**.
Ramzoff, 85.
Raphael, 218.
Rasomovsky, Razoumofski (Razumovsky), Prince Andrey Kirilovich, 35, 124, **243**, *258*.
Rastrelli, Bartolommeo, architect, 84, *236, 253*.
Ratafia, 44, **245**.
Razomofsky (Razumovsky), Count Kiril Grigor'yevich, 99–101, 104, 209, *241*, **255**.

Rembrandt, 45.
Reni, Guido, 45.
Repnin, Prince Nikolay Vasil'yevich, 36, 80, **244**.
Reval (Tallin), Estonia, 49, 54, 59, 77, *258*.
Reynolds, Sir Joshua, 45–6, 72, **251**.
Ribas, Admiral Giuseppe de, 57, **247**.
Ribbing, Adolf Ludvig, Count, 7, 8, 14–15, 18–19, **235**.
Richelieu, Armand-Emmanuel-Sofie-Septimanie du Plessis, duc de, 53, 87, **247**.
Rickhausen, 8.
Riga, Latvia, 23, 102, 220, 224, *244, 256*.
Rimsky-Korsakov, Ivan Nikolayevich, 102, *246, 252*.
Robespierre, 53.
Rochford, 4th Earl of, Secretary of State for the Southern Department, 1770–75, 13.
Rodney, Admiral, 88.
Rogerson, Dr. (sometimes as Rogers), xii, 32–3, 35–6, 60–1, *240*, **242**.
Rohan, Duke of, Louis-Marie-Bretagne-Dominique de Rohan-Chabot (1710–1801), 219.
Romanzoff (Rumyantsev), Marshal Count Pyotr Aleksandrovich, 41, 84, 128, 201–2, 204–7, *238, 240*, **263**.
Romanzoff (Rumyantsev), Count Sergey Petrovich, 41, 92–3, **244**, *245*.
Roscolnicks, 201, **263**.
Rouble, value of, 68, 70.
Rousseau, Jean Jacques, 87, 130, *259*.
Routh, Dr., xiv.
Rubens, 45, 93.

St. Andrew, Knights of, 62–3.
St. Anthony, catacombs of, 199–201, **262**, *263*.
St. George, Knights of, 58–9.
St. Ivan, 201, **262–3**.
St. Petersburg, xii, xv, 11, 20–95 (chapter 3), 96, 124, 128, 130, 140, 150, 161–2, 180, 214–15, 218, 221–8 (chapter 18), *236–7, 241–2, 244–5, 247, 250–3, 255, 264–5*;
— Academy, Russian, 61, 64, *241*;